Hispanic Muslims in the United States

Hispanic Muslims in the United States

Agency, Identity, and Religious Commitment

VICTOR HUGO CUARTAS

WIPF & STOCK · Eugene, Oregon

HISPANIC MUSLIMS IN THE UNITED STATES
Agency, Identity, and Religious Commitment

Copyright © 2020 Victor Hugo Cuartas. All rights reserved. Except for brief quotations in critical publications or reviews, no part of this book may be reproduced in any manner without prior written permission from the publisher. Write: Permissions, Wipf and Stock Publishers, 199 W. 8th Ave., Suite 3, Eugene, OR 97401.

Wipf & Stock
An Imprint of Wipf and Stock Publishers
199 W. 8th Ave., Suite 3
Eugene, OR 97401

www.wipfandstock.com

PAPERBACK ISBN: 978-1-7252-5384-1
HARDCOVER ISBN: 978-1-7252-5385-8
EBOOK ISBN :978-1-7252-5386-5

Manufactured in the U.S.A.   03/17/20

Contents

Abstract	xi
List of Tables	xiii
Acknowledgments	xv

Chapter 1: Introduction   1
- 1.1 Context of Religious Affiliation of Hispanics in the United States   2
- 1.2 Context of Islam in the United States in the Twentieth Century as Religious Minority   5
- 1.3 Context of Hispanic Muslims in the United States   8
  - 1.3.1 Hispanics in Washington, DC Metropolitan and New Jersey   9
- 1.4 Islam in the West   11
- 1.5 Background and Main Problems in Conversion Studies   12
- 1.6 Approach and Theories to Be Considered   16
- 1.7 Rationale and Need   17
- 1.8 Research Problem and Limitations   18
- 1.9 Research Questions   19
- 1.10 Research Methodology and Methods   20
  - 1.10.1 Interviews   22
  - 1.10.2 Demographic Survey   23
  - 1.10.3 Gender   24
  - 1.10.4 Generational Aspects   25
  - 1.10.5 Religious Background   26
  - 1.10.6 Educational Level   26
- 1.11 Rationale for Choosing Case Studies   26
- 1.12 Layers to Be Used   27
- 1.13 Organization of Chapters   28

Chapter 2: Pre-affiliation Stage and Background of Hispanic Muslim Converts   29
- 2.1 Introduction   29

    2.1.1 Rationale for Choosing Case Studies for this Chapter   31
    2.1.2 Defining the Boundaries of the Cases   31
    2.1.3 Explanation of Each Category (Continuum)   32
    2.1.4 Layers   36
2.2 Martina's Case   36
2.2.1 Martina: "I believed that the Qur'an was true."   36
    2.2.2 Family Background and Structure   37
    2.2.3 Previous Religious Commitment   39
    2.2.4 Parental Religious Commitment   39
    2.2.5 Contextual Factors: Personal and Religious   40
    2.2.6 Contact with Muslims   41
    2.2.7 Level of Crisis   41
    2.2.8 Conversion Motives   42
    2.2.9 Reasons for Conversion   43
    2.2.10 Conversion Motifs   43
    2.2.11 Multiple Factors that Shaped Martina's Choices   45
2.3 Similarities and Differences Between Martina, Catalina, and Simón   47
    2.3.1 Catalina: "Islam was so simple"   47
    2.3.2 Simón: "It was an interesting experience"   48
2.4 Similarities Between Martina, Catalina, and Simón   49
2.5 Differences Between Martina, Catalina, and Simón   53
2.6 Case Pairing: Similarities and Differences Between Martina and Lucía   57
    2.6.1 Lucía: "There is one God."   57
    2.6.2 Similarities between Martina and Lucía   58
    2.6.3 Differences between Martina and Lucía   59
2.7 Making Sense of the Relationships Between Important Categories   61
2.8 Conclusion   63

Chapter 3: Diverse Conversion Narratives of Hispanic Muslim Converts   67
    3.1 Introduction   67
    3.2 Analysis of the Conversion Narratives   68
        3.2.1 Description of the Categories   69
        3.2.2 Contextual Factors   71
        3.2.3 Choices of Words and Metaphors   75
        3.2.4 Most Appealing Aspects about Islam   78
        3.2.5 Main Themes that are Emerging   80
        3.2.6 Predominant Discourses   82
        3.2.7 How Discourses are Created By the Converts   86

3.2.8 Integration of the New Religion's Values and Beliefs	87
3.2.9 Degree of Tension between Culture and Religion	90
3.2.10 Reactions of Vicente's Family and Friends	92
3.3 Types of Conversion Narratives	96
3.3.1 Vicente's Narrative	96
3.3.2 Jaime's Narrative	97
3.3.3 Claudia's Narrative	97
3.3.4 Teresa's Narrative	98
3.4 Comparison and Contrast with other Studies	99
3.5 Conclusion	102
Chapter 4: Becoming a Hispanic Muslim	**105**
4.1 Introduction	105
4.2 Identity, Ethnicity, Culture, and Religion	106
4.2.1 Identity Studies	107
4.2.2 Ethnicity	108
4.2.3 Ethnic and Religious Identities	109
4.2.4 Identity Markers and Post-Affiliation Changes	110
4.3 Analysis of the Data: Diverse Examples of the Reconstruction of Identities	111
4.3.1 Introduction of the Selected Cases	111
4.3.2 Identity Markers and Post-Affiliation Changes	113
4.3.3 Institutional Agency and the Development of Collective Identities	121
4.3.4 Values and Beliefs—What Has Really Changed?	122
4.3.5 Religious Beliefs	126
4.3.6 Women and Islam	127
4.3.7 Marriage and the Transmission of Values	128
4.3.8 Tensions between Culture and Religion	131
4.3.9 Self-Identification of the New Muslims	133
4.3.10 Contrasting Self-Identification with Biography	134
4.3.11 Contextual Factors and Present State of the New Hispanic Muslims	135
4.4 Selected Theories	136
4.4.1 Assimilation Theory	136
4.4.2 Integration Theory	138
4.4.3 Link to My Research and Limitations of Selected Theories	139
4.5 Explanation of the Results in Light of Theories	140
4.6 Conclusion	143
Chapter 5: Being a Hispanic Muslim in the United States	**147**
5.1 Introduction	147

5.2 The Nature of Religious Commitment ... 149
   5.2.1 Definitions of Religious Commitment ... 149
   5.2.2 Distinction between Religious Activity, Recruitment, Conversion, and Commitment ... 150
   5.2.3 Conceptualization of Religiosity ... 151
   5.2.4 Limitations of Glock and Stark's 1968 Dimensions ... 153
   5.2.5 Operationalization of Religious Commitment ... 153
   5.2.6 Debates among Muslim Scholars ... 153
5.3 High and Low Levels of Religious Commitment ... 154
   5.3.1 Indicators Used to Measure Religious Commitment ... 154
   5.3.2 Index of Religious Commitment ... 156
   5.3.3 How are These Studies Informing My Research? ... 156
   5.3.4 How Will I Measure the Proposed Indicators? ... 156
   5.3.5 Religious Affiliation of the Hispanic Muslim Converts ... 157
   5.3.6 Indicators of Religious Commitment among Hispanic Muslim Converts ... 159
   5.3.7 Comparison and Contrast between the More Active Converts and the Less Active Converts ... 168
   5.3.8 Ritualistic and Devotional Dimensions of Religious Commitment among Hispanic Muslim Converts ... 171
   5.3.9 The Devotional Dimension ... 178
   5.3.10 Religious Commitment in Relation to the Perspectives of the Converts Regarding the Meaning of a Committed Muslim ... 181
5.4 Discussion of the Findings Considering Theories and Studies Done on Religious Commitment ... 184
   5.4.1 Religious Socialization and Social Networks ... 184
   5.4.2 Similarities and Differences with Other Studies Done on Religious Commitment ... 189
5.5 Conclusion ... 192
   5.5.1 Assessment of High and Low Levels of Religious Commitment 192
   5.5.2 Conclusions Drawn from Socialization and Social Networks Theories ... 194
   5.5.3 Findings Regarding Gender Differences ... 195
   5.5.4 What Is Next? ... 196

Chapter 6: Concluding Thoughts ... 197
6.1 Introduction ... 197
6.2 Summary of the Main Findings ... 198
6.3 Implications and Contributions of the Study ... 201
   6.3.1 Theoretical Implications ... 201
   6.3.2 Literature Implications ... 204

6.4 My Role as Researcher and Reflexivity	205
6.5 Limitations of the Study	206
6.6 Prospects for Further Research	207
6.7 Questions Raised in the Study	208
6.8 Regarding Theory and Approaches (Socialization)	209
6.9 Identity, Community, and Beliefs	209
6.10 Muslim Refugees in the United States	210
6.11 Final Remarks	210
Appendix 1	213
Appendix 2	215
Appendix 3	216
Appendix 4	217
Appendix 5	225
Appendix 6	231
Appendix 7	232
Bibliography	233

Abstract

One of the problems in conversion studies involves the definition of conversion itself. Some researchers argue that conversion is an event; others argue that it is composite and dynamic. Here, conversion is understood as a process, which encompasses pre/post-affiliation stages, but the emphasis is on the post-affiliation stage.

In research on conversion, often the debates among scholars focus on the role of institutional and individual agency. The studies that emphasize the institutional dimension highlight the passive (less active) role of the converts, whereas the others challenge this assumption through recognizing the active role of the convert. The problem with the scholars who concentrate on an institutional agency is that they largely ignore the choices that the less active converts make. The problem with the latter is that even though they recognize the active involvement of the converts, they largely miss the role that is played in making diverse choices regarding religious commitment and practice.

Furthermore, some scholars on conversion have concentrated on biography, largely ignoring the importance of narrative discourses. Several scholars propose the need for a multidisciplinary approach. The significance of combining biography with narrative discourses is that it enables scholars to better understand the process of conversion and the choices converts make while they construct their new identities. These conversions are analyzed considering different factors in terms of social, cultural, and religious contexts. This multidisciplinary approach will facilitate the analysis of not only the content of the narratives but also how the converts create new discourses during the process of conversion; what are their choices and purposes and how they create these discourses?

In addition, most researchers in the last three decades have focused on the New Religious Movements, and there are limited studies on the conversion to Islam and to other religions. The studies done on conversion to

Islam are mostly focused on European countries. Therefore, there is a need to conduct more studies on Islam in the United States.

The empirical case here is that of the Hispanic Catholic converts to Islam in the Washington DC Metropolitan and New Jersey areas of the United States. The central research question is: *To what extent do Hispanic Muslim converts play a role in making different choices regarding religious commitment and practice?*

The argument is that not only do both the more active and even the less active converts play a central role in making choices during the pre-affiliation and post-affiliation stages, but that these choices can often be strategic in nature as they practice the new religion in the United States. These choices are shaped by multiple factors. This contributes to a new understanding of the prevailing debates among Muslims in Europe and the United States on the nature of Muslim minorities in the West—that Muslims here are not merely transplanted but are active participants of diverse expressions of local Islam.

The evidence in my research shows that being less active does not mean converts do not play a role or make choices. Both more active *and* less active converts make choices based on multiple factors. This is especially significant as the main aim of this thesis is to show that the converts make choices and play a role in the post-affiliation stage and that these often have strategic elements.

The primary data for this study are drawn from field-notes, demographic surveys, and fifty-six interviews, including individual interviews, group interviews, and focus group interviews conducted over a period of four years. The research was conducted among Muslim leaders, born Muslims, born Hispanic Muslims, and Hispanic Muslim converts from different stages, levels, and dimensions of religious commitment, locations, generations, previous religious backgrounds, national origins, and genders. Using a qualitative approach, the data will be grouped appropriately and analyzed looking at significant patterns in conjunction with selected cases and existing theories of conversion.

List of Tables

Table 1: Layers, Levels, and Categories (Continua)
for Comparing and Contrasting Selected Cases   35

Table 2: Summary of Similarities and Differences
between Martina, Catalina, and Simón   57

Table 3: Case Pairing between Martina and Lucía   62

Table 4: Summary of Layers and Levels for Comparing
and Contrasting Selected Cases   65

Acknowledgments

First and foremost, I am grateful to God for the opportunity to embark in this study. I am indebted to so many people for their help in this research. I want to express my gratitude to my lovely wife and daughter for their continuous encouragement and prayers. I am grateful for my mother and my two brothers for their constant prayers and encouragement.

I would like to express my deepest appreciation to Dr. Michael Palmer, Dr. Amos Yong, Dr. Wonsuk Ma, Dr. Graham Twelftree, and Dr. Ed Smither. These dear colleagues from different institutions have been very instrumental in this project. They highly inspired me to pursue a PhD. In addition, they encouraged me to continue moving forward during difficult times that I had while I was doing this study.

I owe my earnest gratitude to Dr. David Singh, Dr. Henri Hooren, and Dr. David Cashin for the helpful feedback and supervision they provided throughout the different stages of this project. Also, I am very grateful for the editorial assistance of several teaching assistants from diverse institutions who helped me to improve this study.

Finally, words cannot express my gratitude to all the informants who participated in this research. I am grateful for their willingness and openness to share their stories.

Chapter 1

Introduction

My wife and I came to the United States in December 1997, and since then we have been involved in different areas serving the Hispanic community. We have experienced both the challenges and opportunities of adapting to another culture. I was amazed at the diversity in almost every city we visited. I began to think about the different interactions that take place among diverse peoples in our cities and neighborhoods. This inspired me to research more intentionally about the different dynamics and the diverse challenges that Hispanics face in different areas, particularly religious experiences and affiliations.

The religious landscape has changed significantly in the last thirty years. There is usually a stereotype regarding the religious affiliation of Hispanics. Most people think that Hispanics follow only Catholicism, but the reality is that, due to multiple factors, Hispanics are finding new alternatives regarding religious affiliation, and there is limited research examining the nuances of the experiences of minorities following a minority religion such as Islam.

While researching Hispanic conversion studies, I began to find articles about Hispanic Muslims in the United States. Even though this phenomenon was not well researched at that time and most of the articles that I found had a more journalistic approach, I began to research more about this topic. As a first-generation Hispanic, I started to consider the conversions of Hispanics in the United States to Islam. One of my preliminary questions was how Hispanics—being already a minority—were willing to become part of another minority as Hispanic Muslims within the United States context. This thesis represents my effort to understand the nuances of their conversions and experiences.

In the first section of the introduction I will first describe the context and background of Hispanics in general in the United States. Then, I will briefly concentrate on the context of Islam in the United States. Next, I will focus on the Hispanic Muslims in the United States. I will concisely describe the context of Hispanics, particularly in the Washington DC Metropolitan and New Jersey areas. Also, I will describe the different approaches of Muslim scholars to Islam in the West. In the second section of the introduction I will describe the rationale and the need for this study, including the research problem and the limitations of the study. Finally, I will describe the research methodology and methods.

1.1 CONTEXT OF RELIGIOUS AFFILIATION OF HISPANICS IN THE UNITED STATES

The Hispanic communities in the United States are vibrant and diverse. De La Torre states that "Hispanics are bringing transformation to religious communities in the United States, and also these religious communities are bringing change to Hispanics."[1] The Pew Hispanic Center (PHC) conducted a comprehensive study of religion among Hispanics in the United States which showed that Hispanics express greater commitment to religion (68 percent) than the overall population in North America (60 percent). Nine out of ten Hispanics identify with a specific religion.[2]

The PHC's study also reveals that nearly a third of all Catholics in the United States are now Hispanics and projects that the Latino share will continue to rise. In addition, more than half of Hispanic Catholics identify themselves as charismatics, compared with only an eighth of non-Hispanic Catholics. In the same way, the charismatic renewal movement is very influential among Hispanic Protestants. More than half of Hispanics in this group identify with spirit-filled religion, compared with nearly a fifth of non-Hispanic Protestants. Many Hispanics who are joining evangelical churches are coming from Catholicism.[3]

According to a national study conducted by the Hispanic Churches in American Public Life (HCAPL)[4] in the United States, Hispanic religious

---

1. Pew Research Center, "Shifting Religious Identity," xx.
2. Pew Hispanic Center, "Changing Faiths," 1–4.
3. Pew Hispanic Center, "Changing Faiths," 1.
4. For more information about this comprehensive survey, see Espinosa et al., *Hispanic Churches*. The HCAPL national survey went through ten revisions over a four-month period. Eighteen scholars gave valuable feedback in the construction of the survey framework and questions: Virgilio Elizondo, Jesse Miranda, Gastón Espinosa,

affiliation in the United States is as follows[5]: 70 percent of Latinos are Catholics, translating into 29 million Catholic Latinos in the United States. Twenty-three percent of Latinos are Protestants or "other Christians" (including Jehovah's Witnesses and Mormons). That translates into 9.5 million people. Eighty-five percent of all US Latino Protestants identify themselves as Pentecostals or evangelicals. That translates into 6.2 million people. Thirty-seven percent of the US Latino population (14.2 million) self-identifies as "born again" or evangelical. This figure includes Catholic charismatics, who constitute 22 percent of US Latino Catholics. Twenty-six percent, or 7.6 million, of all Latino Catholics self-identify as being born again. One percent of Latinos identify with a world religion such as Buddhism, Islam or Judaism. And 0.37 percent of all Latinos self-identify as atheists or agnostics.[6]

Despite the surprisingly high percentage (23 percent) of Latino Protestants, the majority of US Hispanics (70 percent) are Catholics, making the Catholic Church the most recognizable institution of Latino religion. In 2005, there were approximately 29 million Latino Catholics in the United States. However, the new immigration of Hispanics from different religious backgrounds and generations are adding new dynamics to the religious landscape in the United States.[7]

The number of Hispanic Catholics in the United States has decreased in the last three decades. According to Greeley, "the Catholic population in the United States among those of Spanish origin in the early 1970s was 78%. By the mid-1990s that percentage had dropped to 67%."[8] Greeley estimates that the defection rate is approximately 60,000 people per year.[9] As the Pew Hispanic Center notes, "Hispanics are transforming the nation's religious landscape because they are practicing a distinctive form of Christianity."[10] In addition, Hispanics are finding new alternatives in other religions such as Islam and Buddhism. The new choices regarding formerly unfamiliar

---

Harry Pachon, Rudy de la Garza, Jongho Lee, Daisy Machado, Milagros Peña, Louis DeSipio, Allen Hertzke, David Leege, María Elena González, Donald Miller, Wade Clark Roof, Dean Hoge, Edwin Hernández, Samuel Pagán, and Elizabeth Conde-Frazier.

5. Espinosa et al., *Hispanic Churches*, 14–15.

6. See Aponte, *Santo!*, 40–45, for a study of Hispanics shifting to Buddhism, Mormonism, and Jehovah Witnesses.

7. For studies about the religious experience of Hispanics, see Cafferty and McCready, *Hispanics in the United States*; Abalos, *Latinos in the United States*; Diaz-Stevens and Stevens-Arroyo, *Recognizing the Latino Resurgence*; Weyr, *Hispanic USA.*; Avalos, *Introduction to the US Latina*; Espinosa et al., *Latino Religions*; De La Torre, *Hispanic American Religious Cultures*.

8. Greeley, "Defection among Hispanics (Updated)," 12.

9. Greeley, "Defection among Hispanics (Updated)," 12.

10. Pew Hispanic Center, "Changing Faiths," para. 1.

religions are in part due to globalization and secularization in the United States. These converts are also contributing to the local expressions of their new religions.

The speedy growth of the Hispanic population over the past thirty years has created a significant shift in the makeup of the Catholic Church in the United States. Studies show that while only 12 percent of US Catholics were Latinos in 1970, today that number is estimated by US Catholic bishops to be 40 percent. Over that same period, though, the percentage of US Latinos who consider themselves Catholic has declined.[11]

More recent studies[12] show that "Hispanics make up a larger share of the US Catholic population than they do of almost any other religious group."[13] According to this study, one-third of Catholics are Hispanic (34 percent), up from 29 percent in 2007. The data suggests that the Hispanic share of the Catholic population is expected to continue to grow rapidly because Hispanic Catholics are far younger, on average, than non-Hispanic Catholics. The median age of Hispanic Catholic adults is forty-two, while the median age of non-Hispanic Catholic is fifty-three.[14] Analyzing the racial and ethnic composition of different religious groups, it is important to notice that there has been an increase of Hispanics following non-Christian faiths, including Judaism, Islam, Buddhism, and Hinduism, from 4 percent in 2014 to 6 percent in 2017.[15] The number of Hispanics interested in Buddhism has doubled from 6 percent in 2014 to 12 percent in 2017.[16]

There is now a shift from Catholicism towards Protestant Evangelicalism in the United States, and especially towards Pentecostal congregations and the Catholic charismatic renewal.[17] This trend evidently shows that

---

11. The Institute for Latino Studies is located at the University of Notre Dame in Indiana.

12. For more details about the Hispanic religious landscape in the United States, see also Pew Research Center, "Shifting Religious Identity," and Nabhan-Warren, "Hispanics and Religion in America."

13. Pew Research Center, "America's Changing Religious Landscape," 51.

14. Pew Research Center, "America's Changing Religious Landscape," 51.

15. Pew Research Center, "America's Changing Religious Landscape," 50.

16. Pew Research Center, "America's Changing Religious Landscape," 50.

17. For conversion studies from Catholicism to Pentecostal Evangelicalism see also Díaz-Stevens and Stevens-Arroyo, *Recognizing the Latino Resurgence*; Avalos, *Introduction to the US Latina*; Portes and Rumbaut, *Immigrant America*; Gooren, "Conversion Careers in Latin America"; Gooren, "Conversion Careers and Culture Politics." For Pentecostal congregations and Catholic charismatic renewal see Portes and Rumbaut, *Immigrant America*; Roof and Manning, "Cultural Conflicts and Identity."

while Catholicism is still the leading religion among Hispanic immigrants, it no longer holds a religious monopoly.[18]

While scholars have done research in the United States on Pentecostalism and charismatic Catholic movements,[19] I argue that there is a need to research Hispanics' experience with other religions as well. Even though there is only a small portion of the Hispanic population who are shifting to other religions such as Islam, Buddhism, and Judaism, the experiences of Hispanics turning from Catholicism and Protestantism to Islam will shed new light on the studies of religious conversion among Muslim minorities in the West. According to research conducted in 2015, religious traditions such as Jehovah's Witnesses, Islam, Buddhism, and Hinduism, are composed largely of racial and ethnic minorities. In addition, more Hispanics in the United States are becoming attracted to atheism and agnosticism.[20]

Due to current demographic changes in which major concentrations of populations now live in urban rather than rural areas, as well as the migration of people to different countries, individuals are more easily finding new religious options for conversion. This is also the case within Hispanic communities. Even though the majority of Hispanics in the United States are still Catholics, limited research has been done to understand the dynamic processes and challenges that some Hispanics experienced when switching to other religions such as Islam. To understand these challenges, it is important to analyze the context of Islam in the United States where Muslims are a minority.

1.2 CONTEXT OF ISLAM IN THE UNITED STATES IN THE TWENTIETH CENTURY AS RELIGIOUS MINORITY

Muslims in the United States experienced significant changes during the twentieth century.[21] The economic hardships during the nineteenth century prevented many Muslim immigrants from succeeding financially in their home countries. Therefore, many Muslim immigrants decided to settle in the United States, particularly in the Midwest in places such as Dearborn, Michigan; Quincy, Massachusetts; and Ross, North Dakota. Muslim

---

18. Althoff, "Migration," 6.

19 For statistics about religion affiliation of Hispanics in North America, see Espinosa et al., *Latino Religions*; Althoff, "Migration."

20. Pew Research Center, "America's Changing Religious Landscape," 51.

21. See Haddad and Lummis, *Islamic Values*; Haddad and Smith, *Mission to America*; Haddad, "Century of Islam"; Curtis, *Black Muslim Religion*; Bowen, "Islamic Adaptations."

immigrants started arriving in small numbers around the turn of the twentieth century and continued in increasing waves throughout the first half of the century. They were "adventurers" who became attracted to the New World for its economic opportunities.[22]

The twentieth century witnessed several favorable developments for Muslims in the United States from a demographic perspective.[23] Haddad states that in the last half of the twentieth century, the number of Muslims in the United States rose substantially due to "immigration, procreation, and conversion."[24] Thus, migration played a significant role in the advancement of Islam during the twentieth century.[25]

According to Haddad and Lummis, the migration of Muslims to North America occurred in five waves as follows: a) the first wave from 1875 to 1912; b) the second wave from 1918 to 1922; c) the third wave from 1930 to 1938; d) the fourth wave from 1940 to 1960; and e) the fifth wave from 1967 to present.[26]

---

22. Haddad and Smith, *Mission to America*, 11.

23. For statistics about the Muslim population in North America, see Smith, "Review."

24. Haddad, "Century of Islam in America," 88.

25. See Haddad, "Century of Islam in America"; Haniff, "Muslim Community in America."

26. This is an important aspect to understand how Muslims began to settle in the United States. 1) The First Wave, from 1875 to 1912. This wave of immigrants "consisted mostly of uneducated and unskilled young Arab men from the rural areas of what now constitutes Syria, Jordan, Palestine, and Lebanon, then under Ottoman rule" (Haddad and Lummis, *Islamic Values*, 14). There were some Christians and Muslims among the immigrants. Most of the immigrants came with the purpose of improving their economic status. They had difficulties in finding jobs. Some had to work in factories for small merchants. Some of them even were forced to return to their countries of origin because of the challenges of learning a new language and the difficulties of adaptation. Progressively, they settled in the eastern United States, the Middle West, and on the Pacific Coast (Smith, *Islam in America*, 1). 2) The Second Wave, from 1918 to 1922. Right after the conclusion of the First World War, immigrants from urban areas from countries such as Libya decided to immigrate to the West due to political and economic reasons. "The majority were relatives, friends, and acquaintances of the earlier immigrants" (Haddad and Lummis, *Islamic Values*, 14). Regulated laws restricted the number of immigrants who were permitted to enter the United States, with preference given to relatives of former immigrants (Haddad, "Century of Islam in America," 89). Later, in 1924, a new US immigration law restricted the number of immigrants by instituting the national origins quota system. Immigration was limited according to the national origin of the foreign-born population of the United States in 1890, later changed to 1920 (Smith *Islam in America*, 2). 3) The Third Wave, from 1930 to 1938. Due to restricted regulations during these years, the movement of Muslims to the United States was very limited. Only relatives of former immigrants were allowed to immigrate. Many immigrants and Muslim families experienced challenges and difficulties due to these regulations. 4) The Fourth

Historically within the United States, African-American conversions to Islam have been more likely than Caucasian conversions. "African-Americans make up about a third of the estimated 4 to 8 million Muslims in the US—conservatively, around 1.5 million, nearly 5 percent of all African-Americans."[27] According to a poll conducted in 2001 by Muslims in the American Public Square (MAPS), 20 percent of African-American Muslims are converts while 80 percent were raised as Muslims.[28] More detailed information about Islam in the African-American community, however, is relatively scarce.[29] The discussion of Islam within the African-American community is important because some first-generation Hispanics were influenced by Muslim minorities, including African-American Muslims in the sixties and seventies.[30] According to recent statistics, Hispanics comprise 1 percent of the Muslim population in the United States. Now, I will focus on the context of Hispanic Muslims in the United States.

Wave, from 1947 to 1960. There was a considerable increase in numbers of immigrant Muslims not only from Middle Eastern countries. This wave also included immigrants from India, Pakistan, Eastern Europe, and the Soviet Union. Some of the immigrants left their countries of origin due to political reasons. Many Muslim families applied for asylum to escape political persecution. Many Muslim children and youth arrived at the United States. "A growing number were the children of the ruling elites in various countries, mostly urban in background, educated, and Westernized prior to their arrival in the United States. They came searching for a better life, higher education, or advanced technical training and specialized work opportunities, as well as for ideological fulfilment" (Haddad and Lummis, *Islamic Values*, 14). 5) The Fifth Wave, from 1967 to the present. Muslim immigrants from different countries have chosen to come to the United States for several reasons. Some of the main reasons to immigrate include the following: economic, educational, and particularly political issues. "Many of the arrivals from Pakistan and the Arab world since the middle of the century have been educated professionals. More newly groups of semiskilled workers have come from Pakistan, Yemen, Lebanon, and Iran" (Haddad and Lummis, *Islamic Values*, 14). This trend of significant Muslim immigration will continue due to the instability in some Middle Eastern and North African countries such as Libya and Egypt.

27. For projections about Muslim population in the United States, see Read and Bartkowski, "To Veil or Not to Veil?"

28. For more details about the discussion on the Muslim population in the United States, see Smith, "Review."

29. Armstrong, "Turning to Islam," 18.

30. Sánchez and Galván, "Latino Muslims," 26.

1.3 CONTEXT OF HISPANIC MUSLIMS IN THE UNITED STATES

As noted before, some Hispanics, particularly the second generation, are finding alternative religions in the United States such as Buddhism, Islam, or Judaism. Moreover, it is difficult to estimate the number of Hispanic Muslims in the United States because the United States Census Bureau does not provide statistics on religion. Additionally, the main focus of researchers has been on Catholicism because historically Catholicism has been the main religion in Latin American countries and still remains as the majority religious group in the United States. Thus, more studies need to be done analyzing the conversion narratives of Hispanics to other religions.

Sources provide a wide range of estimates regarding the number of Hispanic Muslims; however, due to the increase of conversions of minorities to Islam in the United States, different organizations and scholars are focusing on several aspects regarding Hispanic Muslims in the United States. For example, a 2007 study conducted by the Pew Research Center showed that Hispanic Muslims accounted for an estimated 4 percent out of a total of about 2.5 million Muslims living in the United States. That is approximately 10,000 to 15,000 Hispanic Muslims.[31]

According to the Islamic Society of the United States (ISNA) and the Council for American Islamic Relations (CAIR), there are 40,000 Hispanic Muslims in the United States.[32] As recently as 2006, Ali Khan, National Director of the American Muslim Council in Chicago, claimed that this number had increased fivefold to 200,000.[33] The most recent conservative estimates suggest that the US Latina/o Muslim population is somewhere between 50,000 and 75,000.[34]

The majority of Hispanic converts to Islam are women. While the statistics about the precise number of Muslims in general, and Hispanic Muslim converts in particular, are scarce and wide ranging, it is clear that the first large-scale conversions of Hispanics to Islam occurred in the 1960s and 1970s, when many Spanish-language Muslim groups began to emerge and the Black Muslim movement was at its height.[35] Hispanic Muslim communities have emerged in different cities where there is a strong presence

---

31. Pew Research Center, "Muslim Americans: Middle Class," para. 1.
32. Martínez-Vasquez, *Latina/o y Musulmán*, 2.
33. Martínez-Vasquez, *Latina/o y Musulmán*, 2.
34. Martínez-Vasquez, *Latina/o y Musulmán*, 2.
35. Sánchez and Galván, "Latino Muslims," 26.

of Hispanics. such as New York, New Jersey, Chicago, and Miami.[36] I conducted interviews and fieldwork in the Metropolitan DC area and New Jersey. Most of the conversions of the individuals in my study happened after September 11, 2001.[37]

1.3.1 Hispanics in Washington, DC Metropolitan and New Jersey

With more than 750,000 Hispanics present, the Hispanic population in the Metropolitan Washington area is growing.[38] Salvadorians are the single

---

36. Ramirez, "New Islamic Movement," para. 9.

37. The events and the consequences of the September 11, 2001 attacks on the Twin Towers of the World Trade Center in New York significantly transformed the presence of Islam in North America. Within hours of the attacks, an unprecedented rash of intolerable incidents on Muslims and Arabs, along with Sikhs, South Asians, and other individuals who appeared to be of Middle Eastern descent, in the form of discrimination, harassment, and racial and religious profiling was reported (Peek, "Becoming Muslim," 230). It was on this date that America came under attack from a group of eighteen terrorists from the al-Qaeda organization which was under the leadership of Osama bin Laden (National Commission on Terrorist Attacks upon the United States, et al., *9/11 Commission Report*, 56). Nonetheless, an international group of Islamic political leaders and scholars quickly issued a fatwa, defined by John Esposito as "a legal interpretation or judgment" (Esposito, *Islam: The Straight Path*, 38) on September 14, 2001 which condemned the attacks of September 11th and the loss of innocent lives (Esposito, *Islam: The Straight Path*, 148). Furthermore, the Fiqh Council of North America issued another fatwa on September 27, 2001 which stated that "every Muslim has a duty to work to apprehend and bring to justice anyone who planned, participated in, or financed such attacks" (Esposito, *Islam: The Straight Path*, 149). Muslims in North America experienced great challenges. The USA Patriot Act, approved in October 2001, resulted in rounding up about 1,200 Arab, South Asian, and Muslim men on suspicion of potential ties to terrorism. The detainees' names were not released, and they were not even permitted access to a lawyer and were therefore held in jail without being indicted of a crime (Curtis, *Muslims in America*, 100). One of the main challenges faced by Muslims in North America, both indigenous and immigrant, will be to remain as active US citizens without losing their Islamic heritage and culture. The difficulty for Black Muslims will be the possibility of full integration into the North American social and political order (Simmons, "From Muslims in America," 275). Another challenge within the Muslim community is the current tensions and intergroup relations between the immigrant Muslims and the native-born converts. Despite all the difficulties and challenges after September 11, "Muslim Americans of all racial and ethnic origins, their organizations, and institutions became visible players in the American public life to a greater degree than even before" (Curtis, *Encyclopedia of Muslim-American History*, 506). After the terrorist attacks, Muslim Americans emerged in a much different social position from that which they held prior to the attacks. Muslims living in North America today represent diverse movements and identities: immigrant and indigenous, Sunni and Shiite, conservative and liberal, orthodox and heterodox (Smith, *Islam in America*, 1).

38. US Department of Commerce, "Hispanic Population"; Pew Hispanic Center,

largest Hispanic group in the Washington, DC metropolitan area which includes Virginia and Maryland.[39] The Salvadorian population has grown by 152 percent since 2000 and comprises 33.7 percent of the Hispanic population.[40]

Puerto Ricans are the largest Hispanic origin group in Philadelphia, Pennsylvania/New Jersey, the 24th-largest Hispanic metropolitan area, making up more than half (53 percent) of all Hispanics there.[41]

The diversity of Hispanics in this area is significant. In addition to Puerto Ricans, there are Mexicans, Cubans, Dominicans, Guatemalans, and others from South America. This area is the heart of the nation. The capital of the nation is located here, causing interesting dynamics in terms of immigration and religious and ethnic diversity. Thus, the converts from this area will add insightful aspects to the conversion studies.

There is a tendency to see Hispanics in the United States as a monolithic group. This is not the case. According to de La Torre, "Hispanics represent a very diverse population. Some of them are White, some indigenous, others Black, and most somewhere in between. They are a mestizaje (mixture) of cultures, races, and ethnicities."[42] In addition, Hispanics represent all the colors of the human rainbow of skin pigmentation, coming from a multitude of cultural and ethnic backgrounds.[43] My argument is that this diversity among Hispanics facilitates the interaction with other ethnic groups, as well as other religions, in North America.

These interactions have occurred in several cities in the US, particularly in the Washington Metropolitan area during the middle of the twentieth century. While individuals from the small Hispanic population assumed leadership roles and began to organize as a community, they also collaborated with African-American leaders and neighborhood activists. Living side by side in a city that, like other major US cities,[44] was experiencing a period

---

"US Population"; Pew Hispanic Center, "US Hispanic Country-of-Origin Counts."

39. For background and demographics of the Washington Metropolitan area, see Suro, "Latino Growth"; Pew Hispanic Center, "US Population"; Pew Hispanic Center, "US Hispanic Country-of-Origin Counts"; Pew Hispanic Center, "Characteristics"; Pew Hispanic Center, "Hispanic Student Enrollments Reach New Highs"; Cristian, *Who are We?*; and De La Torre, *Hispanic American Religious Cultures*.

40. Pew Hispanic Center, US Hispanic Country-of-Origin Counts," 4, 6; US Department of Commerce, "Hispanic Population."

41. Pew Hispanic Center, "Characteristics," 4.

42. De La Torre, *Hispanic American Religious Cultures*, xv.

43. De La Torre, *Hispanic American Religious Cultures*, xv.

44. Cadaval, "Latino Community," conducted an ethnographic research in Adams-Morgan & Mount Pleasant districts in Washington DC area.

of economic and physical decline, residents from the African-American community and some Hispanic leaders began to organize neighborhood-based commissions and service agencies.[45]

1.4 ISLAM IN THE WEST

There are current debates among Muslims in Europe and the United States on the nature of Muslim minorities in the West. Some Muslim traditional scholars concentrate on the universalism of Islam, that is, there is only one Islam. In general, these Muslim traditional scholars consider that there is no need for contextualizing or adjusting the law for Muslim minorities who are living in non-Muslim countries. Following the *Salafiyya* approach, they are against any jurisprudence (*fiqh*) for Muslim minorities and are in conflict with modernity.[46] Muslim traditional scholars are largely opposed to any local variation on Islamic law based on local praxis.

Conversely, modernist Muslim scholars argue that Muslims in the West are not merely a transplant but are active creators of authentic local expressions of Islam.[47] These modernist Muslim scholars are in favor of jurisprudence for Muslim minorities and *Wassatiyya*. Arguably, their approach is more focused on "centricism" instead of universalistic "one Islam."[48] In general, these modern scholars are in favor of modernity.[49] For a summary of the similarities and differences between these two approaches, see Appendix 1.[50]

---

45. Cadaval, "Latino Community," 236–37.
46. Brown, "After the Ramadan Affair," 7–29.
47. Al-Qaradawi, *Lawful and the Prohibited*, 7.
48. Yusuf Al-Qaradawi is the co-founder of *fiqh al-Aqalliyyat* (*fiqh* of minorities) and *wasatiyya* (centrism) alternative interpretations that laid the foundation for the developments of *fiqh* for Muslim minorities. For more details about the *Fiqh and Wasatiyya* approaches, see Al-Qaradawi, *Lawful and the Prohibited*; Fishman, *Fiqh al-Aqalliyyat*.
49. There are many Muslims who adhere to principles described collectively as "reformed Islam." This is defined by moderation and centrism (*Wasatiyya*) in beliefs and practice.
50. These similarities and differences between these two approaches are based on Ghatas's 2013 findings. Ghatas, "Muslims in Europe?," followed the works of Al-Azmeh and Fokas, *Islam in Europe*; Brunner, "Forms Forms of Muslim Self-Perception"; March, "Sources of Moral Obligation"; Khan, "Islam and the New Europe"; and Shavit, "Wasati and Salafi Approaches."

1.5 BACKGROUND AND MAIN PROBLEMS IN CONVERSION STUDIES

One of the main problems in conversion studies is related to the meaning of conversion itself. The definition of conversion remains a difficult problem among scholars; however, the definition used by many scholars of religion implies a "change in one's system of beliefs."[51] Lewis Rambo, for example, defines a religious conversion as "a process of religious change that takes place in a dynamic field of people, events, ideologies, institutions and orientations."[52] Henri Gooren defines conversion "as a comprehensive personal change of religious worldview and identity, based on both self-report and attribution by others."[53]

According to Stark and Finke, "Religious conversion is the adoption of a new religion that differs from the convert's previous religion."[54] However, this definition does not take into consideration that conversion is a process.[55]

The reason for choosing Rambo and Gooren's definitions is that both definitions include important aspects of conversion: it is a process, and a degree of change occurs in this process. In Gooren's research on religious conversion and disaffiliation, he uses the term "conversion career," which he defines as, "the member's passage, within his or her social and cultural context, through levels, types and phases of religious participation."[56] Conversion career conveys the process that individuals experience at different stages. Therefore, one needs to differentiate conversion from conversion career.

Because conversion is a process that takes place over time, the role of socialization needs to be considered as well.[57] Separating conversion from socialization is unwise. It is important to consider the influence of socialization in the process of conversion. I argue that it is necessary to combine the two models, paying special attention to the response of the converts.

In this research, conversion is understood as a "dynamic and complex personal process of religious change that usually implies the construction of

---

51. Buckser and Glazier, *Anthropology of Religious Conversion*, 136.
52. Rambo, *Understanding Religious Conversion*, 5.
53. Gooren, *Religious Conversion and Disaffiliation*, 3.
54. Stark and Finke, *Acts of Faith*, 114–15.
55. For additional definitions of conversion, see Paloutzian et al., "Religious Conversion and Personality Change"; Rambo, *Understanding Religious Conversion*; Snow and Machalek, "Sociology of Conversion."
56. Droogers et al., "Conversion Careers and Culture Politics," 4.
57. Greil "What Have We Learned?"; Lofland and Stark, "Becoming a World-Saver"; Long and Hadden, "Religious Conversion."

new identities, and also the adoption of new values and beliefs." Thus, my description of conversion is partially influenced by Rambo and Gooren's definitions. However, I will use the term "conversion" in a broader sense in my study. Here, the definition of conversion encompasses Gooren's stage of affiliation: becoming a formal member "without change of identity."[58] In addition, "conversion" encompasses pre/post-affiliation stages, with a particular emphasis on the post-affiliation stage.

The theological legacy of Christian hegemony means that the word "conversion" is generally limited to notions of radical, sudden change.[59] "Evangelical Christians have tended to 'own' the concept for several hundred years, and most conversations about conversion—whether on a popular or scholarly level—are confined to the Pauline paradigm of sudden, dramatic change."[60] However, some scholars consider the Pauline model too restrictive and have supported discarding the word "conversion" in general.[61]

It is also significant to make a distinction between conversion and reaffiliation. Religious conversion is the adoption of a new religion that differs from the convert's previous religion. Changing from one denomination to another within the same religion is usually described as *reaffiliation* rather than *conversion*.[62] According to Stark and Finke, conversion refers to shifts across religious traditions. Lewis Rambo sees "genuine conversion

---

58. Gooren ("Conversion Narratives") proposes that it is necessary to develop a typology of religious activity that includes more dimensions than just disaffiliation and conversion, a typology of religious activity based on a review of existing literature from psychology, social and cultural anthropology, sociology, and religious studies (Bromley and Shupe, "Just A Few Years"; Gooren, "Reconsidering Protestant Growth in Guatemala"; Long and Hadden, "Religious Conversion"; Rambo, *Understanding Religious Conversion*). The five primary dynamic levels of individual religious participation are: 1) Pre-affiliation: the life situation and worldview of person before affiliation or conversion; church term: visitor. 2) Affiliation: Formal membership in a religious group, without change of identity; church term: Member, or baptized member. 3) Conversion: In the limited sense of the conversion career approach, a (radical) change of religious identity, followed by a commitment to a (new) religious group; church term: convert, full member, baptized member. 4) Confession: a core member identity with a high level of participation inside the (new) religious community and a strong evangelism on the outside; church term: leader, core member, deacon, missionary. 5) Disaffiliation (Deconversion): no church membership or visits; church term: inactive member, seeker, unchurched Christian.

59. For a critique of this, see Buckser and Gazier, *Anthropology of Religious Conversion*, especially the chapters by Buckser (ch. 6), Coleman (ch. 2), Farhadian (ch. 5), Glazier (ch. 12), and Reidhead and Reidhead (ch. 14).

60. Buckser and Gazier, *Anthropology of Religious Conversion*, 213.

61. Long and Hadden, "Religious Conversion," 1–14; Richardson, *Conversion Careers*.

62. Stark and Finke, *Acts of Faith*, 114.

as a total transformation of the person by the power of God."[63] Although transformation occurs through the mediation of social, cultural, personal, and religious forces, according to Rambo, "conversion needs to be radical, striking to the root of human predicament."[64]

An additional challenge in conversion studies is to consider whether all changes are related to conversion. Not all religious change is necessarily conversion.[65] In this study, some of the participants might argue that they have not experienced a substantial change regarding their former identities, and there are different levels of change after conversion. I will further explore this dynamic in subsequent chapters. All participants in this study did experience some degree of change. The levels of participation and commitment in the new religion were diverse. In this study, I will use the terms "conversion" and "religious conversion" interchangeably.

Some scholars describe different kinds of conversion: *intellectual conversion* (related to change in beliefs), *moral conversion* (where there is a change in motivation toward morally relevant behavior), and *social conversion* (with changes in actions toward social environment).[66] Falkenberg also mentions *sudden, gradual* conversion, and *religious socialization*. Other types of conversion include active conversion, secondary conversion, deathbed conversion, conversion for convenience, marital conversion, and forced conversion.

There are several lenses for studying conversion. For example, Richardson points out that the conversion studies earlier in the twentieth century were from a psychological perspective. However, Thumma states that "presently a social-psychological orientation dominates the majority of theoretical work."[67] Thumma also states that "the phenomenon of conversion should be re-examined in a broader context, using the historical, cultural, and theological perspectives."[68]

Kuburic and Sremac's *Conversion and its Context* compiles a great variety of articles.[69] The collected articles are divided into two parts: Psycho-Social Approaches to Religious Conversion and Theological-Anthropological

---

63. Rambo, *Understanding Religious Conversion*, xii.
64. Rambo, *Understanding Religious Conversion*, xii.
65. Wohlrab-Sahr, "Symbolizing Distance," 74.
66. Falkenberg, *Psychological Explanations of Religious Socialization*, 2.
67. Thumma, "Seeking to Be Converted," 190.
68. Thumma, "Seeking to Be Converted," 185.
69. For detailed information see Kuburic and Sremac, "Conversion and its Context."

Approaches to Religious Conversion, which are comprised of fifteen texts of different authors.[70]

In addition, the emphasis on concentrated approaches in conversion studies is also problematic. First, clinical psychologists and psychiatrists have used a model of conversion called the *brainwashing model*.[71] According to this view,

> cult members use coercive means and deprivation to exercise mind control over new converts, 'stripping' their previous identities, neutralizing their powers of will, creating dependence on the cult, and programming them with cult beliefs, etc. Converts are thought to be so radically and permanently transformed that only 'deprogramming' will sever their allegiance to the cult.[72]

Traditionally, psychologists and psychiatrists have focused on institutional agencies and agents of change such as pastors, priests, and imams. Conversely, sociologists and anthropologists have focused on the responses and roles of the converts.

The other model that has been implemented is the *social drift* model,[73] a designation stimulated by Matza's image of "delinquent drift."[74] The social drift model proposes that people become converts progressively through the influence of social relationships, particularly during times of personal pressure. Consequently, socialization plays an important role in the process of conversion. "Conversion is viewed as precarious and open to change in response to shifting patterns of association."[75]

The problem with the latter model is that even though it recognizes the active involvement of the convert, it largely misses the role played by the individual in making strategic choices, as well as the changing local expressions of Islam in the United States. Here, special attention will be given to individuals without ignoring institutional agency.

There is a need to broaden the approach in conversion studies, particularly on the conversion of Hispanics from Catholicism to other faith positions, including Islam. The current research tells us something about

---

70. Kuburic and Sremac, "Conversion and its Context," 317–20.

71. Schein et al., *Coercive Persuasion*; Enroth, *Youth, Brainwashing, and the Extremist Cults*; Stoner and Parke, *All God's Children*; Conway and Siegelman, *Snapping*; Clark, "Cults"; Singer, "Coming Out of the Cults."

72. Long and Hadden, "Religious Conversion," 1.

73. First developed by Lofland and Stark.

74. Matza, *Delinquency and Drift*, 1.

75. Long and Hadden, "Religious Conversion," 1.

their conversion to Islam but uses only particular lenses, such as social or cultural ones, or focuses only on one area of the US.[76]

1.6 APPROACH AND THEORIES TO BE CONSIDERED

Researchers have focused primarily on their specific fields, not considering important aspects from other fields that will help to better understand conversion as a dynamic process. I argue that it is paramount to use a multidisciplinary approach combining psychology, social and cultural anthropology, and religious studies.[77] Therefore, I will use a multidisciplinary approach in my research. I will concentrate on the role of the converts without ignoring the role and agency of the imams.

In order to adopt a more balanced ontological/epistemological and methodological approach,[78] I will also consider the following theories based on a survey of literature: religious market,[79] rational choice,[80] socialization and network theory,[81] social constructivism,[82] and role model.[83] Gooren proposes an alternative use of the religious market theory: "This alternative links the options individuals find on the religious market with socialization and role model theory from the conversion approaches."[84]

---

76. Bowen, *Conversion to Islam in Colorado*, analyses the conversion to Islam in Denver, Colorado. He interviewed thirteen converts: white, Latino, and Black, including eight females and five males.

77. Gooren "Conversion Narratives"; Rambo, *Understanding Religious Conversion*; Thumma, "Seeking to Be Converted."

78. For detailed information about these theories, see Gooren, "Conversion Careers in Latin America"; Gooren, "Conversion Narratives"; Gooren, "Conversion Careers and Culture Politics"; Stark and Finke, *Acts of Faith*; Thumma, "Seeking to Be Converted." For feminist ethnography, see Bryman, *Social Research Methods*, 423–24; feminist research and interviewing, see Bryman, *Social Research Methods*, 463–65; and feminist theory, see Patton, *Qualitative Research & Evaluation Methods*, 65, 129–30, 132–33, 549). See also DeWalt and DeWalt, *Participant Observation*, 99–108.

79. Gartrell and Shannon, "Contacts, Cognitions, and Conversion"; Gooren, "Religious Market Model"; Gooren, "Conversion Narratives"; Houtepen, "Conversion and the Religious Market"; Stark and Finke, *Acts of Faith*.

80. Iannaccone, "Voodoo Economics?"; Stark and Finke, *Acts of Faith*.

81. Greil, "What Have We Learned?"; Lofland and Stark, "Becoming a World-Saver"; Long, *Development Sociology*; Long and Hadden, "Religious Conversion."

82. Beckford, "Accounting for Conversion"; Berger, *Sacred Canopy*; Searle, *Construction of Social Reality*; Snow and Machalek, "Sociology of Conversion."

83. Bromley and Shupe, "Just A Few Years."

84. Gooren, *Religious Conversion and Disaffiliation*, 18.

For the purpose of this research, I will pay particular attention to Rambo's model and the conversion career approach proposed by Gooren. The term "conversion career" was first coined by James Richardson, but for Richardson it only referred to serial conversions. Then, Henry Gooren gave new meaning by distinguishing levels of religious participation, identifying five groups of factors involved, and synthesizing the relevant literature on conversion from anthropology, sociology, psychology, history, mission studies, religious studies, and theology.[85]

The conversion career is "the member's passage, within his or her social and cultural context, through levels, types and phases of religious participation."[86] This approach represents a systematic attempt to analyze shifts in levels of individual religious activity: pre-affiliation, affiliation, conversion, confession, and disaffiliation. Gooren suggests that "the key elements of this new approach are: a five-level typology of religious activity, the need for a life cycle approach, and a systematic analysis of the many factors influencing changes in individual religious activity: contingency, individual, cultural, institutional, and social factors."[87]

I will follow Gooren's typology with a minor distinction. I will use "pre-affiliation," "affiliation," "conversion," and "high commitment" instead of the term "confession." Since my focus is on affiliation and conversion, I will not use the disaffiliation stage in this study. Here, the term "conversion" is used in a broader sense and encompasses affiliation.

I will follow Rambo's suggestions of using a multidisciplinary approach focusing on personal, social, cultural, and religious contextual factors. Here, the contextual factors will be considered in the analysis throughout all the stages. I also argue that it is necessary to pay special attention to gender, generational aspects, and previous religious background to analyze the differences and similarities between individuals. Few researchers have focused particularly on the analysis of generational differences, while also considering the previous religious background of the converts.

1.7 RATIONALE AND NEED

The rationale for this research stems from the desire to understand the dynamics and challenges among Hispanics who follow Islam in the United States. Already members of a minority culture, Hispanic Muslim converts are also willing to embrace Islam as another minority in a non-Muslim country.

---

85. Gooren, *Religious Conversion and Disaffiliation*, 143.
86. Droogers et al., "Conversion Careers and Culture Politics," 4.
87. Droogers et al., "Conversion Careers and Culture Politics," 48.

The following are some of the main reasons why this study is relevant today. First, a good number of the existing studies on conversion in the United States focus on New Religious Movements (NRMs), "which is a very small proportion of religions in the United States."[88] According to the Pew Forum 2008, members of NRMs make up only 1.2 percent of the population.[89]

Second, most of the research on Hispanic religious conversion in the United States has been journalistic: "Academic writing on the topic is still fairly minimal and mention of Latino Muslims has largely only been in the context of other topics."[90]

Third, it appears, based on recent sources, the Hispanics (religiously Catholic) in America are finding Islam as a particularly attractive option.[91] As Galván points out, "Most Latino converts are former Catholics who had difficulty with the church hierarchy, which has no counterpart in Islam, and the concepts of Original Sin and the Holy Trinity."[92] The difficulty is largely related to the different roles in leadership: bishops, priests, and so on. Nevertheless, more academic research needs to be done to better understand the nature and extent of the conversion to Islam. For example, what is the role of socialization in the conversion process?

Fourth, it is important to consider the role of domestic religions in the life of immigrants: "Domestic religion plays an important role in the lives of immigrants. For many, home is the cornerstone of religious identity, the setting where personal faith is practiced, expressed, transmitted, and transformed."[93] How do Hispanic Muslim converts practice their faith in the United States?

1.8 RESEARCH PROBLEM AND LIMITATIONS

As stated before, the central research question in this study is to examine the nuances of the role that Hispanic Muslim converts play in making different choices concerning religious commitment and practice in a Muslim minority context, as it is the case in the United States. This proposed study will not treat in depth important theological questions that will emerge for the interviews. Even though these theological questions will be briefly

---

88. Thumma, "Seeking to Be Converted," 189.
89. Pew Forum on Religion & Public Life, "US Religious Landscape Survey," 11.
90. Bowen, "Early US Latina/o-African-American Muslim Connections," 390.
91. Martínez-Vasquez, *Latina/o y Musulmán*, 3.
92. Sánchez and Galván, "Latino Muslims," 27.
93. Mazumdar and Mazumdar, "Articulation of Religion," 74.

described in this study, special consideration will be given to social, cultural, and religious contexts.

There is also a limitation in terms of the different theories that have been used in conversion studies. Most of these theories will not be analyzed in depth. The researcher will focus on socialization and social network theories. There are also limitations regarding data and the number of informants who participated in this research. Gender and generational aspects are discussed in this study, but additional studies need to be done to examine in depth significant similarities and differences regarding the implications of gender and generational factors that play a relevant role in conversion processes. In addition, observations and applications related to Hispanic Muslims are based on the specific locations and contexts in which these conversions took place. Thus, observations and implications to other Muslim minorities in different locations in the United States need to be done carefully.

The conclusions of this study cannot be largely generalized for application in other North American countries such as Mexico or Canada, nor in other countries where there are Muslim minorities with different historical, social, and religious backgrounds. However, insight might be provided for analysis of other cultural contexts. Primary application will be for both Muslim minorities who are living in the United States and for Christians who are serving the Muslim community in different areas, such as interfaith dialogue.

Finally, in no way does this study pretend that the choices Hispanic Muslim converts make in these locations in the United States are always intentional. These choices are shaped by multiple factors. The themes studied in this research—including choices, identity, and religious commitment and practice—are complex. The nuances and processes are far more complex than the scope of this project. Religious conversion is a fluid and dynamic process.

1.9 RESEARCH QUESTIONS

The central question of this research is: *To what extent do Hispanic Muslim converts make different choices regarding religious commitment and practice in the United States?* In order to answer this question, it is necessary to address the following: What role do Hispanic Muslim converts play in different conversion motifs? What are the most significant contextual factors? These questions will be addressed in chapter 2. Then, the following questions will be addressed in chapter 3: What are the choices that converts make regarding the words they used in different types of conversion narratives? What are the predominant discourses?

Another important question related to the central question is: What are the factors that shape the evolving Hispanic Muslim identity? Also, what are the most significant changes that occur during post-affiliation? These questions about choices and identity will be addressed in chapter 4. Then, the central question will be addressed in chapter 5: To what extent do Hispanic Muslim converts make different choices concerning religious commitment and practice in the United States? In addition, the following questions will be addressed in that chapter: What are the nuances of religious commitment and practice of Hispanic Muslim converts? Is it possible for individuals labeled as "low committed" or "moderately committed" to show reasonable or high commitment in some of the dimensions of religiosity? I use the term "convert" in this research to refer to the individuals who converted to Islam. Based on their own perspective, they considered themselves followers of Islam. Thus, I make no distinction between affiliation and conversion.

1.10 RESEARCH METHODOLOGY AND METHODS

This is a qualitative study that includes an in-depth analysis of the conversions within specific contexts, paying attention to the causal mechanisms and providing subjective meaning by privileging the voices and experiences of the converts. I will use different models and theories to interpret the data and will draw from different sources such as demographic surveys, interviews, and field notes to enrich the analysis of the cases. See Appendix 2 for demographic information, such as age, country of birth, religious background, occupation, and education levels of the converts and their parents.[94] Additional questions about language preference, use of the Internet, and identity preference were included and will be used in subsequent chapters to validate some of the information that converts provided during the interviews.

I will use biographical data and conversion narratives to do a comparative analysis approach using a multiple-case, holistic design based on the categories that emerge from the data.[95] See Table 1 for more details about the strategy that will be implemented for comparing and contrasting the selected cases.

---

94. Cuartas/Catalina DS 2012. Demographic Survey conducted by Victor H. Cuartas, 25 February, 2012. Cuartas/Lucia DS 2012. Demographic Survey conducted by Victor H. Cuartas, 13 February, 2012. Cuartas/Martina DS 2012. Demographic Survey conducted by Victor H. Cuartas, 29 February, 2012. Cuartas/Simón DS 2012. Demographic Survey by Victor H. Cuartas, 11 February, 2012.

95. Yin, *Case Study Research: 4th ed.*, 46–47.

Van Nieuwkerk outlines two main approaches to conversion studies: the functional approach and the discourse analysis approach.[96] The functional approach looks at what conversion means in the context of a person's life. The discourse analysis approach looks at how discourses are created and how they achieve their effect.[97] I will follow Van Nieuwkerk's suggestion of combining these two approaches because it enables the researcher to arrive at a more complete understanding of the phenomenon of conversion. Chapter 2 will focus on what conversion means in the context of the selected cases, looking at similarities and differences between these cases. Chapter 3 will describe and analyze how the discourses are created by the converts with a special emphasis on identity construction and strategic choices converts make.[98]

I follow Yin's recommendation of identifying "ideal cases" because it reflects the boundaries of the topic. I have labeled Martina's case as a near "ideal case" because I am analyzing agency and the role of the converts, conversion motifs, and additional variables. This case is a good example of a theoretical construct to develop my argument. Martina was very active during her process of conversion, and her conversion was very intellectual. In addition, it shows the different responses to Islam of the second-generation

---

96. Van Nieuwkerk, "Gender and Conversion to Islam," 10.

97. Zebiri, *British Muslim Converts*, 7.

98. I also follow Kramp's recommendations to analyze the case studies (Kramp, "Exploring Life and Experience," 17). The case stories are the basic unit based on narrative reasoning. Case studies are an example of narrative analysis. The narratives are constructed using the data gathered from the interviews, field notes, and the transcriptions. The story the researcher writes "must fit the data while at the same time bringing an order and meaningfulness that is not apparent in the data themselves" (Polkinghorne, "Narrative Configuration in Qualitative Analysis," 16). Attending to the characteristics of a narrative—plot, setting, characters—researchers construct a story in which the data is integrated.

Hispanics in the United States.[99] I will use pseudonyms in my study.[100] These will be Hispanic names because the selected individuals in this chapter did not change their names after conversion.

1.10.1 Interviews

I have conducted a total of fifty-six interviews, including individual, group, and focus group interviews. I interviewed twenty-five Hispanic converts, fifteen women and ten men. I also interviewed three Hispanics—two men and one woman—who were raised in Muslim families, to better understand the dynamics of Hispanic Muslims in the United States. These Hispanic Muslims (who grew up as Muslims) can reveal important aspects in terms of their role in the socialization process and how they involved other Hispanic converts. Furthermore, I interviewed six imams and two Muslim community leaders from different Islamic centers. In addition, twenty Muslim informant—including six non-Hispanic Muslim converts, two Muslim community leaders, and twelve born-Muslims—participated in focus groups.

I used snowball sampling. With this approach to sampling, "the researcher makes initial contact with a small group of people who are relevant to the research topic and then use these to establish contact with others."[101]

The focus in the interviews is to analyze people's life stories.[102] The point was to listen to their stories beginning with their life previous to conversion,

---

99. I was influenced by Yin (*Case Study Research: 4th ed*) and Miles and Huberman (*Qualitative Data Analysis*). They propose three different types of cases: ideal, unique, and typical. 1) An ideal case reflects a delimitation of the topic. In my case, I am analyzing agency and the role of the converts, conversion motifs, and additional variables. I labeled Martina's case as a near "ideal" case because it allows me to analyze different aspects regarding her individual agency and her active role in her conversion. 2) A unique case is one that shows a different angle and offers a different perspective to the topic being studied. In my case, I have labeled Catalina's case as a near "unique" case because it shows a different angle and response during her process of conversion. She had a passive role and was very motivated by personal and social factors. 3) A typical case refers to common responses of the converts. I labeled Simon's case as a "typical" case because it highlights normal, common characteristics and responses during the conversion process. His role was a combination of passive/active, and he was very influenced by Muslim friends. I will do case pairing between Martina and Lucia to be able to find more generalizations. There are some similarities between Martina and Lucía with regard to active agency and conversion motifs. For more details about types of cases, see to Yin, *Case Study Research: 4th ed*, 47–48; Miles and Huberman, *Qualitative Data Analysis*. See also Prevette, *Child, Church and Compassion*, 116–17.

100. Fetterman, *Ethnography*, 142–43.

101. Bryman, *Social Research Methods*, 184.

102. Bryman, *Social Research Methods*, 440–41; Fetterman, *Ethnography*, 53–54.

the process and circumstances leading up to conversion, the narrative and conversion experience, and the events that occurred after their conversion.

This research is a qualitative study, and some of the methodology implemented in the study includes semi-structured and in-depth interviews, a demographic survey, fieldwork, field notes, and observations.[103] The interviews usually took between fifty and ninety minutes each. I also attended five Friday prayers and spent an average of ninety minutes during each visit. Some of the interviews were transcribed by volunteers. I then coded the interviews using topics coding. After I finished the transcriptions, I numbered the pages and used the F4 software program that has the capability of creating time stamps to retrieve specific data from mapped locations when necessary.[104] This method facilitated the process of including specific quotes in my references.

1.10.2 Demographic Survey

A survey of demographic information, in conjunction with the interview findings, served as an instrument to include relevant information to better understand the process of conversion to Islam among Hispanics in the United States. I began the process by asking the respondents to complete the demographic survey. I was able to clarify some points to make sure that the respondents understood and completed all the questions.[105]

A total of twenty-seven individuals completed the demographic survey. There are two Hispanic Muslim women who still need to complete the demographic survey.[106] Demographic variables such as gender, age, religious background, and education are important social categories that help to account for people's decision to join social and religious movements.[107]

The instruments were available in both English and Spanish. When I asked for the language of preference to complete the demographic survey,

---

103. Bernard, *Research Methods in Anthropology*; DeWalt and DeWalt, *Participant Observation*; Fetterman, *Ethnography*.

104. F4 transcription software is compatible with Atlas TI software. Time markers from the transcript are automatically converted to association anchors. The connected audio or video file is also imported.

105. Smith, *Islam in America*; Tinaz, "Conversion Conversion of African Americans to Islam."

106. Three Hispanic Muslims who grew up in Muslim families are included in this section. They are second-generation Hispanics. Second-generation signifies a person that was born in the United States with at least one foreign-born parent. They are US Citizens by birth (Pew Hispanic Center, "Generational," "Rise").

107. Tinaz, "Conversion Conversion of African Americans to Islam," 267–68.

only four of the respondents preferred to have the survey in Spanish rather than English. Therefore, I also asked the participants about their language preference during the interview. Some Hispanics are fluent in both languages. However, some of them speak very well, but they do not feel comfortable writing in Spanish. Thus, some of the interviews were also conducted in Spanish.

The participants had the opportunity to choose the language of preference to complete the demographic survey and do the interview. I asked the respondents what language they speak and write. They were given different options: Spanish, English, Arabic, and other languages. The respondents had to rank their fluency level by choosing one of the following: fluent, familiar, or none. In my sample, nineteen out of twenty-seven respondents were fluent in Spanish (70.4 perent); eight respondents were familiar with Spanish. In terms of the English language, almost all the participants were fluent in English (96.3 percent). Only one respondent reported that he was not fluent in English. In addition, eleven out of twenty-seven respondents (41 percent) were familiar with Arabic. Some of the respondents also mentioned having some degree of knowledge of other languages such as German, Portuguese, and Turkish.

1.10.3 Gender

Gender is an important aspect in religious conversion studies. "Gender not only intersects with the freedom and reasons to convert, but also with the effects of conversion. It affects the ways in which the person expresses and incorporates his or her new beliefs, and how others react to that."[108]

The sample includes twenty-four Hispanic Muslim converts: fourteen women and ten men. Most of Hispanic Muslim converts are women. This reality is also observed in several studies done with Muslim converts.[109] I found in my research that women were generally more willing to share their stories than men (especially when the men's wives were present).

According to van Nieuwkerk, "Female converts to Islam are confronted with a larger gap than men in the gender positions in the respective religious cultures. A Christian woman converting to Islam has to give up more freedoms (as defined by her culture of birth) than a man."[110] I believe that

---

108. Van Nieuwkerk, "Gender and Conversion to Islam," xii.

109. Bowen, "Conversion to Islam in Colorado," King, "Latina Muslims," Martínez-Vásquez *Latina/o*; McCloud, *African American Islam*; and van Nieuwkerk "Gender and Conversion to Islam."

110. van Nieuwkerk, "Gender and Conversion to Islam," xii.

this is also true in the conversion of Hispanic women. They usually have more pressure from their families in terms of higher expectations to follow the religion and practices of the parents. When they decide to leave their traditional faith (in most cases, Catholicism), they can experience rejection and isolation.

I occasionally had difficulties interviewing some Hispanic Muslim women. For example, one of the Hispanic Muslim women was very willing to do the interview at the beginning; she even helped to set up appointments with other Hispanic Muslim women. Nevertheless, she has not replied to my emails lately, nor has she answered my phone calls. Therefore, this interview is still pending.

However, I was able to interview twelve Hispanic Muslim men, including two who were raised as Muslims. One of the challenges was to find Hispanic Muslim men who were willing to share their stories of conversion. Three men refused to participate in the interviews, but some of them were willing to provide contacts for potential interviews. I found later that one of the Hispanic Muslim men was very shy, hence the reason why he did not want to share his story of conversion.

1.10.4 Generational Aspects

Most of the participants are second-generation Hispanics, meaning that at least one of their parents was born in the United States. Only four converts are labelled as first-generation Hispanics. They came as adults from Latin American countries such as Bolivia, Panama, Peru, and Venezuela.

I will analyze in subsequent chapters some similarities and differences in terms of the different generations. The average age of the converts at the time of their interview was thirty-two. The age ranged between nineteen and seventy-four. The average age when the individual became a Muslim was twenty-two years old. The average time span in Islam of those who converted was ten years (e.g., how long they have been a Muslim thus far since conversion). The average time span it took to become a Muslim was almost three and a half years: the time from when they were first interested to when they converted.

Sánchez and Galván find in their study on Hispanic Muslims that the majority of converts were college-educated women between the ages of twenty and thirty.[111] There are some similarities in my findings. The average age of the converts was thirty-two. The average age when the individual became a Muslim was twenty-two years old. The difference is that my study

---

111. Sánchez and Sánchez and Galván, "Latino Muslims," 22–30.

also includes a good number of Hispanic Muslim men. In addition, the age range in my study is wider since it includes converts between nineteen and seventy-four.

1.10.5 Religious Background

Most of the converts have a Catholic background. However, three individuals have a non-Catholic background, coming instead from Baptist, Episcopalian, and Pentecostal backgrounds. The levels of commitment of the converts in previous religions varied. In addition, the parents of the converts reported different levels of commitment. Overall, the mothers of the converts were more involved at their churches than were the fathers. This is an important aspect, comparing and contrasting the role of the converts and their participation and commitment to previous religions and in the new religion. I will analyze these aspects in subsequent chapters.

1.10.6 Educational Level

The variables included in this section are the following: elementary, high school, associate degree, college degree, master's degree, and doctorate. The majority of the converts were college-educated. Only six out of twenty-seven respondents (22 percent) reported that a high school diploma was their maximum level of education. Some of them have attained associate degrees. This is similar to Sánchez and Galvan's findings. In their research, the majority of the converts were college-educated women.[112] In addition, I found that there were only five respondents out of twenty-seven (18.5 percent) that were currently studying at any level. Also, none of the participants have completed a master's or doctorate program.

1.11 RATIONALE FOR CHOOSING CASE STUDIES

A case study is known as a triangulated research strategy to enhance the validity of the study. Thus, I chose these cases for various reasons, because I was trying to get a wide range of actions and interactions with their conversion stories. I follow Stake's suggestions for selecting cases: Is the case relevant to the study? Do the cases provide diversity across contexts? Do the cases provide good opportunities to learn about complexity and contexts?[113]

---

112. Sánchez and Sánchez and Galván, "Latino Muslims," 25.
113. Stake, "Qualitative Case Studies," 23.

The same rationale will be used in chapters 2 and 3. I will choose selected cases to show the wide range of responses of the converts.[114]

1.12 LAYERS TO BE USED

I will use the following layers to answer the research questions and to resolve the problem of the study: content, context, validity, and reliability. The content will be drawn from interviews, demographic surveys, field notes, paying attention to the biographical data, and conversion narratives.

The context will be considered throughout the analysis of the cases. Thus, these conversions need to be understood within their particular contexts. I will use an interdisciplinary approach suggested by Rambo.[115] I will focus on personal, social, cultural, and religious factors that are significant for the individuals. In subsequent chapters, I will also include some theories and models to make sense of the findings.

Validity and reliability are very important elements for evaluating the quality of research designs. Validity and reliability help researchers to identify correct operational measures for the concepts studied. Kidder and Judd[116] recommend the following aspects to establish the quality of empirical research: 1) construct validity; 2) internal validity; 3) external validity; and 4) reliability. The following are important factors to construct validity: a) use multiple sources of evidence; and b) establish a chain of evidence.[117]

I will draw from several sources such as interviews conducted with converts, field notes, and demographic surveys. I will use pattern matching techniques for the case study analysis. I labelled Martina as an ideal case. The other selected cases will be compared with Martina's story. Thus, this will help to construct internal validity.[118]

Kidder and Judd[119] also make a distinction between internal and external validity. Internal validity is useful for explanatory or causal studies only and not for descriptive or exploratory cases. Explanatory cases seek to

---

114. For additional information about criteria for selecting cases, see also Creswell, *Qualitative Inquiry & Research Design*; Patton, Patton, *Qualitative Research & Evaluation Methods*; Prevette, *Child, Church and Compassion*; Yin, *Case Study Research 4th ed.*

115. Rambo, *Understanding Religious Conversion*, 103–4.

116. Kidder and Judd, *Research Methods in Social Relations*, 26–29.

117. Cited in Yin, "*Case Study Research 4th ed.*," 40–41.

118. See Yin, *Case Study Research 4th ed.*, 136–37 for more details about pattern matching.

119. Kidder and Judd, *Research Methods in Social Relations*, 32–36.

establish a causal relationship.[120] External validity helps to define the domain to which a study's findings can be generalized.

Reliability is also important to demonstrate that the procedures of the data collection can be repeated with the same results. I follow Yin's suggestions for case study tactics to construct internal and external validity and reliability as well. I developed a protocol for the interview guide. Consent forms were also signed by the participants. I include here details and information about the interviews, ethics and consent forms.[121] Having established the methodological aspects of my research, I turn to my findings in the next chapters.

1.13 ORGANIZATION OF CHAPTERS

In the following chapter, I explore the background of the Hispanic Muslim converts, looking at the role that Hispanic Muslim converts play in making choices in different conversion motifs. Special attention is given to the significant contextual factors that shape these choices. This chapter shows the complex-yet-dynamic interplay of several factors that shape the process leading up to conversion.

The rest of the chapters focus on the agency and choices that converts make at different levels by looking at the conversion narratives in chapter 3 and the choices that converts make during the post-affiliation stage, and by analyzing the changes that take place and the evolving Hispanic Muslim identify in chapter 4. The final chapter addresses the central question of the study, focusing on the diverse choices of Hispanic Muslim converts concerning their religious commitment and practice in the United States.

Contextual factors—including social, cultural, and religious factors—are considered in each chapter. In addition, selected cases are presented in chapters 2–4, and all the cases are brought together in the final chapter to facilitate the analysis of this study. Each chapter identifies patterns and emerging themes from the data.

---

120. This is a typology suggested by Yin, *Applications of Case Study Research, 3rd ed.*
121. Yin, *Case Study Research 4th ed.*, 41.

Chapter 2

Pre-affiliation Stage and Background of Hispanic Muslim Converts

2.1 INTRODUCTION

The main argument in this chapter is that there is an individual agency of and an active role played by the converts in making strategic choices in the process leading up to a conversion. My intention is to show the role of the converts in making these choices and the complex-yet-dynamic interplay of multiple factors that shape the process leading up to a conversion (i.e., there is not a single factor that influences this process).

In this chapter, I will focus on the following questions: What is the extent to which Hispanic Muslim converts play a significant role in making choices in different types of conversion motifs, and what are the most significant factors that shape these choices? The central research question here is: What role do Hispanic Muslim converts play in fashioning their local Islamic identity in the US? To answer this question, it is necessary to address preliminary questions regarding the active role Hispanic Muslim converts play in making choices in diverse types of conversion motives, as well as the significant factors that shape these choices. These questions will be addressed in this chapter.

My expectation is that this initial analysis will lead me to a better understanding of the choices that converts make in terms of their identity constructions and the changes during the post-affiliation stage (in chapter 4). This will lead to an analysis of the extent to which the converts are making choices regarding religious commitment and practice in these geographical locations in the United States (in chapter 5).

My purpose is to provide a clearer understanding of the ways in which individual agency of the converts plays out in the process of making choices during the stages leading up to a conversion.[1] The choices of these individuals come into sharper focus through their intersections with multiple factors within particular contexts.

This chapter will critically compare four cases using a multiple-case holistic design based on the categories that emerge from the data. The following are the selected cases: Martina, Catalina, Simón, and Lucía, with special emphasis on Martina to create a contrast due to her religious background and more active agency in the conversion process. The most significant differences and similarities between Martina and the other cases will be identified and analyzed using specific categories to facilitate the analysis.

The following layers will be used to facilitate the interpretation of the cases: a) the context, referring specifically to the most immediate setting of a person's life; b) the content of the experiences of the converts based on biographical data and the demographic survey; and c) validity and reliability. The two levels for comparing the cases (horizontal and vertical) will also facilitate the interpretation of the cases. The diverse responses of the converts in the different types of cases will allow me to compare several categories using the multiple-case design in order to answer the research questions. In addition, the functional approach will help me to analyze what conversion means in the context of the converts.

To provide a clearer understanding of the ways in which individual agency of the converts plays out in the process of making choices, I will initially describe the methods used, the rationale for choosing the selected cases, the boundaries of the cases, the categories that emerged from the data, and the chosen layers to interpret the cases. Then, I will contrast the cases looking at

---

1. Agency in social sciences refers to the capacity of individuals or organizations to act independently and to make their own choices. Role of the converts refers to the style of response during their personal quest. For more details about agency, see Archer, *Structure, Agency and the Internal Conversation*; Rambo, *Understanding Religious Conversion*; Smilde, *Reason to Believe*. For active vs. passive role, see Dawson, "Self-Affirmation, Freedom, and Rationality"; Rambo, "Understanding"; Richardson, "Active vs. Passive Convert." Conversion motifs are the patterns or variations in conversions suggested by Lofland and Skonovd, "Conversion Motifs." They proposed a descriptive system for the study of religious conversion. They proposed six conversion motifs: intellectual, mystical, experimental, affectional, revivalist, and coercive. It is also possible to find a combination of two motifs. The conversion motifs then are related to the motivations (push factors) of the individuals who explore new religions.

the choices of the converts within their specific contexts. Finally, I will point out the most significant factors that shape the choices of the converts.

2.1.1 Rationale for Choosing Case Studies for this Chapter

In this chapter, I chose Martina's story because she is an example of an informant with a non-Catholic background. Since the main focus of this chapter is on describing and analyzing the role of the converts in the process of conversion and the stages leading up to conversion, Martina is an "ideal case" to study due to her context, family background, and her active involvement during her conversion. I chose three additional cases as interpretive tools to analyze similarities and differences.

I think that Catalina's story is interesting because she showed a more passive role in her conversion to Islam since everything about the religion came from her husband. I chose Simón because he was a male experimental conversion case and it is important to listen to the male voices since most research done on conversion narratives has been largely focused on female stories.[2] I chose Lucía to do a case pairing analysis with Martina. There are some similarities in terms of agency, levels of choices, and conversion motifs. However, Lucía's religious background is Catholic and Martina's background is Baptist.

2.1.2 Defining the Boundaries of the Cases

The agency and role of the Hispanic Muslim converts in their conversion to Islam will be addressed in this chapter. The selected cases show a wide range of responses and contextual factors that are significant in the conversion process. There are several categories or continua included in this study that emerged from the data and help to develop criteria for selecting the cases. I will list the categories below.

These categories allow the researcher to analyze and compare the different variables that emerge from the conversion narratives. I will include in subsequent chapters the stories of second-generation Hispanic Muslims who did not convert but grew up in Muslim families in order to understand their contexts and their role in socializing other Hispanics.[3] I will

---

2. For more details about case selection, see Stake, "Qualitative Case Studies," 22–27; Tellis, "Introduction to Case Study," 3–4. For additional information on triangulation, see Stake, "Qualitative Case Studies," 33–38.

3. See Miles and Huberman, *Qualitative Data Analysis*, 25–27; Prevette, *Child, Church and Compassion*, 114–15 for guidelines regarding the importance of defining

include different categories for subsequent chapters to address the research questions.

2.1.3 Explanation of Each Category (Continuum)[4]

Agency

This is a central category and the main focus in chapters 2–4. I discovered a range of responses in terms of agency: some converts expressed individual agency, while others were influenced more by an institutional agency. In some cases, there was a combination of individual and institutional agency.

The Role of the Converts

This is also an important category related to agency in the study. The role of the converts is related to how these converts respond during the conversion process. Some converts had a more active role in their conversion while others demonstrated a more passive role.[5]

Life Course Agency

This category is related to both agency and the role of the converts. Usually, converts with an active role in their conversion who are also actively searching for a religious group show more life course agency than the individuals who are passive.[6] Categories 4–7 are not technically a continuum but were included because the significant relationships needed to understand agency and the role of the converts.

Contextual Factors

While not technically a continuum, the conversion of selected converts was influenced by several contextual factors. This is a very important category in my study to understand the predominant contextual factors (personal,

---

the boundaries of the case studies.

4. I follow Prevette's suggestions for describing the continuum. For more details, see Prevette, *Child, Church and Compassion*, 104–5.

5. For more details about active vs. passive, see Richardson, "Active vs. Passive Convert."

6. Life course agency is understood here as a sequence of socially defined events and roles that the individual enacts over time. For more details about life course agency, see Hitlin and Long, "Agency as a Sociological Variable"; Hitlin and Elder, "Time"; Emirbayer and Mische, "What Is Agency?"

cultural, social, religious, and historical) that play a significant role in the conversion of some Hispanics to Islam.[7]

Conversion Motifs

This category is included based on Lofland and Skonovd's 1981 typology to identify the significant conversion motifs of the converts. The motif is the distinctive or central theme in the conversion process. The typology includes six conversion motifs: intellectual, mystical (not found in the study), experimental, affectional, revivalist, and coercive (not found in the study). This typology also includes five major variations: degree of social pressure, temporal duration, level of affective arousal, affective content,[8] and belief-participation sequence. Special attention will be given to the belief-participation sequence. The most common conversion motifs found in my study are intellectual, experimental, and affectional.

Family Background and Structure

The family structure will be analyzed in this category. There are converts with more structure and others with less structure at the following levels: personal, cultural, social, and religious. The degree of stability vs. instability will be considered as well.

---

7. I follow Rambo's suggestions of looking at different contextual factors to better understand the complex process of conversion (Rambo, *Understanding Religious Conversion*, 8–10). Personal factors include: crises, personality, life course, and changes in an individual's thoughts, feelings, and actions. Social factors are related to the interactions and influence of family, relatives, and friends. Cultural factors include myths, rituals, and symbols. Religious factors include religious expectations, worldviews, doctrines and beliefs, and experiences. Gooren emphasizes five factors influencing religious activity: 1) social, 2) institutional, 3) cultural and political, 4) individual, and 5) contingency factors (Gooren, *Religious Conversion and Disaffiliation*, 51–52). One of the limitations of Gooren's factors is that he does not include clear indicators for cultural factors. According to Rambo, context not only provides the sociocultural matrix that shapes a person's myths, rituals, symbols, and beliefs; it also has a powerful impact in terms of access, mobility, and the opportunity for coming into contact with new religious influences. Thus, there is a dynamic interplay between the social, cultural, and religious factors. Here, I also consider the role of migration, mobility/dislocation, and marginalization in the process of conversion and the choices that converts make. Some scholars emphasize a broader definition of culture that includes symbols, values, beliefs, and worldviews. I will follow this approach in subsequent chapters.

8. Affective content focuses on affect and the content. For example: illumination, curiosity, and affection. For specific details about conversion motifs and the major variations, see Lofland and Skonovd, "Conversion Motifs"; Rambo, *Understanding Religious Conversion*.

Conversion Motives (Push Factors)

This category is included to understand the motives for converting to Islam. There is a range of motives such as crises, Muslim friends, mobility, family dysfunctionality, etc.

Reasons for Conversion and Most Appealing Aspects of Islam (Pull Factors)

I included this category to identify the varied responses of the converts in terms of the most appealing aspects of Islam. What are the main reasons for conversion? What are the most appealing aspects of Islam?

Previous Religious Commitment of the Convert

In this category, the main emphasis was to analyze the degree of commitment and participation of individuals in previous religions. Some individuals were very committed (high commitment) in previous religions while others were very nominal (low commitment), by this I mean that they did not participate at all (nominal) or their participation was limited in religious activities.

Parental Religious Commitment

This category is related to category 9 in that it is the same continuum but focuses on the parents of the convert. In this category, the main emphasis was to analyze the degree of commitment and participation of the parents of the converts. Some parents were very committed (high commitment) in previous religions while others were very nominal (low commitment), by this I mean that they did not participate at all (nominal) or their participation was limited to major religious events or celebrations.

Contact with Muslims (Muslims Friends, Muslim Community Leaders or Imams)

Several converts had contact with Muslim friends or imams before they converted to Islam. This is an important category to identify the influence of Muslim friends in the conversion process of the individuals. The continuum here ranges from more friends vs. fewer or no Muslim friends at all.

Crisis

Some converts had several crises while others did not experience any crisis before their conversion to Islam. Some converts probably experienced crises, but they were not fully aware of the consequences of the crises in terms of their conversions. These categories will serve as tools to facilitate the analysis and comparison of the cases.

Table 1: Layers, Levels, and Categories (Continua) for Comparing and Contrasting Selected Cases

Layers Context, Content, Validity, and Reliability
Two Levels of Comparison Horizontal (between types of cases: case 1, case 2 and case 3) Vertical (case pairing between case 1 and case 4)

12 Categories (Continua)
  1. Agency
  2. Role of the converts
  3. Life course agency
  4. Contextual factors
  5. Conversion motifs
  6. Family background and structure
  7. Conversion motives
  8. Reasons for conversion
  9. Previous religious commitment of the converts
 10. Parental religious commitment
 11. Contact with Muslims
 12. Crises

	Four Selected Cases	
Case 1: Martina	Case 2: Catalina	Case 3: Simón
Horizontal ←		→
Case 4: Lucía (Case pairing with Martina)		
Vertical ↑↓		

2.1.4 Layers

As I described it in the previous chapter, I will use the following layers to address the research questions of this study: content, context, validity, and reliability. Table 1 below summarizes the different aspects to facilitate the analysis of the cases. Having established the methodological aspects of my research, I turn to my findings in the next section.

2.2 MARTINA'S CASE

2.2.1 Martina: "I believed that the Qur'an was true."

Martina is a second-generation Hispanic American born to a Chilean mother and a father born to Baptist missionary parents in Chile. She was twenty-five years old at the time of the interview. Her parents immigrated to the United States from Chile to attend college. Her mother did not speak English, and her father spent time as a Baptist minister. Nonetheless, he had left the ministry by the time Martina had been born. Upon leaving the ministry, he spent time as a social worker before deciding to return to school to receive his Law degree, which moved the family to the east coast of the United States.

Martina's family lived in an upper-middle-class, mostly African-American neighborhood, where the children rarely spent time outside. Yet, Martina still managed to find friends, including a Bengali Muslim girl around fourth or fifth grade. This friendship first introduced Martina to Islam, especially as the girls remained very close until high school when Martina's friend moved away with her family.

Martina maintained a love for religion, taking this love to college where she majored in religion. Over the winter break of her first year, Martina decided to pick up a copy of an English version of the Qur'an, which began to reshape the world as she knew it. During her time of reading, Martina determined that she believed everything stated in the Qur'an. Once she had determined this, she knew that she could never remain a Christian. At her university, she developed a relationship with the Muslim chaplain, who answered all of her questions and inspired her to recite the *Shahadah* [declaration of faith] on the first day of Ramadan in the year 2005.[9] Conversion to Islam was the natural next step in her life. She was seventeen years old at the time of her conversion. Her family responded to her conversion

---

9. *Shahadah* is the declaration of faith, sincere pronouncement of which renders someone a Muslim. For more details about the *Shahadah* see Dutton, "Conversion to Islam"; Esposito, *Islam: The Straight Path*; Van Nieuwkerk, "Gender, Conversion, and Islam," 113–14.

with full acceptance, believing, like her, that perhaps this conversion really was her natural next step. Her brother, though friends with many Muslims, seemed to be the only one in need of an adjustment period. For Martina, her transition has been met with nothing but support.

2.2.2 Family Background and Structure

It is paramount to analyze the family background of the converts and the context to be able to understand the conversions of these individuals in their geographical locations.[10] Martina is a second-generation Hispanic. She was born in the United States; both parents are from Chile. She was raised as a Baptist. When I asked her about the description of the neighborhood in which she grew up, she stated "I grew up in a Baptist suburban middle-class neighborhood. Both my parents were born and grew up in Chile. My father's parents were Baptist missionaries there. My mother grew up Catholic but became Protestant around college years. Then, they met and moved to the United States, while my parents were attending college."[11]

Her mother had several challenges while trying to adjust to life in the United States. In regard to her parents, Martina comments, "They got married. My mother could not speak English at that point. She had completed college, but she was just working odd jobs in Kentucky. She was the only Latino that some people have ever met."[12] She mentioned on several occasions that she and her mother were the only Latinas in the neighborhood. She

---

10. I will pay particular attention to the local setting in this chapter. According to Rambo, "context encompasses a vast panorama of conflicting, confluent, and dialectical factors that both facilitate and repress the process of conversion" (Rambo, *Understanding Religious Conversion,* 20). In addition, Rambo makes a distinction between macro-context and microcontext. The macrocontext refers to the total environment ("the big picture") in which the conversion takes place (political, religious, economic, etc.) and the microcontext ("local setting") is the more immediate world of a person's family, friends, ethnic group, religious community, and neighborhood. Each plays its own role in the convert's experience (Rambo, *Understanding Religious Conversion,* 21–22).

11. Cuartas/Martina 2012:1. I use the following system for citations from the interviews conducted during the research. Example: Cuartas/Martina 2012:1. First, I include the last name of the interviewer (Cuartas), followed by the name (pseudonym) of the interviewee (Martina). Then the year of the interview (2012), and finally I include the page number (1). The transcriptions are in the possession of the researcher. However, when I include information from the demographic survey that I conducted, I will add the word "DS" (Demographic Survey). For example: Cuartas/Catalina DS 2012. Demographic Survey conducted by Victor H. Cuartas, 25 February, 2012.

12. Cuartas/Martina 2012:1.

states, "I grew up in almost an entirely African American neighborhood. I was one of the few people who were not African American . . ."[13]

Martina met people from different cultures and backgrounds, including the Bengali Muslim girl at her school. Martina's experience of living in a neighborhood with a high level of diversity increased her awareness of her own identity. When I asked Martina about her personal preference in terms of identity, she mentioned that she identified first as Muslim, then as an American, then as white, and finally as Latina/Hispanic. This preference regarding her identity was confirmed later in the interview.[14]

Martina made comments about her own dual identity being white American and also Chilean. "My identity was far more informed by what I was not than what I was."[15] This quote reflects her consciousness as a minority living in an ethnically diverse neighborhood. She experienced some degree of isolation and marginality. Martina did not play out in the streets. In addition, it is normal in Hispanic families to be more protective with girls than with boys. Usually, boys have more freedom to choose their friends and play sports outside, whereas girls are more encouraged to stay at home or to invite their friends to come to their home. Thus, gender plays a significant role as part of the background and context of the convert.

Her family had some degree of mobility. They lived in Kentucky for many years, and then they moved to the Washington, DC Metropolitan area. Mobility usually has an impact on families in terms of dislocation. This is particularly true when children begin to build relationships with other children. Even though children usually adapt quicker than adults, frequent mobility in families has diverse consequences.[16]

Regarding structure, Martina's family was quite stable. Martina affirmed the following: "Family was so close-knit, we always did things together and it was a good support network. They are always supportive. My parents were never very strict either, although I never tested those boundaries, you know, it was generally a positive upbringing."[17] In general, she believed that she grew up happy. She had close relationships with her parents and received support from them even after she converted to Islam.[18]

---

13. Cuartas/Martina 2012:2.

14. Cuartas/Martina DS 2012:1.

15. Cuartas/Martina 2012:2.

16. For more details about the effects of mobility on children, see Booth and Crouter, *Does it Take a Village?*

17. Cuartas/Martina 2012:2.

18. Chaves analyzed the role of family structure and Protestant church attendance. For more details, see Chaves, "Family Structure."

Hence, Martina did receive much support from her family. This is an aspect that needs further consideration. Normally, when individuals from a Catholic background convert even to other expressions of Christianity, there is much tension with relatives and friends. One can imagine that if an individual converts from being a Baptist to being a Muslim, it would bring a lot of challenges and different reactions from immediate family and friends.

2.2.3 Previous Religious Commitment

Religious experience encompasses both affiliation and conversion. It also includes the diverse experiences of the individual in her religious quest.[19] Thus, it is important to analyze the previous religious experience of Martina and her family. Martina's background was Baptist, and she considered herself active in the Baptist church before converting to Islam. She actively participated in Sunday school and Wednesday services at church. She also was active in Vacation Bible School during the summer. Vacation Bible School for children and youth is an important program in Baptist congregations. Her attendance and participation at church were higher than in the cases of Simón and Catalina for example. To assess the level of religious commitment, I asked questions about the time individuals spent weekly attending church, praying, having discussions at home or in groups, reading the Bible, and going to meetings or other activities with other Christians. She spent an average of four hours weekly in prayer, reading the Bible and attending services. Overall, Martina was very active in the Baptist church.

Martina also mentioned that for several years, her participation at church was very low. She did not offer any further explanation why this happened.[20] Her participation at church was higher than her parents' participation. These aspects of commitment and participation will be further analyzed in chapter 5.

2.2.4 Parental Religious Commitment

Martina's father was a Baptist minister but quit before Martina was born. They went to church only on Sundays. "We generally didn't participate outside of that. I would go to Vacation Bible School, and I would go to kid's

---

19. For more information about religious experience, see Medina, "Women"; Taves, *Religious Experience Reconsidered*; Yamane, "Narrative and Religious Experience."
20. Cuartas/Martina 2012:4.

activities on Wednesday night, but they didn't do much of that."[21] It is not clear why her father decided to quit his vocation as a minister to explore other alternatives such as social work and law. One can assume that he was not entirely happy in his earlier vocation.

Martina's mother was initially Catholic and then she became Baptist. Martina mentioned the following, "We went to church most weekends at a Baptist church, about two-hundred members. My family was generally very spiritual, so even when we did not go to church we would read a passage from the Bible instead. But my family never used like religious rhetoric or anything."[22]

Some of the factors that may help Martina to justify her own conversion to Islam were the switching of her mother to another denomination and the drastic change of vocations by her father. The changes that her parents made were important for Martina and her brother. In some cases, children tend to follow closely the examples and decisions of their parents. This fact also helps to explain the positive reaction of her parents when Martina converted to Islam. Another important aspect to analyze is the structure and stability of the family.

2.2.5 Contextual Factors: Personal and Religious

The most significant contextual factors in Martina's conversion are personal, religious, and social. At the personal level, Martina's beliefs and values were very significant. She was actively searching for the truth. Martina's family background influenced her decision to convert to Islam because of the religious changes of her parents. As I mentioned before, this made it easier for Martina to justify her own conversion.

Based on her biographical information, Martina had some theological questions. She stated, "I was generally interested in religion. I was a religion major in college. So, I definitely had that interest and understanding of religion, but mostly my own. But I had no desire to change religion or to learn to consider changing religions."[23] Thus, the religious aspect was relevant.

Martina commented that imams and Muslim friends answered her questions about Islam. It was important for her to believe before participating in the new religion. Islamic values matched with her personal values. For instance, family and community. Social factors were important due to her friendship and contact with two Muslim girls. Later, she mentioned her

---

21. Cuartas/Martina 2012:3.
22. Cuartas/Martina 2012:3.
23. Cuartas/Martina 2012:4.

contact at college with a Muslim chaplain who encouraged her to recite the *Shahadah*. Hence, personal and religious factors were the most relevant in Martina's conversion.

2.2.6 Contact with Muslims

Martina met two Muslim girls growing up. First, she met a Bengali Muslim girl during fourth or fifth grade (ten to eleven years old) in elementary school. Then, she met a Muslim woman during high school. Martina developed a close relationship with the Muslim girl she met in elementary school. She stated, "She was my best friend through part of middle school and I knew one in high school who was a practicing Muslim."[24] These Muslim friends were the initial advocates who helped Martina in the process of being introduced for the first time to Islam.[25]

Later, Martina had personal contact with a Muslim imam and other Muslim students at college. The imam encouraged her to recite the *Shahadah*. Due to her active searching and individual agency, as well as high life course agency, the influence of Muslim friends was limited in comparison with individuals who have a more passive role. She was the one asking questions and responding in the process. This fact will be further discussed later in this chapter.

2.2.7 Level of Crisis[26]

Martina acknowledged that she had a crisis during her senior year at high school:

> I do not know if I want to elaborate on it too much. I guess I am not sure how much it might help this interview. I do not think it had an impact on my conversion later. And my family was certainly supportive throughout it; my friends were supportive

---

24. Cuartas/Martina 2012:4.

25. Rambo refers to this stage as the encounter. He suggests that in every encounter between advocate and potential convert, the real details of their interplay are extraordinarily complex (Rambo, *Understanding Religious Conversion*, 87).

26. According to Lofland and Stark, "Becoming a World-Saver," crisis is a felt discrepancy between some imaginary ideal state of affairs and the circumstances in which these people saw themselves caught up. Cited in Rambo, *Understanding Religious Conversion*, 47.

throughout it. The impact was more internal, but it did not really affect me spiritually.[27]

Martina emphasized several times that her crisis had no bearing on her decision to become a Muslim. Nonetheless, the impact of the crisis she experienced needs further analysis. Based on Martina's biography, one can perceive that there was discontent with the previous religion and probably some theological questions to be answered. The nature of the crisis is also shaped by the contextual factors.[28] In Martina's case, the personal and religious factors were significant.

2.2.8 Conversion Motives

Motives are factors or motivations that facilitate the conversion process.[29] These motivations are part of the background experiences of the individuals before their affiliation or conversion to Islam. There were several motives that contributed to Martina's conversion to Islam. She was actively searching for the truth. She mentioned that her questions were answered by different Muslim contacts. Martina was first introduced to Islam by Muslim friends. However, she was the one who initiated the process later by asking questions of imams and participating in the Islamic student association in college. Martina was very active during her religious quest.

Martina's conversion was motivated by theological concerns. That is why she decided to read the Qur'an and began to research deeply about Islam. According to her, she found that Islam was true. This fact was confirmed by the emphasis of Islam on there being only one God and the sense of urgency for doing good works. The theological dissatisfaction is related in some degree to Martina's desire for transcendence.[30] She was always interested in religion; thus, she was motivated to seek beyond herself for meaning and purpose. Martina was looking for more in terms of religion. Therefore, she pursued transcendence. We find evidence for the significance of the personal and religious factors in Martina's conversion. Now, I will concentrate on the reasons for Martina's conversion.

27. Cuartas/Martina 2012:3.
28. Rambo, *Understanding Religious Conversion*, 20–32.
29. Some scholars refer to the motives as push factors. For example, see Allievi, "Pour Une Sociologie des Conversions"; Jindra, "How Religious Content Matters."
30. According to Rambo, *Understanding Religious Conversion*, 50–51, and Beckford, "Restoration of 'Power,'" the search for transcendence is a primary motivation for conversion. Rambo, *Understanding Religious Conversion*, 63–65 emphasizes the importance of motivational structures.

2.2.9 Reasons for Conversion

It is significant to analyze the reasons for conversion because it offers valuable insights into why people convert and what factors attract them to a specific religious group. In addition, one can observe the strategies that diverse religious groups use for recruitment.

Even though Martina met Muslim girls when she was in fourth grade at school, her real introduction to Islam as a belief system was by reading the Qur'an. She added, "What led me to convert was deciding to pick up an English version of the Qur'an from the library and reading it over winter break of my first year in college. That is what I consider more of my introduction to Islam."[31] Thus, socialization and contact with Muslim friends were important, but it was not the most significant reason for Martina's conversion.

Martina responded based on her own convictions. She stated, "the Qur'an was true, and so I had no choice but to act on that. I believed that God had communicated to me and to humanity and I could not continue to be Christian."[32] Martina's response is related to the religious factors previously described. She was looking for the truth and focused on reading the Qur'an. She recited the *Shahadah* during the first day of *Ramadan* in 2005.[33] The fact that she said the *Shahadah* during the *Ramadan* fasting period enhanced her experience because this is a special time of community and consecration for Muslims.

2.2.10 Conversion Motifs

The conversion motifs typology suggested by Lofland and Skonovd[34] focused on the most important patterns of the conversions based on intellectual, physical, and emotional dimensions by considering five major variations: 1) degree of social pressure; 2) temporal duration; 3) the level of affective arousal; 4) the affective content, and 5) belief-participation sequence.[35]

---

31. Cuartas/Martina 2012:4.
32. Cuartas/Martina 2012:4.
33. *Ramadan* is a special time for Muslims to fast and consecrate themselves. It occurs during the ninth month of the Islamic calendar. *Ramadan* is a very significant time for Muslims to gather as a community. Fasting is mandatory, usually for adult Muslims, although there are some exceptions for women (during pregnancy and breastfeeding) and individuals with diabetes and other illnesses. For more details, see Esposito, "Religious Life."
34. Lofland and Skonovd, "Conversion Motifs," 375.
35. The six conversion motifs typology was proposed by Lofland and Skonovd,

Martina began to read the Qur'an during one of her breaks at college. She picked up a version of the Qur'an in English. Martina was seeking knowledge about religious or spiritual issues primarily via the Qur'an and searching on the Internet. She was actively seeking out and exploring religious alternatives by conversing with the Muslim chaplain and attending the Muslim student organization at college. Her conversion was intellectual, and the affective content, or the primary content accompanying the experience, was "illumination."[36] Martina's experience is close to mystical conversion according to Lofland and Skonovd's typology.

One of the variations in this typology is the sequence of belief and participation. It was very important for Martina to believe prior to active participation because she was looking for the truth. She stated, "I think as soon as I started reading the Qur'an is when I discovered I found truth in it. And so there was already a level of conversion . . . I was accepting Islam to be true."[37] Martina's level of participation began to increase when she found answers to her questions about Islam. Reading the Qur'an and having periodic conversations with the Muslim chaplain were important factors for her.

Martina described her experience as a gradual process: "I think reconciling that and what it meant for my life and what it meant for how I label my faith and how I practiced it. From there on out, it was a slower process."[38] The length of time from interest to conversion was one year.

"Conversion Motifs," 376–83. This is a description of the motifs. Intellectual: the person seeks knowledge about religious or spiritual issues via books, lectures, and other media that do not involve significant social contact. The person actively seeks out and explores alternatives. Belief generally occurs prior to active participation in religious rituals and organizations. Mystical: some consider this to be the prototypical conversion, as in the case of Saul of Tarsus. It is generally a sudden and traumatic burst of insight, induced by visions, voices, or other paranormal experiences. Experimental: it has emerged as a major avenue of conversion in the twentieth century because of greater religious freedom and the multiplicity of available religious experiences. It involves active exploration of religious options. The potential convert has a "show me" mentality, essentially saying, "I will pursue this possibility and see what spiritual benefits it may provide to me." Affectional: first identified by Lofland and Stark (Becoming a "World-Saver"). This motif stresses interpersonal bonds as an important factor in the conversion. Central to it is the direct, personal experience of being loved, nurtured, and affirmed by a group and its leaders. Revivalist: it uses crowd conformity to induce behavior. Individuals are emotionally aroused and new behaviors and beliefs are promoted by the pressures exerted. Example: revival meetings feature emotionally powerful music and preaching. Coercive: This is relatively rare. Brainwashing, coercive persuasion, thought reform, and programming are other labels for such a process (Rambo, *Understanding Religious Conversion*, 14–16).

36. Lofland and Skonovd, "Conversion Motifs," 376.
37. Cuartas/Martina 2012:6.
38. Cuartas/Martina 2012:6.

Martina said she did not experience social pressure to convert to Islam. She was always active in searching and making choices. Following, I will analyze how Martina's choices were shaped by several factors.

2.2.11 Multiple Factors that Shaped Martina's Choices

Martina was very active searching and pursuing her quest for the truth. The individual agency was significant because she was in control of the process and she made intentional decisions. The institutional agency was limited. Martina was the one who asked questions of her Muslim friends. When needed, she also approached the imam at college. She participated at college in different activities organized by the Muslim Student Association as well.[39]

Personal, religious, and social factors were significant in her conversion, particularly personal and religious ones. She was always interested in religion, and one of the motives was her search for the truth. Even though she had contact and developed friendship with two Muslim girls during elementary and middle school, her inclination toward searching showed a degree of theological dissatisfaction with her previous religion. One might argue that the theological questions of Martina could be related to the religious factors that include different aspects about doctrines and beliefs of the individuals.[40]

Martina's conversion was intellectual, and it seems that she had a new revelation or illumination in the process of searching as described in the conversion motifs typology by Lofland and Skonovd. Martina engaged in a religious quest, looking for an option that was somehow compatible with her previous orientation. She mentioned that she was not looking to change religion, that her faith was very much legitimate.[41] According to Martina, "moving to Islam was more of a natural step for her."[42] She stated that submission to God is an important aspect for her, even when she was Baptist.

---

39. Martina/Cuartas 2012:7–8.

40. With regard to quest, Rambo, *Understanding Religious Conversion*, 56 suggests that the notion of quest begins with the assumption that individuals seek to maximize meaning and purpose in life to erase ignorance and to resolve inconsistency.

41. Rambo emphasizes intellectual and religious availability as part of the structural availability. Structural availability is "the freedom of a person or persons to move from previous emotional, intellectual, and religious institutions, commitments, and obligations into new options" (Rambo, *Understanding Religious Conversion*, 60). For more details regarding structural availability, see Snow et al., "Social Networks and Social Movements"; Rambo, *Understanding Religious Conversion*, 60–62.

42. Cuartas/Martina 2012:5.

There is also a need for transcendence in the life of Martina. She mentioned that Islam helps her to see the reality of life and the importance of deeds because life is short. According to Rambo[43] and Beckford,[44] transcendence is a primary motivation for conversion. She is currently very involved in advocacy initiatives with the Muslim community.

Life course agency is also a very important factor to consider because it is related to individual agency and the degree of searching. Martina showed active life course agency by influencing her life at important moments, making intentional choices. As emphasized before, she took the initiative to read the Qur'an and to ask many questions of different Muslim leaders. She was very thoughtful in her process of searching.[45] There is a dynamic interplay between different factors such as contextual factors, conversion motifs, motives, and reasons for conversion that are significant in the life course agency as well.

Martina identified herself first as Muslim, then as a Latina. She realized that she was different growing up in a context where the majority of the neighbors were African-American. The challenges that her parents experienced by immigrating to the United States, particularly her mother learning English and not having many friends, were important factors that shaped Martina's choices later in life.

In addition, the choices parents make about religion and vocation also have implications for their children. This was the case for Martina; it was easier and acceptable for her to convert to Islam because her parents changed religion and vocation before she did. A significant issue that deserves further examination is what happened in high school even though she says it was not important. The fact of denial indicates importance. All these factors interplay and shape the choices that converts make.

Thus, the individual agency, the active role, the high level of life course agency, alongside parental choices and contextual factors, played a significant role in shaping Martina's choices. She was looking for meaning in her life, and these choices helped Martina to accomplish her specific purpose. Following, I will analyze the differences and similarities between Martina, Catalina, and Simón.

---

43. Rambo, *Understanding Religious Conversion*, 64–65.

44. Beckford, "Restoration of 'Power,'" 13–14.

45. For more details about life course agency, see Crockett, "Agency in the Life Course"; Hitlin and Elder, "Time"; Hitlin and Long, "Agency as a Sociological Variable."

2.3 SIMILARITIES AND DIFFERENCES BETWEEN MARTINA, CATALINA, AND SIMÓN

As has been described before in the methods section, the strategy that I will use for comparing and contrasting the cases includes the following aspects: a) similarities in terms of the selected categories; b) differences in terms of the categories; c) finding relationships between the main categories; and d) pairing gives generalization, for example comparing Martina and Lucía (similarities in terms of agency, active role in conversion, and life course agency).[46] See Table 1 above for more details about the layers and the levels that will be used for comparing and contrasting the cases. Before I begin to analyze the similarities and differences, I will introduce Catalina and Simón.

2.3.1 Catalina: "Islam was so simple"

Catalina grew up in Brooklyn in a mostly Hispanic community among a large, traditional, Puerto Rican extended family. She was twenty-seven years old at the time of the interview. In her family, the mother was more religious than the father, but the mother never actually attended church regularly enough to be active. The father would attend only if he could be convinced to go. However, no further explanation was offered about how they convinced him.

Catalina remembers only a happy childhood. She enjoyed staying at home spending time with family. Most of her friendships involved members of her family. As a baby, Catalina had been baptized, but she never attended a church service, never received her first communion, nor did she participate in a confirmation ceremony. She never knew that she was religious until she asked her mother in about the fifth grade and learned that her family subscribed to Catholicism.

In her pre-conversion years, she enjoyed the idea of praying to God, even though she did not understand what it meant to pray. A friend of her cousin, who later became her husband, introduced her to Islam. Before then, she understood nothing about most religions. After a few months of interaction in March 2004, Catalina felt it necessary to convert. She was twenty years old at the time of her conversion.

In October 2004, she married her cousin's friend, as she thought it would be best for their potential children to have both parents be Muslim.

---

46. These factors for comparing and contrasting the cases also improve the validity of the research, as suggested by Yin, *Case Study Research: 4th ed.*, 40–41. Pairing gives generalization, see Prevette, *Child, Church and Compassion*; Yin, *Applications of Case Study Research: 3rd ed.*

She said that her husband never pushed her to convert. One aspect of Islam that Catalina enjoys is the emphasis that it places on family. She believes that the woman is meant to be the wife and the mother, and so sees no need for women to have any part in leadership, such as leading prayer. Her family and friends supported her decision to become Muslim, as long as they felt that it was a decision she made for herself and did not happen as a result of getting ready to marry her husband.

2.3.2 Simón: "It was an interesting experience"

Simón is the son of an African-American father and a Mexican-American mother. He may be considered a 2.5 generation Hispanic because his mother was born in the United States, but her background is Mexican-American.[47] Simón was twenty-four years old at the time of the interview. His childhood time was split between Colorado and Virginia where the father's family resided, and Texas where the mother's family resided. The communities he spent time in varied, being split between African-American and Caucasian and predominantly Mexican-American ones.[48]

Though his mother could not speak Spanish, Simón still grew up exposed to the language because of his father's ability to speak the language. Around the age of eleven, the family moved to Virginia to be close to relatives from both sides of the family. Simón grew up as an Episcopalian, which was the religion of his father's family. The mother's family professed Catholicism, but later she decided to attend an Episcopalian church.

Simón was very close to his paternal grandfather, and the death of the grandfather played a major part in the life changes that put Simón on the path that led to his conversion. Another major factor which played a role in Simón's life is that he always had been an artistic person. Attending a school that specialized in the sciences made life slightly stressful for Simón. During sophomore year of high school, he was introduced to Islam through a movie about the pilgrimage (*Hajj*) to Mecca in Saudi Arabia.[49]

---

47. For more details about the difference between the second generation and 2.5 generation, see Ramakrishan, "Second-Generation Immigrants?"

48. Lester Murad, "Politics of Mothering," studied the complex dynamics in ethnically and religiously mixed families. In the context of mixed families, the choices of the converts become more difficult in terms of constructing their new identities.

49. *Hajj* is one of the most important pillars of Islam. According to Islamic teachers, the *Hajj* should be an expression of devotion to God. For more details about *Hajj*, see Hammoudi, *Season in Mecca*.

After Simón graduated from high school, he decided to take a year off of school to join AmeriCorps as it was similar to the Peace Corps.[50] Before entering AmeriCorps, Simón decided to pursue his interest in the Arabic language by taking a class at a local community college. After a year in AmeriCorps, Simón spent some time at George Mason University and became part of an ambassadorial program that allowed him to teach English in Turkey.

During this time, Simón had participated in a conversion journey that moved him from Christianity to Buddhism, to Hinduism briefly, and into learning about other world religions. In Turkey, Simón met a German convert to Islam, who took him to various lectures and gave him various materials pertaining to Islam. Even as a nonbeliever, Simón tried participating in *Ramadan* and finally, he converted to Islam in Istanbul in 2007.

Simón was nineteen years old at the time of his conversion. His family, perhaps used to his conversion history, tried to be supportive while waiting for his next move. The one thing they did not seem to take much issue with was his aversion to eating pork, as two years previously he had become a vegetarian.

Now that I have provided a description of Catalina's and Simón's stories, I will analyze the differences and similarities between Martina, Catalina, and Simón.

2.4 SIMILARITIES BETWEEN MARTINA, CATALINA, AND SIMÓN

The most significant similarities between Martina, Catalina, and Simón are the following: a) family background and structure; b) parental religious commitment; c) contacts with Muslims before conversion; and d) crisis.[51]

These converts experienced a degree of diversity in their neighborhoods, particularly Martina and Simón. Catalina's case was a little bit different; yet, her cousin was the one who introduced her Muslim friend to her, who later became her husband. In general, all of them had stable families

---

50. AmeriCorps is a US federal government program that promotes community service within the country and also in different countries in need. For more information about AmeriCorps, see: http://www.nationalservice.gov/programs/americorps. For information about the Peace Corps, see http://www.peacecorps.gov/.

51. The analysis of similarities and differences between the cases will be based on different continua (categories), so even though there are significant similarities, I will also point out when necessary, the degree of differences within these categories. I will do the same when I focus on the differences. I will underline some similarities as well. This shows the complexity and dynamics of the conversion process.

and reported being happy during childhood. Catalina and Simón particularly mentioned that they were looking for more structure and they found that structure in Islam.

The family structure of the converts was similar. These families experienced a degree of stability but had to deal with different issues and challenges. The following aspects were observed in the families of the converts that had little religious structure: minimum religious participation and commitment in previous religions, as well as some degree of mobility and traveling. Some of them also experienced challenges in terms of adaptation and learning English (e.g., Martina's mother). Martina's family, for example, did not have a lot of religious structure. She grew up in a middle-class home in a predominantly African-American neighborhood, and "she was very happy."[52] She also mentioned that her family was "very spiritual but never used religious rhetoric."[53]

Catalina's family grew up with minimum religious structure. She grew up in a stable family though, with a close relationship with her parents and extended family. Catalina's main focus was to spend time with her family. When she was growing up, she played outside with cousins but spent a lot of her time at home. She was a very nominal Catholic. She did not receive her first communion, nor did she participate in a confirmation ceremony. The only aspect that she did by herself was prayer. Overall, she did not attend church regularly.[54]

Parental religious commitment in each case was similar. Martina's family was Baptist, Simón's family was Episcopalian, and Catalina was Catholic. Regardless of the religious background of the parents, their attendance in church was low. Some of them went to church only on Sundays. This was the case of Martina's parents. She stated that her family was "very spiritual."[55] However, her parents only went to the Baptist church on Sundays.

---

52. Cuartas/Martina 2012:2.

53. Cuartas/Martina 2012:3.

54. Jindra conducted significant research that included informants from different religious backgrounds who converted to different religious groups such as Christianity, Jehovah's Witnesses, Islam, and Baha'i. Jindra reported in her research the importance of family structure in the process of conversion. Jindra identified three different categories of converts based on the religious and cultural structure: Category 1: If one's familial and/or sociocultural milieu was experienced as disorganized, more "closed" milieus were attractive. Category 2: If the familial, religious, and/or sociocultural milieu was experienced as too narrow and closed, the person was generally attracted by more "open" conditions. Category 3: Those who felt comfortable in a milieu that was neither too enclosed nor too wide open tended to convert within their own religious tradition (Jindra, *New Model of Religious Conversion*, 63).

55. Cuartas/Martina 2012:2.

Catalina's family only went to church on special occasions such as Easter, Christmas, or weddings.[56] Frequently, the mothers of the converts were more involved in more religious aspects than the fathers. Simón's parents also went to church occasionally.[57] In terms of attendance and participation in activities at the church, all the parents showed low or minimum levels of participation. To a certain extent, the converts participated in more activities at church than their parents did. For example, Simón's grandparents were very influential in his life. They lived in Texas, and they encouraged him to participate in activities at their church. Later, his parents stopped going to the Episcopalian church, but he did not discuss the reason for doing so.[58]

Martina's mother was initially Catholic and then became Baptist. Also, her father was a Baptist preacher, then he decided to do social work, and later he became a lawyer. Martina's father experienced several transitions in his vocation and personal development. These changes and transitions in both parents are significant because they may facilitate the switching of children to other religions later in life. Perhaps Martina was affected somehow by the previous shifting of her parents both at the religious and vocational levels.

All of the converts had contact with Muslim friends. Martina and Simón also had contact with imams and Islamic student organizations during college. Catalina was first introduced to Islam by a second-generation Hispanic Muslim who later became her husband. She subsequently learned more about Islam through her husband. Catalina stated, "He was very open about his religion. He was the first Muslim I have met, and it just intrigued me. He was very honest, very humble, very family-oriented which I like because that's what I grew up with. He was very respectful, and it just made me interested to learn about it and he was very open."[59]

The degree of socialization by Muslim converts is shaped by the agency, the role of the converts, and the conversion motifs. I will discuss this relationship further in this chapter. Next, the similarities regarding crisis experienced by the converts will be analyzed.

To some extent, all of them experienced a degree of crisis. However, the degree of self-awareness and intensity were different. The one who experienced more crises was Simón. His grandfather passed away while he was in high school. Then, he was very frustrated at the end of high school because he

---

56. Cuartas/Catalina 2012:2.
57. Cuartas/Simón 2012:3.
58. Cuartas/Simón 2012:3.
59. Cuartas/Catalina 2012:5.

was unable to practice his talents. He was very oriented toward arts and music. However, he was enrolled in courses to specialize more in technology.[60]

Simón experienced much frustration during this period of his life. Martina acknowledged her crisis, but she did not share specific information about it. There are some details that are missing in her conversion narrative though. I previously analyzed Martina's crisis in the section where I first introduced her case. Catalina did not mention details about a significant crisis before her conversion.

Other similarities that are not part of the main categories were identified among the four cases. The age of the converts was similar: Martina, twenty-five; Catalina, twenty-seven; Simón, twenty-four. The age at conversion was similar: Martina, seventeen; Catalina, twenty; Simón, nineteen. They got interested in Islam at college (Martina and Simón). All of them converted to Islam after September 11, 2001. Martina and Catalina are second-generation Hispanics; Simón may be considered 2.5 generation. Generational differences will be further discussed in later chapters.

Overall, the reactions of the families after their conversion were positive. Some of them received more support than others. Martina, for example, waited for a period of time before telling her extended family about her decision.

Simón's family, perhaps used to his extended conversion career, tried to be supportive while waiting for his next move in terms of religion. The one thing they did not seem to have much issue with was his aversion to eating pork, as two years previously he had become a vegetarian. Catalina's family wanted to make sure that she was not converting because of the influence of her Muslim friend. Later, Catalina married him. He is a second-generation Hispanic Muslim. He was raised in a Muslim family. Overall, these converts did not experience a lot of resistance from their parents or siblings.

There were some similarities with regard to the preferences and choices of the converts. All of these individuals expressed a degree of comfort with the term "convert" rather than "revert." None of these converts changed their names after conversion. Prayer was important for all the converts. It seems that these individuals were looking for a more structured religion. These aspects of changes will be further addressed in subsequent chapters.

However, there were some differences as well. For example, the frequency of the use of the *hijab* was different. Martina uses the *hijab* occasionally, only to pray and in certain settings, whereas Catalina decided to wear it

---

60. Cuartas/Simón 2012:3; Cuartas/Simón DS 2012.

permanently. Martina is still trying to understand fully why she needs to wear it. She mentioned that "she has not gotten to that level of understanding yet."[61]

Catalina's rationale for her choice of wearing the *hijab* is expressed in her comments. "I did not begin to cover my hair right away because I feared how people would react towards me. So, it took me about four to five months to wear the hijab because I was afraid of how people would see me. But once I made the decision to cover my hair, I actually felt more comfortable being outside. I kind of felt safer."[62]

Martina, Catalina, and Simón made intentional choices prior to their conversion to Islam. Even Catalina, who had a more passive role and was very influenced by her husband, was very intentional about her decision to marry a Muslim man to be able to raise their children in the same religion. Thus, all these converts made choices at different levels with different purposes and motivations. On the other hand, what were some of the differences between Martina, Catalina, and Simón?

2.5 DIFFERENCES BETWEEN MARTINA, CATALINA, AND SIMÓN

The following are the most significant: agency of the converts, the role of the converts, life course agency, contextual factors, conversion motifs, conversion motives, reasons for conversion, and previous religious commitment of the converts.[63]

As I argued earlier, the individual agency was significant throughout Martina's religious quest. With Catalina and Simón, there was a degree of institutional agency that is reflected in their contacts with Muslims, particularly with Simón. He traveled to Saudi Arabia, Morocco, and Turkey. He met several Muslims in these countries. An English Muslim encouraged him to say the *Shahadah* in Istanbul.[64] Nevertheless, we observe an individual who was actively responding to these contacts with Muslims even though he was

---

61. Cuartas/Martina 2012:9.

62. Cuartas/Catalina 2012:9.

63. Other differences are found regarding education and hobbies of the converts. Martina earned a BA in religion; Simón earned a BA in global affairs; and Catalina holds an associate degree. Martina, Catalina, and Simón were at college when they began to know more about Islam. This was a significant period in their lives. The hobbies and interests of the converts also differ. Martina enjoyed time with friends, watching movies, and she was very interested in religion. Catalina spent most of her time at home playing with bikes and enjoying time with her family. Simón was very artistic; he enjoys music, traveling, painting, and swimming.

64. Cuartas/Simón 2012:9.

very influenced by the institutional agency. He experienced firsthand the context of Islam in a country where Islam is the most important religion.[65]

The role of the converts was different. Contrasting these individuals, Martina was the most active. Simón's role was more passive than active. Catalina's response was also more passive. There is more individual agency in Martina's case, while there is a degree of institutional agency in Simón and Catalina's cases. The institutional agency was more relevant in Simón's case because Simón had several contacts with Muslim friends and Muslim scholars.

Personal and social factors were important for all of them. Nonetheless, religious factors were very significant for Martina in addition to personal and social factors. In Catalina's case, cultural factors also played a significant role. Contrasting all these cases, Catalina was the individual who was most influenced by cultural factors. Simón was influenced more by personal and social factors. As described earlier, he was strongly influenced by Muslim friends and scholars.

Martina's parents are from Chile; they immigrated to the United States to attend college. Catalina's parents are from Puerto Rico; they traveled back and forth between Puerto Rico and New York. The most diverse family is Simón's. His mother is Mexican-American, and his father is African-American. The family of Simón's mother was active in the Air Force, and his father's vocation involved geology. Later, Simón traveled overseas often and developed friendships with people from different nationalities and religious backgrounds.

There are significant differences with regard to the conversion motifs. Martina's motif was more intellectual. The affective content based on Lofland and Skonovd was illumination.[66] It was important for Martina to believe first and then to participate.

Since I have previously analyzed Martina's motifs, I will concentrate here on Simón's and Catalina's motifs. Catalina's conversion motif was more affectional. The affective content was affection, based on Lofland and Skonovd's typology.

Catalina did not experience social pressure during her conversion. She spent six to eight months from the time of interest to conversion. It was a relatively quick process in comparison with Martina (one year) and Simón (two years). Catalina was greatly influenced by her husband. The fact that

---

65. Cuartas/Simón 2012:8–10.

66. See Appendix 3 for more details about the conversion motifs and the major variations according to Lofland and Skonovd. Affective arousal is related to the degree of emotional arousal accompanying the experience. The affective content is more concerned with the main content in the experience. The main focus of both is on affect (Lofland and Skonovd, "Conversion Motifs," 376).

he is also Hispanic helped Catalina to consider Islam as an option. She converted first, and then months later she got married.

Conversely, Simón's conversion motif was more experimental. The affective content was curiosity. He had a "show me" mentality. This helps to explain the extensive conversion career of Simón. He tried different religions. He spent two years from early interest to his conversion to Islam. He was probably the one who experienced more social pressure since he traveled very often to Muslim countries and had several contacts with Muslims. Both Catalina and Simón first began to participate and then to believe. It was important for these individuals to participate and establish relationships with other Muslims because of the affection and experimental motifs. See Appendix 3 for a summary of the conversion motifs of the converts.

The conversion motives of these individuals vary. The motives are related to the motifs that were described earlier. Martina believed that the Qur'an was true. Her motivation was influenced by personal and religious factors and the intellectual pattern. Conversely for Catalina, conversion was a convenient decision so that her future children would have two Muslim parents. She wanted to be a good wife and a good mother. The example of her mother was very important as well. Here, we observe that social and cultural factors were important. One of the main motivations for Simón was his curiosity about religion and the influence of Muslim friends. His structural availability was higher than that of Martina and Catalina. These motivations are shaped by the contextual factors and conversion motifs. Thus, there is a relationship between these factors.

The reasons for the conversions of these individuals are diverse. They include the factors that appeal the most to the converts to Islam (pull factors).[67] Martina had a revelation from the Qur'an. She believed that God had communicated with her and she could not continue to be Christian.[68] However, the main reason for Catalina was not religious or theological, but rather because she liked Islam's emphasis on the family. She had questions, and her husband answered her questions. She did not look for additional contacts with other Muslims. She stated, "Islam was simple, straightforward, it made sense, it was clear."[69] Catalina spent much time at home during her childhood. She did not have a strong background in the Catholic tradition. Thus, it was easier for her to embrace Islam. She also mentioned that "you

---

67. See Allievi, "Pour Une Sociologie des Conversions"; Jindra, "How Religious Content Matters."

68. Cuartas/Martina 2012:6.

69. Cuartas/Catalina 2012:7.

can pray in the privacy of your home . . . no need to go to church."⁷⁰ Thus, Islam was a suitable religion and fulfilled her expectations.

Simón was drawn to Islam by the sense of community and friendships. According to him, it was an "interesting experience." He used the word "interesting" several times in the interview to describe his experience. The experimental motif was very consistent in his account. Simón observed Muslims while he visited the United Arab Emirates and he was attracted by their integrity, conduct, and concern for other students.⁷¹ Thus, fellowship and friendship were important factors for Simón.

The previous religious commitment of the converts was also different. These individuals had different religious backgrounds: Martina's background was Baptist, Catalina was a nominal Catholic, and Simón's background was Episcopalian. Martina's participation and commitment levels at church were higher than those of Catalina and Simón. Martina went to church on Sundays and Wednesdays and participated in Vacation Bible School. She was active with the Christian community only at church. Conversely, Catalina considered herself inactive at church. She began her awareness of being Catholic during fifth grade.⁷²

Simón was raised in an Episcopalian church. However, Simón mentioned that he was inactive. He tried different religions. Then, he went to a Presbyterian church. Later, he was influenced by friends, and he became interested for a period of time in Buddhism and then in Hinduism.⁷³ According to the biographical data, Simón was influenced by his peers, and that is why his role was more passive than active. Table 2 summarizes the similarities and differences between Martina, Catalina, and Simón.

---

70. Cuartas/Catalina 2012:7.

71. Cuartas/Simón 2012:10.

72. For a study about religious identification and mixed marriage and conversion, see Salisbury, "Religious Identification." Salisbury stated that "religious patterns of conversion are shown to differ depending upon whether the spouse was Catholic or a Protestant, a wife or a husband. Patterns of conversion were mediated to some extent by the social status of the husband as suggested by the occupation of the husband" (Salisbury, "Religious Identification," 1).

73. Cuartas/Simón 2012:3–4.

Table 2: Summary of Similarities and Differences
Between Martina, Catalina, and Simón

Similarities	Differences
• Family background and structure	• Agency of the converts
• Parental religious commitment	• Role of the converts
• Contact with Muslims	• Life course agency
• Some degree of crisis	• Contextual factors
	• Conversion motifs
	• Conversion motives
	• Reasons for conversion
	• Previous religious commitment
	• Different level of socialization by Muslim friends is shaped by agency, the role of the converts, contextual factors, and conversion motifs.

2.6 CASE PAIRING: SIMILARITIES AND DIFFERENCES BETWEEN MARTINA AND LUCÍA

2.6.1 Lucía: "There is one God."

Lucía is also a second-generation Hispanic-American. She was born to a heroin-addicted mother and a Colombian drug lord father and came from a large family consisting of ten sisters. She was twenty-four years old at the time of the interview. The first eight years of her childhood consisted of money and status, including the caregiving of a nanny, because of her father's illegal activities.

They lived in Houston, indulging in constant vacations and living a life of privilege. After the arrest of her father when she was around the age of ten, Lucía and her family lived in and out of hotels. By age twelve, Lucía's mother had passed away in her sleep, leaving the family without a parent.

Resentment settled in upon Lucía against the aunts who then took over her care and forced her to become a baptized Catholic, when her mother had never once forced religion upon her. She left her aunt's care by the age of fifteen, and by the time she had turned twenty, Lucía had given birth to her second child.

Lucía lived a party lifestyle, indulging in things like drinking and drugs, though she said she never fully became addicted. Returning to the Catholic Church did not seem to curb her behaviors, but eight months after leaving the Christian church, a Colombian friend began to introduce her to Islam, and from there, Lucía's journey to conversion began.

Lucía converted to Islam at the age of twenty-two. She began to study about it and grew to love the idea of worshipping one God, without the consideration of Mary, Jesus, and the Holy Spirit. After studying for six months, Lucía recited the *Shahadah*, thus professing her belief in the ideology of Islam. In 2011, she married a Yemeni Muslim man who was a friend of her cousin. The conversion for Lucía has not been easy. She enjoys the strict nature of Islam and believes in wearing her *hijab* (headscarf) appropriately, but because she has children from a previous relationship, she has had to fight against the perceived nature of such a "crime" within the community.

Her previous study has made her very conscious of what she considers to be the difference between cultural variations within the different communities and what is really part of the religion. To transition, Lucía has learned to make sacrifices to follow the rules and tenets of the religion, but she also knows that this is her preference. To be a Muslim, you have to be a good person and follow the words of the prophet Muhammad.[74] For Lucía, whose previous lifestyle had been at odds with the Qur'an, this became a good thing. Next, the similarities between Martina and Lucía will be examined.

2.6.2 Similarities between Martina and Lucía

The similarities between Martina and Lucía are the following: a) individual agency; b) active role; c) contextual factors; d) conversion motifs; and e) contact with Muslims before conversion. Since I already extensively analyzed all the categories in Martina's case, I will concentrate more on Lucía's case.

Martina and Lucía had more individual and active roles in their conversions. They both were in control of the choices they made. Both believed it is important to be educated and thus educated themselves about what it means to be Muslim. Martina and Lucía enjoyed the community aspect of the religion. They both had contacts with Muslims. They asked questions about Islam, but they took the initiative to contact imams and Muslim

---

74. Cuartas/Lucía 2012:5.

friends when necessary. In other words, they were not pressured by the Muslim contacts.

Both were influenced by personal, social, and religious factors. In addition, there was a close interplay of social and religious factors in Lucía's case. The intensive crises that she experienced were significant. These crises caused her to have a mixture of active and passive roles. Due to her intellectual approach in the religious quest, she was more active than passive. Martina was more active than Lucía. Thus, there is also a degree of contrast in regard to their role. In general, both have more active roles in comparison with Simón and Catalina.

Martina and Lucía's approach to Islam was more intellectual. Martina was motivated by her intellectual and theological views. Lucía also took the intellectual approach in that she decided to research Islam as a religion, but her experience was motivated by her emotions after the death of her mother. In her own words, she wanted to leave something for her son should she herself die early.[75]

Martina and Lucía had Muslim friends who introduced them to Islam. She stated, "I have a friend who is Colombian as well and she just started bringing me around."[76] She had problems with the Trinity and the fact that she had to pray to statues. She accepted the invitation of her Colombian friend because she was looking for an alternative religion. Both Martina and Lucía made intentional choices. These choices were motivated by their active agency, the contextual factors, and conversion motifs.

2.6.3 Differences between Martina and Lucía

There is a contrast between Martina and Lucía regarding the following categories: a) family background and structure; b) intensity of crises; c) conversion motives; d) reasons for conversion; e) previous religious commitment; and f) parental religious commitment.

In contrast with Martina, Lucía grew up in a very unstable family. Her mother was addicted to heroin. In addition, her father was a drug lord. Lucía has two children and she essentially lived as a single parent. Lucía considers her experience very upsetting because she was forced to be baptized by her aunts after the death of her mother. Perhaps this is why she has a very negative view of Christianity.

Lucía's story is a narrative of drama and tragedy. She had intensive crises due to the lifestyle of her parents. Her father was arrested when she

75. Cuartas/Lucía 2012:7.
76. Cuartas/Lucía 2012:5.

was ten. Her mother died in her sleep when Lucía was only twelve. One can imagine the impact of the passing of her mother and the absence of her father at that age. She mentioned, "the birth of my son—after losing my mother I didn't real care for anything else. You know, I did not have a person. I felt ashamed. I was very bad in school. I was very bad in school and very disrespectful in school. I had no respect for my aunts because they raised me by themselves."[77]

A turning point occurred in her life when her first son was born. Her son gave her a different perspective of life. In her own words, "I came to meet my aunts after my mother passed way before that she was always apart from her family. So, when my son was born it gave me something to care about."[78]

As I mentioned earlier, the intellectual motif is a point of commonality in Martina and Lucía's experiences. However, the difference is that the affective content of Lucía was affection and emotional, whereas for Martina it was illumination, a kind of a revelation from the Qur'an. Lucía experienced dissatisfaction with Christianity in general. She went to an evangelical church that she was invited to by her nannies. Lucía mentioned that she was disappointed with the pastor's lifestyle.[79] She did not mention the name of the church or denomination. Overall, the intensive crises and dissatisfaction with her previous religion motivated her to look for another religion.

Lucía actively wanted to convert to Islam because she wanted to raise her son in the same religion as his father, whereas Martina's conversion was more motivated by theological concerns. She decided to read the Qur'an and began to research deeply on Islam. According to Martina, she was satisfied with her previous religion, and she was not trying to convert to another religion.[80]

The main reason for Lucía's conversion was that she liked the emphasis of Islam on one God and the same routine every day. Lucía was looking for a religion with more structure because she lacked that in her life. She also liked the idea of seeing her mother in heaven.[81] This is related to the teachings of Islam about paradise (*Jannah*). This word literally means "garden." There is a high regard for mothers in Islam. According to Islam, "Paradise lies under the feet of mothers."[82]

---

77. Cuartas/Lucía 2012:3.
78. Cuartas/Lucía 2012:3.
79. Cuartas/Lucía 2012:4.
80. Cuartas/Martina 2012:3–4.
81. Cuartas/Lucía 2012:6.
82. Ahmed-Ghosh, "Ahmadi Women," 42.

To a certain degree, the religious factor observed in both Martina and Lucía is significant in that it shapes the motivations and reasons for why people convert. The beliefs and doctrines of the new religion also play an important factor.

The previous religious commitment of the converts differed. Martina was active in her previous religion while Lucía was nominal as a Catholic. Her aunts forced her to become baptized at the age of thirteen. She went to church only for Easter, Christmas, or weddings. Her nannies were evangelical Christians. Lucía mentioned that she did not follow the rules in the church.

Lucía's parents were nominal Catholics. Lucía's mother went to church with her children only during special occasions. She did not mention the role of her father in terms of religion. She was always focused rather on her mother. The passing of her mother at an early age had a great impact on her life. This crisis may help us to understand her urgency for thinking about the importance of religious legacy for her children in case of a sudden death like her mother's. Lucía stated, "If I was going to leave, my children would have a belief that I left them—I did not want anyone else giving them their beliefs."[83] Table 3 summarizes the contrast and comparison between Martina and Lucía. Table 1 shows the layers and levels used in this chapter for contrasting and comparing the selected cases.

Based on these findings, one can observe that regardless of the types of converts with different conversion motifs, they both made strategic choices that were shaped by multiple factors. See Appendix 4 for a summary of the findings in each category.

2.7 MAKING SENSE OF THE RELATIONSHIPS BETWEEN IMPORTANT CATEGORIES

How do we make sense of the relationship between the role of the converts, the contextual factors, and the conversion motifs? This present research is one of the few empirical studies that include both male and female converts, analyzing several categories such as agency, the role of the converts, motifs, and contextual factors.

Richardson's research on the active and passive role of converts included a helpful analysis emphasizing that a new paradigm has emerged in contemporary studies of religious conversion. He argues for a more active role of the converts. He also acknowledges Lofland and Skonovd's

---

83. Cuartas/Lucía 2012:3.

conversion motifs but did not consider the relationship between the role of the converts and the conversion motifs.[84]

Table 3: Case Pairing Between Martina and Lucía

Similarities	Differences
• Individual agency of the converts • Active role of the converts • Life course agency • Contextual factors • Conversion motifs • Contact with Muslims before conversion • Low level of socialization by Muslim friends • Lucía's conversion motifs: Intellectual/ affectional. Her crises had a significant impact.	• Family background and structure • Conversion motives • Reasons for conversion • Previous religious commitment • Parental religious commitment • Intensity of crisis

Rambo underlines the importance of focusing on different contextual factors such as personal, social, cultural, and religious ones, and not only on

---

84. According to Richardson, "Conversion and recruitment research has been directed for years by a traditional paradigm assuming a passive individual being converted by external powers over which no control is possible. The traditional model is also rather psychological and deterministic. A new or alternative paradigm has been developing, derived largely from studies of recruitment to new religions. It suggests a more active, meaning-seeking subject who exercises volition in deciding to convert to a new religion. The conflict between the new and the old paradigms is discussed including characterizing the so-called brainwashing model as a modern variant of the traditional paradigm" (Richardson, "Active vs Passive Convert," 1–2). For more details about the role of the converts, see Richardson, "Active vs Passive Convert," 172–75. For Active and Passive Paradigm, see also Rambo, *Understanding Religious Conversion*, especially ch. 4 on "Quest." For an example of the passive role of converts, see Conway and Siegelman, *Snapping*. Robbins, "Constructing Cultist 'Mind Control,'" assesses varied arguments with regard to the "brainwashing" model of conversion. For arguments in favor of active role of the converts see Dawson, "Self-Affirmation, Freedom, and Rationality"; Goody, "Religion"; Rounds, "Curing What Ails Them." Kuburic and Sremac, "Conversion and its Context," compiles several articles with different approaches: Psycho-social and theological-anthropological approaches. Long and Hadden, "Religious Conversion," proposes the integration of both models psychological ("brainwashing") and sociological ("social drift").

social or personal factors. He also acknowledges the conversion motifs in the context stage of his conversion model. Nonetheless, he did not offer any explanations about the relationships between the agency of the converts, contextual factors, and conversion motifs.[85]

In light of the data collected in my study, the most significant conversion motifs among my informants were intellectual, experimental, and affectional. These findings were also reported in Kose and Loewenthal's 2000 study. They assessed Lofland and Skonovd's 1981 conversion motifs by analyzing the conversion biographies of seventy British-born converts to Islam. The coercive and revivalist motifs were almost absent.[86]

One can observe that some of the more active converts are greater influenced by personal and religious factors, whereas converts with comparatively passive roles might be influenced more by social and cultural factors. Intellectual or experimental conversion motifs might be more prevalent in individuals with more active agency. Affectional conversion motifs might be more frequent in women's conversion accounts than men's, as well as in individuals with more passive agency. Affectional motifs among women's narratives were also reported in Loewenthal's 1988 study on religious commitment. Here, I have focused on the individual agency of the converts without ignoring institutional agency. A clear relationship between these categories has been demonstrated. In subsequent chapters, I will compare the results with additional theories to make sense of the findings.

2.8 CONCLUSION

The analysis of the selected cases shows that there is individual agency and a more active role played by the converts in making strategic choices in different types of conversion motifs. Martina, Catalina, Simón, and Lucía made intentional choices in the process leading up to their conversion to Islam. Even the individuals with a more passive role made intentional choices. For example, Catalina was very intentional about her decision to marry a Muslim man so as to be able to raise their children from the same religious perspective. Simón studied Arabic, traveled on several occasions to Muslim countries, and met several Muslim friends.

One also encounters a significant degree of institutional agency through Muslim contacts and imams, particularly in the case of Simón and to a lesser degree in Catalina. The degree of incorporation into Islam is heavily impacted by personal agency, the role of the converts, conversion

---

85. Rambo, *Understanding Religious Conversion*, 22–35.
86. Kose and Loewenthal, "Conversion Motifs among British Converts," 106–10.

motifs, and institutional strategies for recruitment. The strategies for institutional recruitment will be discussed in subsequent chapters.

In general, family background and structure, alongside the previous religious affiliations of the converts and the parental religious commitment, are significant factors in shaping the role of the converts. Conversion motifs are also significant. In addition, converts with less religious structure have the tendency to join groups with more structure like Islam.[87]

In many cases, the diverse choices of these individuals are partly influenced by the choices of the parents. With regard to conversion motifs, the predominant conversion motifs are intellectual, experimental, and affectional. The affective contents are illumination, curiosity, and affection respectively. These conversion motifs are related to different motivations and reasons for conversion.

In light of the collected data, it is evident that personal, social, and religious factors shape the processes leading up to a conversion. Cultural factors play a more significant role in individuals with a more passive role. Another salient factor is the interplay between the role of the converts, the contextual factors, and the conversion motifs. Converts that are more active might be more influenced by personal and religious factors, whereas converts with more passive roles might be influenced more by social and cultural factors. Intellectual or experimental conversion motifs might be more prevalent in individuals with more active agency. Affectional conversion motifs might be more frequent in individuals with more passive agency. These generalizations emerge by way of inference, comparing and contrasting the cases, and by doing case pairing between Martina and Lucía.

As I have argued, there is the individual agency and a more active role played by the converts in making strategic choices in the process leading up to a conversion. This does not mean that more passive converts do not play a role in making choices. On the contrary, these converts, though they are more passive and influenced by Muslim friends, still make strategic choices. The process is complex, and there is a dynamic interplay of multiple factors that shapes the process of conversion. Additional relationships between the categories selected will be further analyzed in subsequent chapters.

Here, choices are important to the extent that they become contributions to the local Islamic culture. These choices of the converts in the post-affiliation stage also lead to further choices as they construct their new identities.

---

87. This fact was also observed in Jindra's study on converts from different religions. For more details, see Jindra, *New Model of Religious Conversion*.

Table 4: Summary of Layers and Levels for Comparing and Contrasting

Layers
Context, Content, Validity, and Reliability
Two Levels of Comparison
Horizontal (between types of cases: case 1, case 2 and case 3)
Vertical (case pairing between case 1 and case 4)
12 Categories (Continua)
1. Agency
2. Role of the converts
3. Life course agency
4. Contextual factors
5. Conversion motifs
6. Family background and structure
7. Conversion motives
8. Reasons for conversion
9. Previous religious commitment of the converts
10. Parental religious commitment
11. Contact with Muslims
12. Crises

	Four Selected Cases	
Case 1: Martina — More active role, individual agency, Intellectual/ Illumination conversion motif, Personal and religious factors	Case 2: Catalina — More passive role, individual/institutional agency, Affectional/ Affection conversion motif, Social and cultural factors	Case 3: Simón — Passive/ Active role, institutional agency, Experimental/ Curiosity conversion motif, Social and personal factors
← Horizontal →		
Case 4: Lucía (Case pairing with Martina) More Active than Passive role, individual agency, Intellectual/ Affectional conversion motif, Personal and religious factors		
↑ Vertical ↓		

In the next chapter, I will concentrate on the choices that converts make as they share their conversion narratives and the different choices converts make regarding chosen words. This will lead to an analysis in subsequent chapters of how these converts make choices concerning their religious commitment and practice in the context of the United States. The same methods used in this chapter will be used in subsequent chapters with the added feature of different themes that emerge from the data analyzing different patterns.

Chapter 3

Diverse Conversion Narratives of Hispanic Muslim Converts

3.1 INTRODUCTION

I described the methods for analyzing the conversion narratives in chapter 1, and I argued that converts play an active role in the conversion process starting from their pre-affiliation stage. This chapter will show that the converts continue to display active agency even when retelling their conversion narratives; this review of the past, in light of the present, is an essential ingredient in the development of their identities.

The intention is to analyze the various personal and religious choices, and the emphases converts make as they tell their conversion stories. Special attention will be given to those aspects converts emphasize in their narratives, looking at the content of their conversion narratives and how they share their conversion stories; that is, key words and metaphors or analogies they use in different types of conversion narratives will be discussed. The following issues will also be addressed: the themes and discourses emphasized by these converts, the integration of Islamic beliefs, the tensions between religious and cultural aspects, and the role of family values.

It will be argued that there are different types of conversion narratives that are shaped by multiple contextual factors, present circumstances, institutional discourses, and the integration or nonintegration of the newly adopted religious beliefs. There are predominant discourses in their narratives; each individual has different purposes in telling their stories. Their religious and ethnic identities are reflected in their stories as well.

This will be accomplished in three ways. First, the conversion narratives of four Hispanic Muslims—Vicente, Jaime, Claudia and Teresa—outlining the various emphases they make in their narratives will be analyzed.[1] Second, the diverse types of conversion narratives will be compared and contrasted. And third, the findings will be compared and contrasted with additional research done on conversion studies, paying special attention to the different discourses emphasized by the converts, the aspects that converts find most appealing in Islam, and the reactions of the families upon conversion.

3.2 ANALYSIS OF THE CONVERSION NARRATIVES

Conversion narratives need to be analyzed within the contexts and present realities of the converts. There are different contexts, religious backgrounds, and religious experiences. Special attention will be given to the narratives by contrasting the different personal and religious choices and the emphases these converts make in terms of words, themes, and discourses. These personal and diverse stories are told in different ways.

Then, how the discourses are created by the converts with a special emphasis on present circumstances and choices of words, metaphors, and discourses that converts make will be analyzed.[2] According to van Nieuwkerk, "Most conversion stories contain a biographical narrative (why they as individuals took the path to Islam), a religious discourse (why Islam), a gender discourse (why they as women chose Islam), and finally an ethnic or national discourse (why they as Dutch/Western women chose Islam)."[3] The institutional discourse (what Islamic teachings and principles are emphasized by imams and Muslim converts) has been largely ignored in the conversion accounts. Thus, I will also identify and analyze the institutional discourse in the conversion stories. I will follow the discourse analysis approach in this chapter.[4]

---

1. I selected these cases carefully to show the variety of emphases in their conversion narratives to strengthen my argument in connection with primary data and interviews. These converts show a wide range of types of narratives. Most of them are second-generation Hispanic Muslims and they accepted Islam during their last years of high school and college. The age of the converts ranged between seventeen and twenty years.

2. Lieblich et al., "Holistic-Content Perspective," 62–87; I will concentrate on the following aspects suggested by Lieblich et al., *Narrative Research*: the themes that emerge from the stories, choice of metaphors or words, and how they shed light on the entire development.

3. Van Nieuwkerk, "Gender, Conversion, and Islam," 95–96.

4. Zebiri, *British Muslim Converts*, 7; For more details about the methods, see the methodology section within the introduction.

Converts usually emphasize, in different ways, one or several of these discourses. Van Nieuwkerk suggests that "these four discourses give insight into Islam's appeal to women in the West. Whereas the biographical narratives are heterogeneous, the other discourses show recurrent patterns. The religious discourse, in particular, shows a high level of congruency."[5]

There is a process of reflexivity as these individuals tell their conversion stories. Van Nieuwkerk also argues that "conversion narratives are created backward, that is, they are written at the time of or after becoming Muslim. Past events are reinterpreted in the light of current convictions. This reconstruction process takes place not only at the individual level but also at the group level."[6] Conversion is a product of the interactions among the convert's aspirations, needs, and orientations, the nature of the group into which she or he is being converted, and the particular social matrix in which these processes are taking place.[7]

To facilitate the analysis of the conversion narratives, I selected nine categories drawn from extensive literature on conversion narratives and conversion studies.[8]

3.2.1 Description of the Categories

The following is a description of the nine selected categories. The first category is the contextual factors that are important to understand the conversion narratives and the construction of identities, including personal, social, cultural,

---

5. Van Nieuwkerk, "Gender, Conversion, and Islam," 96; Van Nieuwkerk, "Gender and Conversion to Islam," 10 outlines two main approaches to conversion studies: the functional approach and the discourse analysis approach. The functional approach looks at what conversion means in the context of a person's life. Discourse analysis approach looks at how discourses are created and how they achieve their effect (Zebiri, *British Muslim Converts*, 7). I will follow Van Nieuwkerk's suggestion of combining these two approaches because it enables the researcher to arrive at a subtler and complete understanding of the phenomenon of conversion. I also found very helpful Riessman's recommendations about the structural analysis of discourses because it focuses more on how the narratives are organized and put together to achieve a narrator's strategic aims. How does a speaker attempt to persuade a listener that a sequence of events "really happened" with significant effects on the narrator? These questions shift attention from "the told" to the "telling" and from exclusive focus on a narrator's experience to the narrative itself (Riessman, *Narrative Methods*, 77).

6. Van Nieuwkerk, "Gender, Conversion, and Islam," 97.

7. Van Nieuwkerk, "Gender and Conversion to Islam," 8–9.

8. For additional information about methods and categories selected, see the introduction.

religious, and historical ones.[9] Second, the choices of words and metaphors used; the preference between conversion and reversion; the emic (insider) vs. etic (outsider) perspective[10]; how converts use analogies or narratives as "cultural tools" to provide coherence to individual religious experience.[11] Third, the most appealing aspect(s) about Islam.[12] Fourth, the main themes that emerged from the narratives, for example: religious seeking (wandering), discovery, and fulfillment.[13] Fifth, the predominant discourses in the conversion narrative: biographical, religious, gender, ethnic, and institutional.[14] Sixth, the varied purposes of the converts in telling their stories and how the discourses are created by the converts.[15] Seventh, the integration—or lack thereof—of the new religion's values and beliefs or continued integration of the previous religion's values and beliefs. I will analyze the continuity or discontinuity with the previous religion.[16] Also, I include important Islamic practices (pillars) such as prayer, fasting, almsgiving, and *Shahadah*. Eight, the degree of tension between culture and religion, high vs. low.[17] Ninth, the post-affiliation reactions of family and friends of the converts.[18]

Following, I will concentrate on the analysis of the conversion narratives by looking at the selected themes. I will begin each theme with Vicente, followed by Jaime, Claudia, and ending with Teresa. For more information about the profile of the converts and demographic information, see Appendix 2.

---

9. See Gooren, *Religious Conversion and Disaffiliation*; Rambo, *Understanding Religious Conversion*.

10. See Harris, "History and Significance."

11. See Edgell, "Cultural Sociology of Religion"; Jindra, *New Model of Religious Conversion*; Lieblich et al., "Holistic-Content Perspective."

12. See Allievi, "Pour Une Sociologie des Conversions"; Rambo, *Understanding Religious Conversion*.

13. See Morton, "Embracing Islam."

14. See van Nieuwkerk, "Gender, Conversion, and Islam"; Zebiri, *British Muslim Converts*.

15. See van Nieuwkerk, "Gender, Conversion, and Islam"; Zebiri, *British Muslim Converts*.

16. See van Nieuwkerk, "Gender, Conversion, and Islam."

17. See Bagheri, "Qualitative Investigation," Kraft, Kraft, *Searching for Heaven*.

18. See Kraft, *Searching for Heaven*; Zebiri, *British Muslim Converts*.

3.2.2 Contextual Factors

Vicente's Contextual Factors

Vicente's parents came to the United States in the late seventies. Vicente was born in Jersey City and raised in Union City, New Jersey. Vicente's parents raised their son according to the Ecuadorian culture and norms with which they were familiar. With regard to the neighborhood where he grew up, Vicente explained,

> Union City . . . although only 40 blocks long, is broke up into 3 sections, downtown, midtown and uptown. Downtown was the toughest area, more like you would say the ghetto. You know, there is a lot more crime. And you would have a lot of people who were a lot lower class people, a lot of [im]migrants, so I was raised around Puerto Ricans, Dominicans, Ecuadorians, there were not many Caucasians or even African Americans. There were a lot of Latinos in that area. That was pretty much all I knew.[19]

There are several contextual factors that are important to understand in Vicente's conversion narrative. First, theologically, Vicente expressed his disagreement in the past with some theological doctrines such as the Trinity and the role of Jesus in the Trinity. Second, Vicente previously had questions about what he believed in, especially as he started having new experiences with new people and new beliefs. He also expressed disappointment about the selfish attitudes of some Catholic priests. Vicente mentioned that "some priests live in nice houses and they have nice things."[20]

Third, culturally, he was interested in learning more about Hispanic culture and what it meant to be Hispanic both culturally and politically. He was very interested in politics, religion, and social issues. Islam gave him a chance to broaden his perspective.

Fourth, socially, his friendships with Muslims allowed him to participate in several meetings related to his topics of interest.

Fifth, historically, on several occasions Vicente mentioned the historical links of Islam with Andalucía, Spain. Also, the fact that his conversion was on September 11, 2001 is very significant. He chose this date because he wanted to make a statement about his commitment to Islam. It is interesting that, even though Vicente mentioned this historical link with Spain, he does not use the term "reversion" in his conversion story.

---

19. Cuartas/Vicente 2012:2.
20. Cuartas/Vicente 2012:3.

Jaime's Contextual Factors

Jaime's mother is from the Dominican Republic, and his father is from Puerto Rico. Jaime converted in January 1999. Jaime's parents are still married. He has one younger sister. They lived in a residential area in Miami,, where he sometimes went out to play, but mostly liked to stay indoors. Jaime received good support from his parents.

At a personal level, Jaime tends to be a loner, and he was not very religious. Jaime considered himself very artistic and sometimes suffers from depression, going back and forth between wanting to relate to society and friends and not wanting to relate with others. Because of his primarily loner status, Jaime is very conscious of the world around him. Because he experienced depression during childhood, he was searching for something that would give his life meaning. He is aware of the difficulties of practicing a minority religion.

Jaime's parents were diverse religiously. His father was nondenominational and not very active. His mother was Catholic and was more active than her husband. Jaime's mother was the one who took him to Sunday school at the Catholic Church. He explained,

> I always believed in God. I think I always had more of a Christian swing, and more of a Protestant belief. Put it that way. My intermediate family was kind like that. But my dad is not Catholic, he was more like, I would say non-denominational. My father is evangelical. When he grew up, his father was very strict, so with us, he was not that way. My mother is Catholic, but she is not like a stone Catholic [religious]. She is more like barely Catholic [nominal]. We believed in God. I considered myself Catholic up until high school. However, [I was] never really comfortable with the idea of praying [to] the saints.[21]

At the social level, Jaime spent much time with his best friend during high school (tenth to eleventh grade) who spoke to him about what it meant to be Muslim. From her, he began to embark on the journey of discovering things for himself. He does not fully recognize in his narrative the influence of other Muslim friends or imams. His level of socialization was moderate. One of the reasons for this is that he decided to learn by himself, and he spent considerable time with his female Muslim friend.

Theologically, Jaime found that he did not understand the Christian Bible and that it left him with too many questions that needed answers. Jaime stated, "I went to Sunday school. I grew up as a Catholic. I would not

---

21. Cuartas/Jaime 2012:2.

say I was a very devout Catholic who knew all the prayers. I would not say that, but we would attend Sunday school. We attended Mass on Sundays for a while. In middle school, I probably stopped going."[22] During his period of searching, Jaime was forced to think about his beliefs because his Muslim friend asked questions and he did not know how to respond to her. Then, he began to see Islam as a continuation of Christianity instead of thinking that Islam was a completely new religion.

Culturally, Jaime was heavily influenced by American culture. He has partially assimilated into the way of living in the United States. Because of the diverse beliefs of his parents and the lack of socialization with other Hispanic friends, the Hispanic values with which he was raised were not well retained. He stated, "I am not the type to make a lot of friends. I am the type to make a couple of friends, and just stay close with them, so I was not like the social butterfly."[23]

Claudia's Contextual Factors

Claudia's father is from Argentina and her mother is from the United States. Her parents were young when they had her, and it was a very happy home. Her grandparents also lived nearby. The family loved to play sports, especially soccer.

The following contextual factors are important in Claudia's case. First, the theological factor—she did not like that many of the questions she had about Christianity were not being answered by the pastor of her youth group. She also has never understood the Trinity or believed in the idea that Jesus was born fully a man and fully God.

Claudia lacked biblical training when she really needed someone to help provide the answers to her questions. The youth leaders in the church wanted her to find the answers for herself. Instead, Islam provided all the answers to her questions about faith and religion. Claudia stated: "There was always somebody to answer questions or talk to. And, they were my age; they understood. And, I think, their responses just always made sense. And, if it did not, I would just dig deeper and they were never trying to push me off and say . . . stop asking so many questions, they welcomed it."[24]

Second, personally, she needed something that would not only make sense to her but would also answer the questions that she had about God.

Third, the social factor was also important during her conversion to Islam. Claudia met several Muslims and developed friendships with them,

22. Cuartas/Jaime 2012:1.
23. Cuartas/Jaime 2012:1.
24. Cuartas/Claudia 2012:9.

but she did not simply rely on her friendships for answers about Islam. Instead, she knew that she had to do her own research. Claudia was first introduced to Islam by Muslim friends at college. She affirmed this, stating,

> Yes, there were a few Muslims at college. I think they had learned that I was interested. And, they were welcoming any questions that I had. They wanted to show me how to pray and more about their culture and, you know, what they do in Ramadan and what that is like at night and the fasting and the breaking of the fast, going to the various prayers and Friday prayers. Through this process, they invited me to Islam and wanted to definitely teach me as much as they could about it.[25]

However, Claudia initiated some of her contacts with Muslims because she wanted to ask questions. She had been observing them as well. Claudia directed her own socialization process.

Fourth, the cultural factor was also noteworthy because the relationship with her father was very important to her. Claudia mentioned the emphasis of Islam on family. She wanted to maintain the relationship of love and respect that she had with her father. Moreover, during high school and college, Claudia was surrounded by friends from other ethnicities and religions. Thus, she was very familiar and felt comfortable talking with people from other religions, particularly since she majored in anthropology in college.

Teresa's Contextual Factors

There are several contextual factors that are important in Teresa's case. First, at a personal level, Teresa arrived in the United States at the age of four. Her mother is American, and her father is Peruvian. She was the only child at that time. They had a lot of mobility within the country, and they worked hard to be able to adjust in the United States. Teresa stated: "My parents, you know, began to work and we moved to Miami. Then, we have family here in Virginia, so we moved to Virginia. My parents started working very hard and, you know, I had more family kept up coming from Peru, so we had more family around us. I thought that they were very hard workers you know. I had a normal childhood and every day was good."[26]

Teresa is considered a member of the 1.5 generation. She had a lot of confusion about Christianity during her adolescence. Additionally, she experienced several crises that had an effect on her: by parents' divorce when she was around seven years old and the death of her grandfather from cancer.

---

25. Cuartas/Claudia 2012:7.
26. Cuartas/Teresa 2012:1.

Second, the social factor was also significant. Because of her job at the auto dealership, she had consistent interaction with mature, practicing Muslims. Working among Muslims gave her many chances to see and do what they did. Then, she began to have questions and later she decided to find a new Muslim class where she was able to learn more about Islam. The level of socialization by Muslim coworkers was high, but she said she was always in control of her choices. She also worked in an Islamic center performing administrative tasks.

Third, the religious factor was important because Teresa's family was very religious growing up. As Teresa explained,

> My family was very strong Catholic . . . I feel like my family was more religious when I was younger; you know, we were going to church every Sunday and I went to Sunday school. I remembered getting baptized. I was not a baby, I was older, so I got baptized in Peru and when we came here, I did everything, you know, confirmation everything. I went to Sunday school . . . I went to classes. I went to classes every Sunday you know; I did everything in the Catholic Church.[27]

Fourth, with regard to cultural factors, she was dissatisfied with some cultural values as a Hispanic. She mentioned that some of her relatives were drinking alcohol and that this is related to the Hispanic culture. She stated, "I did not like what alcohol did to certain people in my family, so I saw some things really bad that happened. And I really liked the fact that in Islam you are not supposed to drink. So, I was like you know this is perfect . . . in Islam you are not supposed to drink."[28] She wanted to change her lifestyle and become different from the rest of her family.

3.2.3 Choices of Words and Metaphors

There is a movement in Vicente's story from non-Muslim to Muslim. There is relatively little emphasis on reciting the *Shahadah*. Vicente used Islamic or Arabic words on only a few occasions. Vicente lived in Egypt for almost

---

27. Cuartas/Teresa 2012:2; Apparently, Teresa had many questions unanswered by the previous religion. Teresa mentioned that she was missing something. She went back to church and asked questions, but she got no answers. At that time, she began to interact with Muslims at the auto dealership, and this was the beginning of her interest in Islam. Teresa does not elaborate in her story about specific theological issues that she had. She is still in the process of answering some questions. She is working to construct her new religious identity.

28. Cuartas/Teresa 2012:11.

one year and learned Arabic there. He said he can read and speak Arabic well. He has been following Islam for almost eleven years.

When I asked him about the most appealing aspects of Islam, Vicente answered "there are no mysteries in Islam . . . it is clear as light in day."[29] Vicente used Christian vocabulary on several occasions. For example: "God" instead of *Allah* (only twice), "salvation," "reading the Bible," and "Jesus." Vicente also repeated the word "perspective" several times. He only mentioned the prophet Muhammad once.

Some of the repeated phrases within Vicente's story are the following: "I learned," "I became very interested," "I became very involved," and "I became very intrigued." He sometimes mixed Spanish and English in his narrative. Regarding Vicente's preference about conversion or reversion, he stated, "I am not very [hung] up on being a revert or a convert, it depends on what point of view you look at it. Many people say convert, because it will [imply] a way of life that a lot of people have."[30] He prefers to use the phrase "embrace Islam."[31] In his narrative, Vicente used, on several occasions, phrases such as "embraced Islam," "accepted Islam," and "followed Islam."

Jaime used the word "sculpture" in his story. He explained, "In a sense, sometimes I look at it as . . . more like a process of self-discovery as well as more as . . . sometimes I look at it as a sculpture."[32] Jaime paused before using words such as "prophet," "like," and "you know." Jaime also laughed frequently during the interview and used a lot of Christian vocabulary; for example, "God" instead of *Allah* (used only one time), "salvation," "reading the Bible," and "Jesus." There was no emphasis on reciting the *Shahadah* in Jaime's narrative.

Jaime also quoted from the Bible on several occasions. For example, "When Jesus says 'I am the way, the truth and the life' [quoted from John 14:6], He is the role model. He is the way; He is the truth; He is the light; He is the bridge of the salvation."[33] Jaime mentioned Jesus several times in his narrative.

Claudia did not use metaphors or analogies in her conversion narrative. She repeated phrases such as "I enjoyed watching people, observing

29. Cuartas/Vicente 2012:6.

30. Cuartas/Vicente 2012:6.

31. Vicente added, "A lot of Muslims would say revert because they were born Muslims, they believe that they were born Muslims and that is a side, that is adopted different way of thinking, and is coming back to [what] we were. To me, I would like to say 'embrace' Islam. I do not say I converted or reverted [to] it. I would say 'I embraced Islam'" (Cuartas/Vicente 2012:6).

32. Cuartas/Vicente 2012:6.

33. Cuartas/Jaime 2012:8.

them, asking questions; you know." Claudia mentioned God several times and she never used *Allah* to refer to God. Also, she did not mention the prophet Muhammad in her narrative. Claudia did not emphasize reciting the *Shahadah*.

In terms of her preference for conversion or reversion, she stated, "Some people say reversion because they say you are born Muslim. Your parents are the doctrinarians; or your community changed you. I am comfortable with either. I am comfortable with conversion; I am comfortable with reversion. I mean, I will refer to myself as a convert and a revert."[34]

Claudia rarely used the term "reversion" in her conversion narrative. She used phrases such as "when I converted . . . when I learned about Islam, embracing Islam."[35] She was very careful about not labelling what she is. When she participated in Christianity, she considered herself non-denominational. She did not really define whether she considers herself a convert or a revert because she will tell people either depending upon the circumstances. As a Muslim, she does not subscribe to one of the schools of thought unless she feels that she has to, but she really only considers herself to be a Muslim instead of a Sunni or a Shi'ite.

Teresa was very relaxed and open in the interview; she laughed all the time. Before the interview, she was not wearing the *hijab* and she asked me to give her time to be ready for the interview. Then, she wore the *hijab* during the interview. There were several phrases repeated in her conversion narrative, for example: "you know," "I was like," and "I feel like." There were many pauses in the interview as well. Teresa used simple language to answer the questions, and she did not use Arabic in her narrative. Also, she did not use analogies or metaphors to describe her religious experience. Teresa mentioned God several times and she never used *Allah* to refer to God. Furthermore, she did not mention the prophet Muhammad in her narrative. In her conversion narrative, Teresa did not mention details about saying the *Shahadah*.

When I asked Teresa about her preference for using the term "conversion," she stated, "I do not mind, but they say that in Islam everybody is born a Muslim, so you are supposed to say I am reverting to Islam."[36] She stated in the quote that she is not defined by these terms. Additionally, she explained that "some people tend to be focused [on] the little things, but I tend to be focused on the big important things, you know."[37] She did not ex-

---

34. Cuartas/Claudia 2012:5.
35. Cuartas/Claudia 2012:7.
36. Cuartas/Teresa 2012:12.
37. Cuartas/Teresa 2012:12.

plain what the important things were that she was referring to here. Teresa did not use the term "reversion" at all in her narrative.

3.2.4 Most Appealing Aspects about Islam

Vicente mentioned several appealing factors about Islam:

> The simplicity and clarity of Islam. There are no mysteries, everything is what it is, is clear as light in day, there are no mysteries or ambiguities, there is no confusion. For me, the biggest thing was... you know when they say there is one God, there is one God, there is no three in one or one in three, there is no egg, yolk, shell or anything like that, there is no trying to explain a divine... a trinity in one.[38]

Vicente emphasized the simplicity of Islam. He affirmed, "for me, it was this simplicity, understanding who Jesus was, and who were the previous prophets, their missions, they were all the same... and the... so that simplicity of things, made me really realize that whoa, this is it."[39]

Vicente was not satisfied with the responses of the priest in his previous religion. He claimed, "because one of my biggest questions, when I began to question Christ, [was] Catholicism, if this is the religion of God, why is this so complicated to follow or complicated to understand? Why is it that when I asked a priest my questions [he couldn't] answer, he says: 'son you just have to have faith'? Well, how can I have faith when I cannot understand?"[40]

Jaime apparently gained a new perspective about the wider role of religion (Islam) in life. Jaime stated,

> Many people entered Islam through a major shift in their lives; they have a lot of... I do not want to say drama or... something that causes them to think about their lives; something bad or something hard. For me, I was thinking deeply about my life,

---

38. Cuartas/Vicente 2012:6.
39. Cuartas/Vicente 2012:6.
40. Cuartas/Vicente 2012:6–7; Vicente also mentioned the importance of historical and scientific proofs. He explained, "so when I learned about Islam, it was not just about having faith. The faith was just one aspect. But the other aspect is the historical proofs. For me, that did it. Also, I studied for Mechanical Engineer, so I spent a lot of time in science and math. So, when I learned about the scientific findings, the scientific proofs of the Qur'an... that solidified more its acceptance. So, when I started realizing that the Qur'an describes how the stars are formed; how the babies are formed; the barriers and the water. All these different scientific proofs that are found much later it just made me realize, how is it possible that somebody who did not know anything could know about it, except that it was revealed from God" (Cuartas/Vicente 2012:6–7).

but it came as a result of being next to someone else who was. Not through my own direct problem, but rather through somebody else's problem. Then, I became awakened to the fact that there is just more. And, so for me, like the most valuable thing is maybe the new perspective on the awakening I got. Religion and life in general that came about through accepting Islam.[41]

Jaime was attracted by the new perspective that he gained though Islam. Based on his narrative, this was a religious perspective that allowed him to see Islam integrated with other aspects of life. He mentioned the relationship between religion and science because it was something new for him.

Claudia found a sense of continuity between Islam and her previous religion, Catholicism. Claudia explained, "For me it was the familiarity. It was something foreign to me, but it still felt very familiar to me at the same time. I was reading about something that I had never heard of or learned of before. But, a lot of it spoke to me. And a lot of it kind of related to the way that I had lived my life . . . the way that I wanted to continue to live it."[42]

One of the most important aspects for Claudia is to become a better person. She explained, "So, for me it was really a guide in how to be the best person that I want to be—How to be the best daughter, the best sister, the best mother, the best wife and the best friend. It was really a book of guidance for me."[43]

Claudia was a good observer of people when she was at college. She affirmed, "So, those two years outside of, you know, attending class and sports and everything else, a lot of it was just research. I graduated with an anthropology degree. So, I enjoyed watching people and learning about their ways and just kind of being an observer. And, I was just always a people watcher. I would sit in the main halls and the Johnson Center and I would just watch people in how they interacted with one another."[44]

41. Cuartas/Jaime 2012:7.

42. Cuartas/Claudia 2012:7.

43. Cuartas/Claudia 2012:7.

44. Cuartas/Claudia 2012:9; Claudia was impressed by the behavior of her Muslim friends and the structure of daily prayer. She felt attracted to public interruptions of daily prayer to express piety. Claudia stated, "Something that really struck me while a lot of my non-Muslim friends in college were more interested in what is the next party we are going to go to and what we are going to do tonight, my Muslim friends would stop, we would be playing a game of cards, and they would stop in the middle and say, 'I have to go pray . . . I will be right back'. And, to me that just shocked me because I'm #1 growing up Christian and you pray whenever you want; there is no set time. You know, I can pray before I go to bed. I can pray on my way to work or whatever. But, to have somebody who is my age usually engrossed with looking good and you know self-image and not wanting to feel awkward or weird in front of others, you know, it was

Teresa liked some things that she heard from her Muslim friends. She also observed Muslims at work. Teresa affirmed,

> A story that one of my associates told me about their gathering is that . . . I mean, this is one of the reasons why Islam was appealing, but it was not my favorite thing, but they had a party in the house and the women were in a top, second floor, and the men were in the basement, so I was like, 'why do you do that?' And you know, I was asking the guy, why you guys do that, and they explained all the reasons why. It was very interesting . . . that makes so much sense. I was like . . . you do not have, you know, jealousy or people like you just do not have . . . and it just started to click . . . Islam tries to avoid all those things happening because things happen, and we are humans.[45]

Teresa is talking about relationships, marriage, and being faithful. The separation between men and women during times of fellowship provided a sense of structure for Teresa. She added, "by avoiding these things then everybody is happy, so that is something that attracted me."[46]

Another aspect that was important for Teresa was something that she was taught in the courses for new Muslims. Teresa stated, "the fact that Islam was the last religion to be revealed—that was appealing to me, and I was like . . . 'well then, it must be the right thing to do.'"[47] This theological aspect of ongoing revelation from God was significant for Teresa and Jaime as well.

3.2.5 Main Themes that are Emerging

Vicente had unresolved questions before his conversion to Islam. He experienced a time of religious seeking (wandering) at the end of high school and during college.[48] Vicente stated, "I became very intrigued with what he [a Muslim friend he met in college] was saying, because many of the aspects, that I grew up wondering, or confused about, he answered it, and

---

their faith first. So that really, it really grabbed me" (Cuartas/Claudia 2012:9).

45. Cuartas/Teresa 2012:11.

46. Cuartas/Teresa 2012:11.

47. Cuartas/Teresa 2012:11; Teresa always wanted to know more about new things, so this theological aspect appealed to her.

48. The literature refers to this season of wandering as religious seeking. The people who do it are called seekers. For more details about religious seeking, see Buxant et al., "Free-Lance Spiritual Seekers"; Guzik, "Search for Meaning"; Roof and Greer, *Generation of Seekers*.

what amazed me was that he was only eighteen years old. And I thought he had the answers that I was looking for."[49]

Then, apparently, Vicente began to discover new relationships between Islam and Hispanic values. He explained, "that made it easy for me to adapt within the religion, because as a Latino I already had many of those morals, such as the respect you have for your parents. And even culturally, you have a lot of other things that came from Andalucía, Spain."[50] He looked back on history to try to make sense of his own conversion. This is also part of the institutional discourse taught in some Islamic centers. This historical link gives a sense of familiarity to new Hispanic converts.

Finally, there is a sense of fulfillment in Vicente's story with a high degree of choices observed in his conversion account. Vicente affirmed, "how Islam is a shared religion, you know, the interaction with different things that dealt with just living."[51] Vicente gained a new perspective with Islam and he emphasized the fact that Islam is a way of life. Vicente was highly socialized by Muslim friends due to his choices. Muslim friends caused him to think about social and political views with religion. He controlled the level of his socialization by virtue of the fact that he made certain connections to talk about his political and evolving religious views.

Jaime experienced a religious seeking period during his final years in high school. Jaime had unresolved questions before his conversion to Islam; he was raised Catholic, but he considered himself nondenominational. Jaime stated,

> I started thinking I do not really believe that praying to saints is correct. I did not really believe that confessing to a priest is right. I guess I am not really Catholic. Because to me that is what really defines Catholicism. I do not even think too much about the Pope. Not that I am liberal . . . At that point, from the 10th grade forward, I considered myself non-denominational Christian.[52]

Jaime then went through a process of self-discovery and personal searching. He began to accept Islam as a continuation of Christianity. Regarding fulfillment, there is a low level of fulfillment and involvement in Islam. For example, Jaime is not participating in the Friday prayer meetings (it is required for male Muslims), and his socialization with other Muslims is very limited. Jaime is still in the process of reconstructing his religious identity. Perhaps this is in part due to the fact that he has isolated himself

49. Cuartas/Vicente 2012:5.
50. Cuartas/Vicente 2012:7.
51. Cuartas/Vicente 2012:6.
52. Cuartas/Jaime 2012:5.

from the Islamic community. In addition, there is a lower degree of choices observed in his conversion account in comparison with other converts.

Claudia experienced a period of religious seeking before her conversion to Islam. She had unresolved questions before her conversion. She then went through a time of discovery. She mentioned that she was already living it. She found connections with the way she was living before she embraced Islam. Analyzing her conversion narrative, there is also a sense of fulfillment, and there is a sense that she is still constructing her religious identity. A high degree of choices was observed in her conversion account.

The level of Claudia's socialization by Muslim friends was high due to her choices. She had several Muslim friends in high school and college. Once she was interested, Claudia decided to go to the Muslim Student Association to gather more information and to learn what it was she was supposed to do as a Muslim.

Teresa experienced several crises before she accepted Islam. She also had unanswered questions when she was Catholic. She tended to always ask questions, but she was very disappointed at the lack of answers from the people at church. This was a period of religious seeking.

Teresa stated, "I was in a point in my life where I didn't want to do what everybody was doing. You know, at nineteen, you know, like party and things like that. I just [got] over it very quickly, and I saw that I realized that I didn't want to keep doing that anymore even though I was really young. I don't know. It was weird."[53] Teresa experienced difficult times and she said her life was a mess.[54] Then she began to interact with Muslim coworkers. She discovered that "Islam was the last religion to be revealed."[55] According to her conversion narrative, she has a low level of fulfillment in Islam. Teresa is still in the process of learning, finding answers, and making changes because she has been following Islam for only three years. Thus, the level of fulfillment is yet unclear in her narrative. Teresa was highly socialized by Muslim coworkers and friends. She also worked in an Islamic center. Teresa worked for an auto dealership with older Muslim men and women. She took a class for newly converted Muslims.

3.2.6 Predominant Discourses

The most predominant discourses in Vicente's story are ethnic and religious. He began his story by emphasizing the fact that he was very interested in

---

53. Cuartas/Teresa 2012:9.
54. Cuartas/Teresa 2012:9.
55. Cuartas/Teresa 2012:11.

Hispanic culture. In addition, he emphasized the importance of family and respect for parents. He stated that, because he found connections with Islamic values, it was easier for him to follow Islam. With regard to the religious discourse, Vicente shared some of the reasons why he decided to follow Islam. He was looking for answers and found simplicity and clarity in Islam.

The institutional discourse is also present in Vicente's narrative. He learned from imams and Muslim friends that Islam offers historical and scientific proofs. Vicente's socialization was high and came through his participation in conferences, meetings, and living in Egypt. The biographical discourse is included in his story as well. Vicente discussed significant aspects of how he began to follow Islam. The gender discourse is very limited. He briefly mentioned some perceptions from born Muslims with regard to Muslim converts. Vicente explained,

> When you tell them [born Muslims] that you are Latino, and you accepted Islam, they are the most welcoming people. Some of them had come to me and say: you are so lucky that Allah choose you to become Muslim, I was born Muslim, so they feel like you [Muslim converts] are better than [born Muslims], and not in the sense to diminish themselves, but is in a way to encourage you and welcome you.[56]

The most predominant discourses in Jaime's narrative are biographical, religious, and institutional discourses. Jaime provides many details in terms of the crises and unresolved questions he had before accepting Islam. He also explained some of the reasons for his conversion to Islam. He found continuity between Christianity and Islam.

Jaime found something that suited his need to stay in the home and to not have to participate publicly. Nonetheless, he does not say when he decided, or even how he decided, other than his friend helping him to make sense of it without fully challenging him to convert to Islam.

The institutional discourse is very significant as well. Jaime sees Islam as a continuation of Christianity. "I thought that I was doing my Christian duty by accepting Islam."[57] He felt a need to respond at that point. Jaime stated,

> The idea that there was a covenant and we were obligated to accept the message whenever it continued. It never occurred to me up to that point. So, I was supposed to pray. God might have given another message; another prophet, and the message continued. Whatever the perspective is on Jesus is another story,

---

56. Cuartas/Vicente 2012:12.
57. Cuartas/Jaime 2012:7.

but you know . . . the message already continued. So, I need to validate if it is true. I looked at it from that perspective.[58]

Jaime considers himself a Muslim of the Sunni tradition. He explained,

> I have always thought I identify myself as Muslim. I think it is better to avoid terminology and separation, in the Quran says not to bear sects, no accept divisions . . . if someone wants to know, if there is a particular perspective that I follow, just to make it easier to understand where I come from, I would say Sunni tradition *Hanafi Fiqh*. It is just like the perspective of what you practice. The Sunni tradition that kind of more affects the legislation, the sort of legislation.[59]

Jaime mentioned that it was like a spiritual awakening for him. The Islamic teachings and institutional discourses were very significant for Jaime. For example, the messages and revelations continue, as Jaime explained, "so my perspective on some of the things that I read in the past was expanded. The idea that the message did not stop with Jesus and that actually it continued afterward, it was something new for me."[60] Ethnic and gender discourses are not prevalent in Jaime's story. The aspects of gender will be further analyzed in upcoming chapters.

The predominant discourses in Claudia's narrative are religious, gender, and institutional. Claudia had unresolved theological questions from her previous religion. She did not believe in the Trinity or in the role of Jesus. Perhaps her issue with the Trinity is an expression of deeper dissatisfaction with Catholicism. Claudia was looking for discipleship and someone able to help her with her spiritual journey because there was so much unknown about Catholicism.[61] Claudia ended up disappointed with Catholicism, the faith she was supposed to have.

---

58. Cuartas/Jaime 2012:6.

59. Cuartas/Jaime 2012:8; The Hanafi school of jurisprudence was founded by Abu Hanifa an-Nu'man. It is followed by Muslims in the Levant, Central Asia, Afghanistan, Pakistan, India, Bangladesh, Western Lower Egypt, Iraq, Turkey, the Balkans, and by most of Russia's Muslim community. There are movements within this school, such as Deobandis and the Tablighi Jamaat, which are all concentrated in South Asia and in most parts of India. Some of the differences with other schools are the following: a) Hanafi permits one who does not speak Arabic to pray in another language; and b) Hanafi permits appointing female judges. For more details about the different schools of jurisprudence, see Rahim, *Principles of Muhammadan Jurisprudence*.

60. Cuartas/Jaime 2012:7.

61. Here, discipleship is understood as a steady spiritual growth and increasing knowledge of Scripture.

In high school, she met many friends, many of whom were Muslims and she enjoyed talking to them about being Muslim. She was beginning to find her missing answers. There was a movement in the story from the previous religion to the new one. Claudia embraced Islam because she needed more structure, and she was comfortable with the choices she had made because they allowed her to continue to be connected with her family, especially with her father.

The gender discourse is particularly evident in Claudia's narrative. Claudia is a *feminist activist*, and she wants to be able to focus more on raising her kids. She fully justified her involvement in sports to become connected with the community and with Muslim sisters. She is also very devoted to raising her children as Muslims. She elaborated in terms of the use of the *hijab*. This was a critical decision for Claudia because she began to wear the *hijab* right after 9/11.[62] Her father was concerned about her safety. Claudia also decided that she would not change her name. She explained, "I like my name too much. That is me. That is who I am, and I thought that I had changed enough of myself, you know, like wearing the scarf [anytime], and covering my clothes and prayer that I did not want to change anything else. And also, I did not want it to be a negative influence on my father. I thought of keeping it even when I got married."[63]

Due to the high level of socialization into Islam, there is also an institutional discourse in Claudia's story. The Islamic teachings influenced Claudia's belief system during the process of socialization. She stated, "I was reading about something that I had never heard of or learned of before. But, a lot of it spoke to me. And a lot of it kind of related to the way that I had lived my life . . . the way that I wanted to continue to live it."[64]

For Teresa, the predominant discourses are biographical and ethnic or national. There are some aspects that are incomplete or missing from her story. She did not explain in her narrative why she left her previous religion or why she followed Islam. Teresa included some details about why she, as a woman, chose Islam. One of the aspects she observed from her Muslim friends was the separation between men and women during activities of fellowship. The way in which her Muslim friends managed relationships provided a sense of structure for Teresa.

The main emphasis in her narrative is her need to change and become different. One of the aspects that was underlined in her narrative from the beginning was the tension between religion and Hispanic culture in terms

62. Cuartas/Claudia 2012:15.
63. Cuartas/Claudia 2012:13.
64. Cuartas/Claudia 2012:7.

of drinking alcohol. There were many problems in her family with drinking alcohol. She found later that Islam is very strict about alcohol use, and this provided a sense of structure for her because she was partying too much.

3.2.7 How Discourses are Created By the Converts

Vicente's account is reconstructed in light of his interest in Latino culture, politics, and religion. He was impressed by the presentations and answers he heard from a young Muslim man during his second year of college. He found a sense of empowerment, relevancy, and influence in Islam. He is very motivated by *dawah*. He used his narrative to dramatically communicate the choices he made to follow Islam and how difficult it was for him to make that decision on September 11, 2001. He also used analogies to make sense of his religious experience.

Vicente is the only Hispanic Muslim convert within this study who has shared his faith with his family and relatives and actively influenced them in their conversion to Islam. He married a Hispanic Muslim convert. He explained, "my brother accepted Islam months later after I accepted Islam, and then two years later my mom accepted. My cousin accepted Islam back in 2004. I have a younger cousin that accepted Islam in 2004. My dad accepted Islam earlier or late last year."[65] Unfortunately, Vicente did not give details about the dynamics of his family's conversion to Islam. He is also intentionally keeping his Hispanic name to be able to share his faith among his Hispanic friends. Thus, he is very active in doing *dawah*.

Jaime's story is constructed in light of his understanding that Islam is a continuation of Christianity. He was looking for belonging and friendship as well. Jaime only nominally practiced his previous religion. Through his relationship with a Muslim girl, he was forced to rethink his belief system and found continuity between his previous religion and Islam. With regard to participation in and commitment to Islam, he recognized his challenges and limitations to becoming more active publicly. He is more focused on his personal relationship with God and not on rituals.

In Claudia's story, her motivation was all about needing to find the answers to the questions that she had about religion. The nondenominational youth group she attended was all about finding answers personally, most likely through prayer, reflection, and reading the Bible. For Claudia, there was a serious need to learn more about the Bible and about God because when she was younger, she did not know basic histories from the Bible including

---

65. Cuartas/Vicente 2012:9.

the stories of Adam and Eve.⁶⁶ According to her, "she had been living the life of Islam."⁶⁷ Claudia was motivated by this acceptance, as well as Islam's structure which enabled her to learn. She was looking for a sense of meaning. Islam was familiar, but different. Being the best person she could be was a significant aspect. She was impressed by the behaviors of her Muslim friends.

Teresa was looking for meaning, stability, and structure. No alcohol, no pork, and no partying. Teresa said she was tired of partying too much.⁶⁸ Charity and giving back were important for Teresa. There is a sense of partial fulfillment as she is still working out her conversion. She received help from Muslim friends to explore job opportunities while she was adapting to the country. Teresa always wanted to know more about spiritual things, so that is reflected in her conversion narrative. She was very honest answering the questions. Teresa's discourse is still under development.

3.2.8 Integration of the New Religion's Values and Beliefs

Vicente mentioned the significance of family values, respect for parents, and emphasis on morals. His parents emphasized these values while he was growing up. Thus, the most important aspects of Islam for Vicente were monotheism and the emphasis on family values. He affirmed,

> for me [it] was the devotion and dedication to your family, and it appealed to me because being Latino, one already has strong family values. One, my family came here without anything, without knowing anyone, so we were very close to each other. Islam strengthened that bond . . . because Islam teaches you values and morals regarding family, your mother and father.⁶⁹

Vicente found a sense of congruency between the Hispanic values and the Islamic values he was taught. Vicente explained, "That attracted me very much. That made it easy for me to adapt within the religion because as a Latino I already had many of those morals, such as the respect you have [for] your parents. And even culturally, you have a lot of other things that came from Andalucía, Spain. The biggest thing that really did it was the monotheism and the values for my family as well."⁷⁰

---

66. Cuartas/Claudia 2012:4.
67. Cuartas/Claudia 2012:5.
68. Cuartas/Teresa 2012:9.
69. Cuartas/Vicente 2012:7.
70. Cuartas/Vicente 2012:7.

With regard to the pillars of Islam, Vicente noted that most important pillar is prayer. He stated,

> so, of course I believe that God is one and he is the only one worthy of worship and that Mohammed is his final messenger, also accepting all the messengers that came before. Prayer is the biggest thing. Prayer is the probably the most important thing, next to believing in monotheism. Then you have of course your other obligations as far as other activities as learning Arabic, learning how to read the Qur'an, learning where you should put the Qur'an.[71]

As previously explained, there is a sense of continuity and familiarity with the previous religion. Vicente said he was a devoted Catholic before his conversion. Vicente faithfully served as an altar boy from fourth to eighth grades. According to him, this became part of his lifestyle.[72] He and his wife are both very active in Islam.

Jaime has partially integrated the new values and beliefs of Islam in his conversion narrative. In part, some aspects still remain the same. For example, he is not interested in building relationships with other Muslims. He is very focused on his wife, who is also a Muslim. Jaime believes that it is important to listen to and help other people. His biggest emphasis was on prayer. He did not emphasize family like the other converts. Overall, there is a sense of continuity with the previous religion because Jaime saw Islam as having continuity with Christianity.

An important value for Claudia throughout her life has been respect for her father, and she is always looking for his approval. She did not mention her mother. Claudia shared:

> Yeah, I mean a lot of it is respect for others. Respect for yourself. Something that I think I gained more of once I learned more about Islam was patience. And just helping out and giving back more specifically to my family and ones that have given so much to me. Like giving back instead of being selfish; thinking more of others than just of myself.[73]

Claudia wanted to be sure of the facts about life and how to become a better person. She also spent time researching the Trinity and the oneness of God. She was very rational in her approach of accepting Islam. Looking for proofs about life and religion became a personal value for her. She affirmed,

---

71. Cuartas/Vicente 2012:8.
72. Cuartas/Vicente 2012:1.
73. Cuartas/Claudia 2012:8.

"for me it was a lot of 'show me the facts.' I want to see the facts. I want to see the proof of the reasoning behind it. I do not want to believe it blindly."[74]

Claudia was comfortable with her values as a Latina. She explained,

> I think a lot of it was what related to the way I was raised. And I think a lot of it had to do with the Latino values. A lot of it was respecting your elders, and your family is key and important. And it was the oneness of God, and that can play a large part of your life. So, I think that took a lot of the love I had growing up and just having it centered around my family and I think learning that that was also a big part of Islam, that spoke to me as well.[75]

There is a sense of continuity with the previous religion in Claudia's narrative. When I asked Claudia about her experience with Islam, she replied,

> I think I had been living the life of Islam for some time before that. And I think one day it just, it really clicked that I was very living it in my heart and I felt like, you know, between me and between God, like we knew I was living it. I just kind of wanted to make it official. And still even in 2000 I was really only saying the *Shahadah* privately with myself and only telling a few friends. And, then, a year later, I did it publicly at school.[76]

She then added, "So, it took a little bit longer to make it more public. But my close friends at school knew."[77]

It was the opposite for Teresa. There is a sense of continuity between the old and the new religion in Teresa's narrative. Teresa was not aware of changes in terms of her worldview. She explained, "I did not know about Islam before, so it made me think about obviously more people in the world that are Muslim, but that is not . . . there is nothing changed in terms of world view. Like, I mean, it just . . . it is just a religion."[78]

74. Cuartas/Claudia 2012:8.

75. Cuartas/Claudia 2012:8.

76. Cuartas/Claudia 2012:6.

77. Cuartas/Claudia 2012:7; Analyzing Claudia's story, I noticed that Claudia was looking back, reflecting on and explaining her conversion and already integrating the new religious beliefs. For example, when I asked her about her previous religious experiences, she affirmed, "it was practically little to none. My mother was very religious, and my grandmother was Roman Catholic . . . You know, my grandmother went to church all the time. My father not so much and my mother as well not so much. So, when I was raised, it was I knew I was Christian because we believed in God and it was the law of the land and I was not growing up on the Trinity. I was not growing up on, you know, Jesus as God. There was really one God. I never associated Jesus with Him being God" (Cuartas/Claudia 2012:2).

78. Cuartas/Teresa 2012:17.

Some of the pillars that were important for Teresa were prayer and charity. Teresa affirmed,

> They were like praying all the time, you know, and not [eating] certain food and explained to me they're like a family gathering. What they will do? Why give to charity this amount? I was like, oh my God, this is so cool, like you know . . . this [is] so interesting like I really want to know more, because that is how I am . . . I want to know everything. So just to know, and they started telling me and on my own gradually, gradually, you know, a few months were passing by, I researched on where I can get classes on Muslims, you know, Islam, and that is it. And you know obviously they are Muslim, so they are telling me the good stuff about, you know, the Islam and encouraging me. Charity . . . just giving back and learning from people you know and learning from experiences.[79]

3.2.9 Degree of Tension between Culture and Religion

Vicente experienced a low degree of tension between religion and culture because, based on his account, his Latino culture fit with his perspective on family values, monotheism, and prayer. However, one of the most difficult issues for Vicente was dealing with the negative reactions of some of his friends after embracing Islam. He has learned to navigate these mild tensions.

Vicente recognized some of the tensions between culture and religion, but he saw Islam in a holistic way that transcended culture and reinforced his personal values. Vicente explained, "I do not think it is part of Latino culture per se, I think it is part of what has been accepted as normal within the Latino culture. Like, for example, in the Latino culture we find that alcoholism [drinking alcohol] is very preeminent. It is something that is wrong . . . This is actually a problem in society nowadays. There are more commonalities than differences."[80]

Vicente mentioned that Islam provides clear guidelines with regard to abstinence from drinking alcohol, relationships, and diet. Vicente explained,

> when I was growing up my dad, Latino, my dad would be like [Spanish] *'consíguete una novia'* [you need to date somebody] and it was normal but in Islam there are certain methodologies on how to marry an individual, and it was an adjustment in that,

---

79. Cuartas/Teresa 2012:9–10.
80. Cuartas/Vicente 2012:12.

but those are really the only very things and [eating] pork. There is more commonality than differences.[81]

The degree of tension between religion and culture for Jaime was high. Perhaps one of the reasons for this is the differing ethnicities of his parents. He converted at the age of seventeen during high school. Of the converts within this study, Jaime is the one that has been following Islam for the longest period of time. However, Jaime also assimilated more to American society. For example, individualism and hard work are important American values he embraced as his own.

Jaime decided not to be involved with his Muslim community, and he justified this because the nature of his job largely prevents him from becoming more involved in the Muslim community. He became more concerned about his responsibilities at work and did not make much of an effort to be more involved with the Muslim community. He has not resolved this tension, and he is fine with it. Jaime is a good example of a low-commitment Muslim who is more active privately than publicly. His major focus is on prayer.

Claudia did not have any problems being Hispanic and Muslim. There was a low degree of tension between religion and culture because most of Claudia's choices about religion were based on her cultural and personal values. She learned to navigate the tensions between culture and religion. She found shared values between Islam and Hispanic culture, for example, the emphasis on family and respect of parents. The support from her father was significant because she made decisions based on her father's approval. Claudia was raising her children in a Muslim community, but she was still very much Hispanic in the things that she did. For example, she was very protective of her children. She stated,

> Like a lot of that culture is still very strong in our life. I mean, we still get together, you know, when the weather is good on every Sunday at my father's house. I mean every weekend we are with my family for dinner. They come over for dinner. The fare, if my dad's cooking usually, it is usually Argentine food. Especially when it is nice outside, he usually has an *asado* and *molleja* [typical Argentinian barbecue]. He mixed everything. You know, there he has got the tango [Argentinian music] in the background, and he has the Argentine grill. So, you know, that part of culture is still very much in my life and my kids' life. You know, my kids call my parents *abuelo* [grandfather] and *abuela* [grandmother].[82]

81. Cuartas/Vicente 2012:12.
82. Cuartas/Claudia 2012:14.

Claudia's family all hug regardless of a person's sex, her husband included. Claudia's husband (unknown nationality) adjusted to Claudia's family traditions.

Teresa learned to navigate the tension between culture and religion. She acknowledged the cultural tension from the beginning of her story by identifying some aspects about her family, such as drinking alcohol, and she found in Islam a way to balance the conflict by following the clear rules and structure. Teresa made choices that fit her values and purposes. She is comfortable keeping things separate when navigating culture and religion. For example, Teresa mentioned that she is willing to eat pork and drink alcohol.[83] According to Teresa, "Islam . . . is just a religion."[84] Thus, she did not fully express the idea that Islam was part of her daily life. Additionally, she does not have any problem having non-Muslim friends. She is very open to building relationships with non-Muslims.

3.2.10 Reactions of Vicente's Family and Friends

Vicente's mother supported his decision to follow Islam. He stated, "When I came home, and I told my parents that weekend . . . and told my mom that I accepted Islam, my mom said . . . if that is what you want to do, then go ahead, as long as you found God, you found something that brings you closer God, I am okay, it does not matter. My mom was very religious . . . she was Catholic."[85] Vicente probably did not share all the details of his mother's reaction.

With regard to Vicente's father's response, he had questions and was more concerned about the safety of his son. Vicente shared, "my dad was like, 'why are you accepting it during this time, it is okay, you do it, you can do it, you can do whatever you want but do not do it now. I am worried about you.'"[86] Apparently, his brother was supportive as well as other relatives. He explained, "My brother was, he was ok too, but he did not want to tell him anything or forcing to become a Muslim. He told me, 'that is cool, but I do not want to become anything.' And those were my immediate family. I had other family that did not make a big deal of it, because other family members became Muslim."[87]

---

83. Cuartas/Teresa 2012:20.
84. Cuartas/Teresa 2012:20.
85. Cuartas/Vicente 2012:9.
86. Cuartas/Vicente 2012:9.
87. Cuartas/Vicente 2012:9.

Vicente's friends did not fully support his decision. Vicente stated, "my friends felt much more, because I stopped doing things that I was not supposed to do. I stopped going to parties and I started doing other things. I started practicing Islam and adding values of how to treat women."[88] What about additional concerns of his friends after his decision, especially on such a significant day in history? There are details that are missing or softened here.

Jaime's father cautioned his son not to try to convert him. Jaime explained, "I was very blessed; I have to say very blessed, that everybody was very open."[89] Jaime's father's response after his conversion was noteworthy. His father told him, "Ok, I am ok with it, as long as you do not try to convert me."[90] Jaime's mother showed some concerns about her son leaving Catholicism. Jaime stated, "My mom was the one who is the most taking it back, you know as Catholic she felt like I was kind of leaving . . . leaving Catholicism, leaving her faith . . . but she was very respectful."[91] Because of Jaime's relative isolation, he was not affected by the reactions of friends. He explained, "I did not have too many friends, so that was pretty easy."[92] He did not give any further details about the reaction of his friends. However, his female Muslim friend was surprised when Jaime decided to follow Islam.

Claudia's father had some initial reservations about her conversion and had some questions at a restaurant one day. She stated,

> I am a daddy's girl. So, one day he ordered it for me and I came and sat down, and he said, 'Oh, I ordered you your soup.' I was like, 'oh, I cannot eat it anymore.' And, he was like, 'Why? You're on a diet?' I was like, 'No. It has bacon and I don't eat pork anymore.' And he was like, 'Why?' I was like 'because I am Muslim.' He is like, 'Okay.' He was not mad. He definitely had questions. But, I think he kind of took it kind of slow.[93]

Claudia does not give details about the reaction of her mother; she focused on her father instead.

Regarding Claudia's extended family (her uncles), she affirmed "they used to joke around; but nobody ever gave me a hard time about it."[94] She also told her closest friends and they reacted well. She expressed in her

---

88. Cuartas/Vicente 2012:9.
89. Cuartas/Jaime 2012:9.
90. Cuartas/Jaime 2012:9.
91. Cuartas/Jaime 2012:9.
92. Cuartas/Jaime 2012:9.
93. Cuartas/Claudia 2012:9–10.
94. Cuartas/Claudia 2012:1.

conversion narrative her desire to see her parents and younger brother following Islam. She shared,

> I am hoping, you know, definitely my parents. They have really embraced it; they do not drink in front of us; they do not eat pork in front of us. It definitely was a learning process . . . They do not cook pork around us at all. They do not drink around us at all. So, they really embraced it. So, I am hoping that they will and my brother. And, I joke about it sometimes with them. And, my mom is on a diet.[95]

Claudia emphasized in her story that her brother admired Muslims, but he married a dedicated Catholic woman. She explained,

> My brother is younger. So, he is like three years younger, he is almost twenty-seven. But his role models growing up were all Muslims. So, he used to like Mohammad Ali, Malcolm X. So, I used to always try to make connections, but it is hard because he just married—it is not just married; it has been two years and just had a baby, she is really a devoted Catholic. So, I mean, they are getting their son baptized in a few weeks. So, I am like okay. So, it is going to be really hard now. But, you know, I am just trying to live the way I live and, then, include them in it and educate them as much as I can.[96]

With regard to the reaction of her mother, Teresa stated,

> I was very lucky, the night I converted, I did not tell anybody, but the next morning I was with my mom in the car, and we went to the doctor's appointment and I was like . . . 'hey mom I got to tell you something do not be mad,' and she was like . . . 'ok,' and I was like 'I converted to Islam' and she is like . . . 'oh really,' she is like okay. I was like 'so you are not mad?' She goes: 'I do not care as long you are happy.' So that is what she said.[97]

Teresa did not fully discuss the details of her conversion with her father. She stated,

> My dad . . . he did not say much; I did not really tell him you know formally. I do not remember. I think I might have told him, but he is . . . I mean . . . if my mom said that he will be like ten times like I . . . whatever you want you know. My dad, but it

---

95. Cuartas/Claudia 2012:11.
96. Cuartas/Claudia 2012:12.
97. Cuartas/Teresa 2012:15.

does not mean that he is not going to say any jokes you know, but he is going to say whatever you want, whatever you want is your life you do whatever you want you know as long you are happy.[98]

Teresa was perhaps concerned about the reaction of her father. She expected a favorable reaction from her father, but it is not clear whether or not she shared about her conversion to Islam with him.

With regard to the reaction of her extended family, she explained,

I did not announce it to my family (laughter). I definitively did not do that. I only told my parents. So, the only thing my mom said to me was do not tell your grandmother because she is really hardcore Catholic, she is like very like . . . She said do not tell her. I said 'why?' 'Because she is older, and she is not going to understand,' so I said it is okay.[99]

However, in time Teresa's grandmother began to notice her granddaughter's new practices. Teresa shared,

It was a process, and my grandmother realized some things . . . I mean, certain things, they kind of knew and my family started to realize 'ok she is doing this, she is not doing this, she is wearing this, ok, ok, ok . . . ' so I mean whatever happened in the transition was definitively for the better, so there is nothing I can say. So gradually my grandmother started to realize. She did not want to believe it, but she started to realize and obviously you know . . . good.[100]

As noted, there is shared repetition of words between the narratives such as, "you know," "I was like," "I feel like," and "I became very interested." Furthermore, there are similar themes that emerged in the narratives, for example, religious seeking, discovery, and sense of fulfillment. The use of God instead of Allah, infrequent mention of Muhammad, and minimal emphasis on reciting the *Shahadah*. Some of the converts used Christian vocabulary. However, there are also differences in terms of the predominant discourses and how these discourses are created by the converts.

Some of the elements of the present that informed these emphases by the converts include their religious experiences with the previous religion(s) and the new religion, the institutional discourse, the current jobs, and education level, and the reactions of their families. Now that I have analyzed

---

98. Cuartas/Teresa 2012:15.
99. Cuartas/Teresa 2012:15.
100. Cuartas/Teresa 2012:15.

the conversion narratives looking at different patterns, I will compare the diverse types of conversion narratives.

3.3 TYPES OF CONVERSION NARRATIVES[101]

3.3.1 Vicente's Narrative

Vicente is a second-generation Hispanic American. He was born to Ecuadorian parents who immigrated to the United States in the late 1970s. They were Catholics and raised their children accordingly. Vicente was born and raised in the New Jersey area. He was thirty-one years old at the time of the interview. He earned a BS in mechanical engineering and converted to Islam during his second year of college on September 11, 2001. He was twenty years old at the time of his conversion. The length of time from Vicente's first introduction to Islam to the *Shahadah* was two years. He has been following Islam for almost eleven years. Vicente's wife is also a Hispanic Muslim convert from Puerto Rico. He works as an instructor of martial arts at his current mosque.

Vicente began talking about the Latino culture and how he became interested in learning about socialism, communism, and ideologies through people such as Emiliano Zapata and Che Guevara. Latino history and culture are important in his account, though it was not extensive at all. He did not mention specific aspects of Islam, such as why he converted or his motivations. His story is dramatic because Vicente included some details about September 11, 2001. However, he did not include specific details about challenges and difficulties with friends or the overall reactions of his extended family. I believe he downplayed some of the consequences and negative reactions of some people in his story.

Vicente definitely integrated his new religious beliefs in his narrative. His narrative described his life in light of the new religion. The historical link with Spain allowed Vicente to gain a sense of continuity in his religious experience. His narrative was used as a cultural tool in that he described the historical link with Spain in order to explain his religious experience of Islam.[102] It did reflect the *dawah* ideology using convincing tools. There was a sense of continuity between the old and the new religion.

---

101. Types of conversion narratives based on different factors. See Jindra, *New Model of Religious Conversion*; van Nieuwkerk, "Gender, Conversion, and Islam."

102. Cultural tools refer to how individuals use religious ideas, symbols, and metaphors in ways that can have both intended and unintended consequences—including consequences for boundary-making or boundary-blurring (distorting) processes (Ann Swidler, cited in Edgell, "Cultural Sociology of Religion," 255). Converts may use

3.3.2 Jaime's Narrative

Jaime is a second-generation Hispanic-American. His mother is from the Dominican Republic, and his father is from Puerto Rico. Jaime's mother is Catholic, and his father considered himself nondenominational. Jaime grew up Catholic but later considered himself nondenominational like his father. Jaime converted to Islam during his last years of high school in January 1999. He was seventeen years old at the time. He was thirty years old at the time of the interview. He later earned a BS in information technology. The length of time from Jaime's first introduction to Islam to the *Shahadah* was only nine months. He has been following Islam for thirteen years. His wife is also a Muslim (unknown nationality), and he currently works for the government as a software developer.

Jaime's account was told in light of his previous religion and the relationship with his female Muslim friend during the eleventh grade in high school. Jaime's story included aspects from his experience as a Catholic and as a nondenominational person. He had never been one to engage in much fellowship with others. Because of this, I think that for him, converting was his attempt to try to find a sense of community. Jaime had a Muslim friend who talked to him a lot, and he found their conversations to be very interesting. Perhaps he was tired of being depressed and tried to find a message that was going to stick and be able to fill his life with meaning. Jaime called his conversion a self-discovery process.[103]

3.3.3 Claudia's Narrative

Claudia is a second-generation Hispanic-American. Claudia is the daughter of an American mother and an Argentinian father. Her parents are Catholics. Claudia was raised in the Catholic faith but later began to attend a nondenominational church. Claudia converted to Islam during her second year of college in 2000. She earned a BS in sociology. She was nineteen years old at the time of her conversion. She married before she accepted Islam (her husband is a Muslim from Palestine). The length of time from Claudia's first introduction to Islam to the *Shahadah* was two years. She was thirty-one

---

words, analogies, or metaphors to describe some aspects of their religious experiences.

103. Jaime had a very personal story to tell, and his personal view of his story made it difficult for him to fully share its totality. He was not looking to convert any individual to Islam. Jaime had partially retained his Hispanic values, for example respect for his parents and compassion for others. Jaime had assimilated more to American culture, for example he is more independent now, he is very rational and a hard worker. His previous values and beliefs were largely retained after his conversion.

years old at the time of the interview and had been following Islam for almost twelve years at that point. She currently works as an information technology recruiter.

Claudia shared her story based on her new religion. Yet, there was a congruency and a sense of familiarity and continuity between the new and the old religion. She affirmed, "Even though Islam was something new, it was still very familiar . . . It was really a guide on how to be the best person that I want to be."[104]

Claudia explained her conversion process by looking at her new religious beliefs. She justified her decision by adjusting her cultural values to her new religious identity. She also explained why she converted to Islam and clearly specified the most appealing factors about Islam.

Family values are emphasized in the narratives of Claudia and Vicente. With regard to motivations for conversion to Islam, there are some commonalities in my research with other studies done. For example, in the study of women's conversion to Islam in the West done by several scholars, van Nieuwkerk found that

> while no single set of factors can explain why Western women are embracing Islam faith traditions, some common motivations emerge. These include an attraction to Islam's high regard for family and community, its strict moral and ethical standards, and the rationality and spirituality of its theology, as well as disillusionment with Christianity and with the unrestrained sexuality of so much of Western culture.[105]

As noted previously, several converts within this study experienced some of these aspects in their process of conversion.

Claudia wanted to see her family converted, but it is also possible that she did not want to risk her family actually changing. She did not want to change the dynamics of closeness and fellowship with her immediate family because that could make them look a little less like Hispanics. Thus, she did not really talk about religion with her family.

3.3.4 Teresa's Narrative

Teresa was born in Peru and arrived to the United States at the age of four. Teresa is the daughter of an American mother and a Peruvian father. Her parents are Catholics, and they divorced when she was around the age of

---

104. Cuartas/Claudia 2012:7.
105. van Nieuwkerk, "Gender, Conversion, and Islam," 95.

seven. Teresa grew up in the Catholic faith. She embraced Islam during her college years in 2009. She is the only individual from the selected cases who converted after September 11, 2001. She was twenty years old at the time of her conversion and twenty-three years old at the time of the interview. The length of time from Teresa's first introduction to Islam to the *Shahadah* was one year. She has been following Islam for several years. Her husband is also Muslim (unknown nationality). She has an AA in business and is currently working as a financial broker.

Teresa was a young Muslim convert. She converted post-9/11, at the age of twenty. Her story was focused on the previous religion, and it reflected partially her new religious beliefs. In part, this was due to the fact that she had been a Muslim for only three years. Teresa's narrative was all about making changes. She admired the things that she saw her coworkers doing as they practiced their faith, and she seemed to enjoy the fact that they had harmony among themselves. The conference she attended developed more of a need within her to make life changes that would allow her to have the structured life she desired. Her family's partying and alcohol abuse certainly played a large role in her feeling the need to make serious changes in her life. Teresa needed to make herself someone brand new, breaking the pattern of her family's choices.

Due to her place in life and her still relative youth, it is easy to see that Teresa's narrative was not fully considered. Teresa went through strong socialization by the Muslims in her workplace. She also had an important life change in trying to organize herself. Most of her story was about her diving into the community in order to try to understand it. However, there was no clear indication of when or why she fully decided to commit to the community. We only know that she was able to find meaning through this experience, especially in light of her family's attitudes toward alcohol and partying and her decision that she did not want to do either. It is clear that she was still very much in the process of learning about Islam.

3.4 COMPARISON AND CONTRAST WITH OTHER STUDIES

One of the most comprehensive studies on the conversion of women who embrace Islam in the West is Van Nieuwkerk. Her work was published as a result of a conference held in May 2003 in the Netherlands. Her book includes the perspectives of several historians, sociologists, anthropologists, and theologians who explored the religious experiences and challenges of non-Muslim women converting to Islam. Van Nieuwkerk's research includes conversion narratives of women from the United States, Europe, and South Africa.[106]

As shown in this chapter, converts emphasize different discourses in their narratives. The most significant discourses among the converts in my study are biographical, religious, and ethnic ones. The gender discourse is more predominant in Claudia's narrative than in Teresa's story. Perhaps one of reasons for this is that Teresa has been following Islam for a shorter time than Claudia. The religious discourse of the informants in my study shows a high level of congruency. Van Nieuwkerk's 2006 research mostly focuses on biographical, gender, religious, and ethnic discourses. Van Nieuwkerk emphasizes that the biographical narratives are heterogeneous and the religious discourse particularly displays a high level of consistency.[107]

However, the analysis of institutional discourse has been largely ignored. I have acknowledged the importance of the socialization process and how the converts actively participated in their own process of socialization. The institutional discourse is reflected in their narratives on how individuals integrated the values and beliefs of their previous religion with their new one. The influence of Islamic teaching is important because it shows the way in which these converts integrate their new beliefs within their narratives.

The imams often teach specific Islamic principles, such as the continuity of the message and revelation, that are communicated by Muslims as they also share their stories with new Muslim converts. These interactions and discourses reflect the development of group identity that also shapes the identity of the individual. These discourses also reflect the diverse levels of socialization by imams and Muslim friends. The identity reconstruction of the converts will be further analyzed in the following chapter.

The institutional discourse is largely overlooked in Martínez-Vásquez's 2010 research on Hispanic Muslims in the United States. His study explores the process of conversion of Hispanic Muslims and how this becomes the foundation for the reconstruction of their US Hispanic identities.

Moreover, in Jindra's 2014 study on the conversion to different religions, she primarily concentrates on biographical discourse using biographical

---

106. For additional research done on conversion narratives, see Allievi's and Badran's studies on feminism and conversion. Badran compared British, Dutch, and South African conversion stories (Badran, "Feminism and Conversion," 192–232). Fisher, "Conversion Reconsidered"; Gooren, "Religious Market Model"; Hermansen, "Roads to Mecca"; Jindra, *New Model of Religious Conversion*; Kraft, "Faith Is Lived Out in Community"; Martínez-Vásquez, "Alianza Islámica"; Van Nieuwkerk, "Biography and Choice"; Wohlrab-Sahr, "Symbolizing Distance"; and Zebiri, *British Muslim Converts*.

107. van Nieuwkerk, "Gender, Conversion, and Islam," 96.

sociology. She conducted a significant study and interviewed converts to various religious groups, ranging in age from nineteen to ninety-five years old, over the last nine years in four cities and one small town in the Midwest United States.[108]

Regarding the conversion experience and the most appealing aspects of Islam, the informants highlighted the following: Vicente mentioned several appealing factors about Islam; Jaime seemingly gained a new perspective about the broader role of religion; Claudia emphasized the familiarity and continuity between Islam and her previous religion; and Teresa was impressed by the behavior of her Muslim friends. Only Vicente mentioned the significance of the Qur'an.

Haddad analyzes the conversion narratives of white American women and notes that some women emphasize their intellectual connection to Islam, while others stumble upon the faith while shopping around for something that makes sense in America's supermarket of religions. Others report that they have been captivated by the scientific aspects of the Qur'an. Still, others tend to emphasize the intellectual appeal of the Qur'an. Another important theme in the conversion narratives relates to the negative experiences the converts have had with Christianity.[109] This was also experienced by some of the Hispanic Muslim converts.

It has been shown in my study that some converts integrate Islamic beliefs into their accounts. Haddad also notes that some converts mention the integration of their deepest beliefs in Islam, such as the following response:

> I discovered the universal theory I had been looking for, the rejection of moral relativism, the explicit rejection of racism and sexism, the rejection of nationalism, and a strong emphasis on personal responsibility and social justice. It is important to make very clear that I converted to Islam because I wanted a sincere connection to God. The main reason for my conversion was a spiritual emptiness that I felt, an emptiness that Islam filled.[110]

One of the nuances that I have found in my study is the post-affiliation reactions of the families. Most of the converts reported positive support from parents and only one (Vicente) mentioned negative reactions from his friends. Perhaps the informants downplayed the negative reactions and tensions experienced by the converts because they wanted to show a level of acceptance by their families. However, this is difficult to understand because especially in families with a Catholic background, conversion to another

108. Jindra, *New Model of Religious Conversion*, 28.
109. Haddad, "Quest for Peace in Submission," 27–29.
110. Haddad, "Quest for Peace in Submission," 29.

religion can be seen as one abandoning the Catholic faith. Teresa said she waited for some time to share the news about her conversion with her extended family. Initially, she only told her parents.

By contrast, Haddad reports that almost all the female converts within the study described the difficulties they had explaining their choice to their families. The reactions of the families ranged from complete acceptance to dramatic stories of rejection.[111] In one extreme example, a woman recounted the loss of her husband, children, and job. Some families saw the conversion of their daughter as a betrayal of their values and culture. Some converts reported that their parents refused to see them after their conversion. Many of the converts experienced some sense of alienation from families and friends. Haddad also mentions that some converts reported that their decision to convert was accepted and even welcomed.[112]

Some individuals in my research shared their faith with parents and siblings, and they converted. That was the case for Vicente. Some, like Claudia, have a strong desire to see her parents embracing Islam, but they have not converted. Haddad also considers converts who were able to convert other members of their family. One woman reported converting her entire family.[113]

I have shown some similarities with additional research done on conversion studies, for instance, the emphasis of the converts on biographical and religious discourses. The most significant difference was the lack of attention on institutional discourses in other studies. There are also some differences in terms of the most appealing aspects of Islam and the post-affiliation reactions of the families of the converts. The informants in my research did not report the difficulties, tensions, and dramatic responses of their parents, though it was predominant in other studies.

3.5 CONCLUSION

The central theme of this chapter is the significant choices and emphases within different types of conversion narratives, the creation of different discourses by the converts, the responses in terms of the tensions between religious and cultural aspects as they tell their stories, and the significance of family values.

There is no single set of factors that can fully explain why some Hispanic men and women convert to Islam. The reasons for conversion to Islam varied among the informants. Vicente was looking for answers and found

111. Haddad, "Quest for Peace in Submission," 31.
112. Haddad, "Quest for Peace in Submission," 31.
113. Haddad, "Quest for Peace in Submission," 31.

simplicity and clarity in Islam; Jaime highlighted the continuity between Christianity and Islam, and Claudia had unresolved theological questions about the Trinity and the role of Jesus. While Claudia needed discipleship and structure, Teresa highlighted her need to change and become different. One common aspect that all of the participants shared was that they had unresolved personal and theological questions before they embraced Islam.

There were varied themes that emerged from the narratives ranging from religious seeking, discovery, and fulfillment. The orientations and horizons of the conversion narratives were different. Some of the interviewed individuals reconstructed their previous identities, integrating the values and beliefs of the new religion. This reconstruction process took place at the individual and group levels, depending on the degree of socialization and participation with other Muslims. Most of these Hispanic Muslims actively participated in their own process of socialization through Muslim friends, coworkers, and imams.

As I have argued, converts emphasize words and use metaphors and analogies to explain their religious experiences. These individuals focus on different themes and discourses that are shaped by multiple factors of ethnicity, culture, gender, and religion. The tensions that converts experience between ethnicity, culture, and religion shape the way they told their conversion stories. These choices, in turn, shape their level of commitment and lead to the possibility of Hispanic converts contributing to the local Islamic community. For example, some of these converts are very committed, and they serve in different positions of leadership such as youth directors, chaplains who are involved in interfaith dialogue, and others who are involved in advocacy projects.

Family values are mainly emphasized in the stories of Vicente and Claudia. Vicente mentioned the respect for his parents, and Claudia highlighted the time she spent with her parents and extended family. She also waited to make decisions until she got the approval of her father.

All of the converts seemed to downplay the post-affiliation reactions by their parents and extended family, particularly in the case of Vicente and Claudia. Vicente converted on September 11, 2001. He did not offer details about the tensions and concerns about his parents. However, he mentioned the negative reactions of some friends. Claudia did not offer details about the concerns and responses of her mother. Her main focus was on the responses of her father. Jaime stated that his father was fine with his conversion but warned him not to try to convert him.

The previous religious experiences of the converts play a significant role. The data shows that converts who had good experiences in another religious tradition were able to make multiple choices according to their own purposes. By contrast, when individuals had previous negative experiences, it impacted the way they made relevant choices.[114] Moreover, some researchers on conversion, such as Lofland and Stark, have largely ignored the importance of previous values and beliefs of individuals. It is of paramount importance to relate the changes and choices to the previous values and beliefs of the converts.

The level of socialization of the converts was high, except for Jaime whose participation with the Islamic community was limited by his own choice. He mainly learned Islam through his Muslim friend during high school. These individuals had multiple interactions with imams and Muslim friends and participated in diverse activities. Some of these activities included: Friday prayer meetings, group meetings, and special courses to learn about Islam. Most of these interactions and contacts occurred at their places of study and work.

As I have shown, there are different types of conversion narratives. One can also find predominant discourses in the conversion narratives, namely biographical, religious, gender, ethnic, and institutional ones. The most important discourses among the informants are biographical, religious, and ethnic. While for some individuals past events are reinterpreted with the lenses of newly acquired religious values and beliefs, for others past events are still conceptualized with the help of previous religious values and beliefs.

The different types of narratives of the converts reflect the tensions between culture, ethnicity, and religion, as well as the integration of new values and beliefs of the newly adopted religion. These converts reconstruct their identities in the process of becoming Hispanic Muslims. Important aspects of ethnicity, culture, and religion will be further explored in subsequent chapters. *What are the choices that converts make as they reconstruct their new identities? What are some significant identity markers of Hispanic Muslim converts? To what extent do these converts experience a complete break with their previous religion and community?* This will be the content of the following chapter.

---

114. This aspect of the converts making multiple choices according to diverse purposes is highlighted by Gooren, *Religious Conversion and Disaffiliation*, in his analysis of parental religion.

Chapter 4

Becoming a Hispanic Muslim

Factors that Shape the Evolving Hispanic Muslim Identity

4.1 INTRODUCTION

The aim of this chapter is to describe and analyze the factors that shape the evolving Hispanic Muslim identity. The main argument is that this identity is neither simple (i.e., it is composite) nor is it completely new (i.e., it is partly continuous with the past). This identity comes into being through the converts' affiliations with members of their family and the wider body of Muslims and Muslim agencies.

My intention is to analyze the following issues: the role of family, marriage, Muslim friends, born-Hispanic Muslims, the most significant post-affiliation changes as identity markers, and the values and beliefs maintained or adopted by the new Hispanic Muslims.

I argue that there is not a complete break with the previous religious beliefs and ethnic values. There is a sense of continuity with previous beliefs even though there is some degree of discontinuity experienced by the converts. Most of these individuals embraced their new religion while maintaining their ethnic values such as family, community, and hospitality, as well as some religious practices such as prayer and fasting. Some of them maintain contact with their previous religious communities.

Conversion does not mean the full rejection of their ethnicities. Full assimilation or integration is absent and often selective. Whilst conversion entails a sort of reconstruction of the religious and social identities, this neither involves full assimilation nor integration into local Islam nor a selective assimilation or integration.

The complex processes of both deconstruction and reconstruction involve tensions, choices, negotiations, and post-affiliation changes that demonstrate the complexities as the converts reconstruct their identities. Some of the aspects in these processes are intended by the converts, while others are unintentional. The responses of these converts with regard to assimilation, integration, tensions between culture and religion, the reactions of family and friends, and the levels of socialization shape the way in which new converts reconstruct their ethnic and religious identities. In turn, the reconstructed identities and multiple factors shape their religious commitment and practice in the United States. These nuances of commitment and practice will be further analyzed in the following chapter.

I intend to do this in three ways: First, I will draw from the literature on ethnicity, religion, and identity studies to justify the selection of themes of this chapter. Second, I will analyze the data using the selected themes, providing different examples of the reconstruction of the Hispanic Muslim identities. I introduce four new cases: María, Héctor, Camila, and Martín. I chose these cases because I intend to show different responses regarding how these converts reconstruct their Hispanic Muslim identities, including both men and women from different generations. In addition, I will interact with previous cases, and some perspectives from born-Hispanic Muslims will also be included. Finally, I will examine the findings in light of theories such as assimilation and integration.

4.2 IDENTITY, ETHNICITY, CULTURE, AND RELIGION

The interplay between religion and identity has been recognized by several scholars and has been a central theme in the sociology of religion since the classical period, even though it is not always labeled in those specific terms. Greil and Davidman state that "a major theme in Durkheim's 1966 sociology of religion is the role of communal ritual in fostering personal and social identity."[1]

According to Greeley and McGuire, meaning and belonging are two of the most important functions of religion. Thus, it is clear that religion is intimately bound up with people's identity, their sense of who they "really"

---

1. Greil and Davidman, "Religion and Identity," 549.

are.[2] The relationship between religion and identity is highlighted by some scholars; for example, Mol makes identity the fundamental concept in his definition of religion. According to Mol, religion is the "sacralization" of identity.[3]

The term "identity" was not used in its modern sense by scholars such as Durkheim, Weber, and Simmel because it was not a scientific term available to them.[4] Gleason states that the term did not become part of the social scientific lexicon until the 1960s.[5] Gleason recognizes both psychological and sociological sources for the integration of identity into the social science terminology. Erikson, for instance, used the terms "identity" and "ego-identity" to refer to a "sense of invigorating continuity and sameness," the development of which is the primary task of adolescence.[6] In this assessment, the achievement of a mature identity is a necessary condition to successful development.[7]

4.2.1 Identity Studies

Making sense of the term "identity" is problematic since "there is no universally agreed-upon definition, even before taking theological perspectives into account."[8] The meaning of identity differs. It generally refers to a sense of self and of belonging. Cook-Huffman suggests that it is related to how people know and understand themselves as individuals, as people who play specific roles, and as members of particular groups.[9]

There are also diverse disciplines that define identity in different ways. While psychologists typically use such terms as "the inner self," anthropologists and many sociologists treat identity as a collective label making out different groups. Social psychologists bridge these conflicting notions, by analyzing "identity negotiation" between individuals and groups.[10]

---

2. Greil and Davidman, "Religion and Identity," 549.
3. Mol, *Identity and the Sacred*, 16–18.
4. Greil and Davidman, "Religion and Identity," 549.
5. Gleason, "Identifying Identity," 910–31.
6. Erikson, *Identity*, 19.
7. Greil and Davidman, "Religion and Identity," 549.
8. Green, "Conversion," 43.
9. Kraft, *Searching for Heaven*, 98; For diverse definitions of identity, see Kraft, *Searching for Heaven*, and Peek, "Becoming Muslim."
10. Green, "Conversion," 43; Some psychologists writing on identity include William James, Erik Erikson, and Galen Strawson; sociologists include Kurt Lewin and Evaitur Zerubavel; social psychologists include Henri Tafjel, George Herbert Mead, and

Another complex aspect to consider is that identities are not fixed and static. On the contrary, identities are shifting and fragmenting under the impact of globalization. The advance of technology, massive amounts of information, communication systems, facility to travel, and the impact of the Internet and social networks facilitate the exposure of people to new religions and worldviews; migration and intermarriage construct new hybrid and multiple identities; and pluralizing societies challenge supposed alliances of faith, ethnicity, culture, and nationality.[11]

Many scholars of conversion have highlighted the notion of identity as a vital concern for converts given the "pace of urbanization, modernization, secularization, and the resulting pluralization of self and community understanding." Thus, old notions of self, relationships, communities, and convictions are under pressure.[12]

In addition, the understandings of identity become more problematic as identities themselves evolve. According to Hall, "In Western thought, the 'Enlightenment definition' of identity was followed by the 'sociological definition' and now the 'postmodern definition' which delights in 'a perplexing, transitory multiplicity of possible identities.'"[13] The debates between individual and collective identities remain significant.

4.2.2 Ethnicity

George DeVos defines ethnicity as the "subjective symbolic or emblematic use of any aspect of culture [by an ethnic group], in order to differentiate themselves from other groups."[14]

Several definitions of ethnicity have appeared in discussions of immigrant adaptation. The first is "primordial ethnicity,"[15] which holds that people have an essential need for "belonging" that is satisfied by groupings based on shared ancestry and culture. Such primordial ethnicity is found to continue to powerfully influence the descendants of immigrants even into the third and fourth generations. Contrary to the "primordial" claim, Herbert Gans argues that ethnic identities are becoming mostly "symbolic,"

Sheldon Stryker; sociologists of religion include Peter Berger and Thomas Luckmann. For more details about the debates on identity, see Greil and Davidman, "Religion and Identity," and Green, "Conversion."

11. Green, "Conversion," 43.
12. Ramirez, "New Islamic Movement," 265.
13. Hall, "Question of Cultural Identity," 273.
14. De Vos, *Ethnic Pluralism*, 25.
15. Geertz, *Interpretation of Cultures*, 290–96; see also Isaacs, *Idols of the Tribe*.

mere vestiges of immigrant cultures and doomed to fade away before the irresistible forces of assimilation.[16]

The third understanding is "situational ethnicity," which regards ethnicity mostly as situational and instrumental for social-political interests.[17]

The fourth and newest conceptualization is the "invention of ethnicity," a phrase first used by Werner Sollors and developed by a group of scholars of ethnic studies. Theorists of the "invention of ethnicity" also agree that "ethnicization is Americanization."[18] Therefore, assimilation eventually seems to have prevailed over ethnic pluralism.[19]

4.2.3 Ethnic and Religious Identities

There is an important link between ethnic and religious identities. Kraft states that "considering the dynamics of Muslim-majority societies among Arabs of a Muslim background who choose to follow a Christian faith, I argue that Islam becomes their ethnicity, while Christianity becomes their religion."[20] As globalization brings increased pluralism, stable identifications are being thrown into doubt. Thus, for people leaving Islam as a faith system, their religious identification as Muslims, which they once experienced as a stable and immutable identity, becomes less essential to who they are. When their Muslim faith is no longer immutable, it is abandoned and replaced by a Christian faith. However, Muslim faith is still important to members of their community and rooted in their own lives, and therefore they discard the religious identity into which they were born at great social risk and often great psychological cost as well.[21]

The dynamic interplay of ethnicity and religion is also relevant in order to understand the process of the construction of identities of Hispanics converting to Islam. Ethnicity can become an identity marker for individuals who are switching religions and reconstructing their identities. Religion, ethnicity, and language are symbols of group identity.[22]

16. Gans, "Symbolic Ethnicity," 1–20; see also Gordon, *Assimilation in American Life*.

17. Espiritu, *Asian American Panethnicity*, 8–15. See also Glazer and Moynihan, *Beyond the Melting Pot*.

18. Fuchs et al., "Comment," 60.

19. Yang, *Chinese Christians in America*, 20.

20. Kraft, *Searching for Heaven*, 101.

21. Hammond, "Religion and the Persistence of Identity," 5.

22. For additional information about ethnicity and religion, see Helbling, *Islamophobia in the West*, 76–77; Herberg, *Protestant-Catholic-Jew*; and Yang, *Chinese*

4.2.4 Identity Markers and Post-Affiliation Changes

Based on research I have on identity and religious conversion, I have identified the following post-affiliation markers: name and dress (e.g., for women the *hijab* [headscarf]) in general, and for men specifically, the *taqiyah* (skull cap), physical features (e.g., beard), and proficiency in Arabic to be able to read the Qur'an, and dietary laws. In addition, relationships with the previous community, and a partial or complete break with previous religion are included here.[23]

Significant markers to analyze as individuals reconstruct their new identities are personal values and beliefs. The retention, rejection, or adoption of values and beliefs help us to recognize what has really changed as individuals embrace the new religion.[24]

While converts embrace their new religion, there are tensions between religion and culture.[25] The level of tension is significant particularly among immigrant converts.[26] Generally, these individuals are forced to make choices as they respond differently to the new challenges.

As noted earlier, the interplay between ethnicity and religion is important. Self-identification has been used by several scholars as an indicator of identity.[27] The self-identification of the individuals and the contextual factors such as social, cultural, and religious ones are important to understand the process of the reconstruction of identities.[28] Contextual factors have been previously used in this study as part of the analysis of the data in the pre-affiliation and affiliation stages of the converts.

Christians in America.

23. Cavalcanti and Schleef, "Case for Secular Assimilation?," 473–83; See also Gooren, *Religious Conversion and Disaffiliation*, 93–112; Haddad and Lummis, *Islamic Values*; Hermansen, "Keeping the Faith," 250–75; Wang, *Uncertain Future*; Zebiri, *British Muslim Converts*.

24. Kim et al., "Latino/a Values Scale," 71–91; Rinderle and Montoya, "Hispanic/Latino Identity Labels," 144–64. See also Gordon, *Assimilation in American Life*; Haddad and Lummis, *Islamic Values*.

25. Hodge, "Social Work," 162–67. See also Haddad and Lummis, *Islamic Values*; Hashmi, "From Ethnicity to Religion"; Yang, *Chinese Christians in America*.

26. Portes and Rumbaut, *Immigrant America*, 124–25; Yang, *Chinese Christians in America*, 57–94.

27. Hashmi, "From Ethnicity to Religion," 34–42. See also Cristian, *Who are We?*

28. Gooren, *Religious Conversion and Disaffiliation*, 93–112; see also Hashmi, "From Ethnicity to Religion"; Rambo, *Understanding Religious Conversion*.

Additionally, institutional agency and the process of developing social and collective identities have been discussed by scholars such as Hermansen[29] and Straus.[30]

4.3 ANALYSIS OF THE DATA: DIVERSE EXAMPLES OF THE RECONSTRUCTION OF IDENTITIES

4.3.1 Introduction of the Selected Cases

María

María is a first-generation Panamanian-American who converted to Islam in Panama. She emigrated to the United States at the age of thirty-two. María's mother is from Panama, while her father is half British, a quarter Scottish, and a quarter Jamaican. She comes from a tradition of Catholicism through her mother (her father converted to the Episcopal tradition during the later years of his life). She was thirty-one at the time of conversion, though she had been struggling to make a decision for fifteen years and has now been committed to Islam for about eighteen years. Before her conversion, she worked as an administrator, close to a local mosque. Since her conversion, she works for her current mosque as a public relations chaplain, doing interfaith dialogue. She has a bachelor's degree.[31] María is married to an immigrant Muslim from the Middle East.[32]

Héctor

Héctor is a second-generation Puerto Rican convert from Chicago. He grew up the son of a Catholic mother and an agnostic father. He had always questioned his faith, such as the role of the Trinity, until he reached college age.

29. Hermansen, "Two-way Enculturation," 188–201.
30. Straus, "Religious Conversion," 158–65.
31. María did not provide detailed information about her bachelor's degree.
32. She did not mention the country of origin of her husband; she just mentioned that he was from the Middle East. It was through her father's influence that she began to question her beliefs about religion. Being in Panama, where it is easy to tell those that do not abide by the Catholic faith, made it easy to begin finding people to ask questions. Her father purchased her first Qur'an, not expecting that she would necessarily convert to another religion but believing that she would benefit from learning and understanding the outside world. He died before her conversion in 1994, but in María's words, her mother's family seemed to have no true reaction to her converting out of Catholicism. The biggest response was from her mother's sister, who questioned why María left her mother's religion.

He converted to Islam at the age of nineteen as a college student after two years of studying Islam. His mother knew that he had been searching for a new religion (focusing on Islam in particular), and so she understood his decision. His father had no problem with the switch, though he disliked religious rules. He obtained his bachelor's degree in history and sociology, and later a master's degree in education. He has been committed to Islam for about seventeen years. He currently works as the Outreach Youth Director of his mosque, teaching the next generation of Muslims about practicing Islam. He is married to a born-Hispanic Muslim from Puerto Rico and has three children, all boys.

Camila

Camila is the daughter of a mother from Switzerland and a father from Puerto Rico. Her family's religious background is nominally Catholic; Camila admits that she did not take Catholicism very seriously. After struggling briefly with the death of her best friend, she entered a pre-med program and became an atheist. As an atheist, she became motivated by social justice issues and through her interests came into contact initially with the Nation of Islam. She changed her major and graduated college with a BA in sociology. She currently works as a health educator and a Zumba instructor. She was twenty-two at her conversion and has been committed to Islam for about six years. At first, her family did not understand her conversion, but after learning a bit about Islam and seeing the positive changes that came over her, they became supportive of her decision. She is married to a Hispanic Muslim convert from Uruguay.

Martín

Martín is a first-generation Bolivian-American. He immigrated to the United States at the age of twenty. He comes from a Catholic background. He converted to Islam at the age of twenty-three under the influence of a friend's brother. He completed four years of systems engineering but did not finish college. He also served briefly in the Bolivian military. His conversion brought about a brief distance from his family, as they were against his conversion. His mother in particular did not speak to him for months. He has been committed to Islam for about eight years and married to a Bolivian Muslim convert; they have two children. His case is interesting because his children do not go to a Muslim school, and instead attend a Catholic school. One of his motivations for sending his children to a Catholic school is that it is convenient for them since the school is very close to their house.

4.3.2 Identity Markers and Post-Affiliation Changes

As I described earlier, the following identity markers have emerged from primary and secondary sources: name, dress, language, dietary restrictions, and relationships.[33] For detailed information about the selected cases, see Appendix 5. Some of the aspects of this section will be expanded in the following chapter looking at the nuances regarding religious commitment and the practices of the converts.

Name

One of the choices that Hispanic Muslim converts face is related to the decision to change or maintain their previous names.[34] When I asked the participants if they changed their names during post-affiliation, the majority reported that they had retained their names. There are diverse motivations observed by the converts to retain their previous names.

For example, Vicente indicated that he did not change his name because his name reflects his Latino heritage.[35] He shared,

> I want people to know that I am Latino. It is a way to open conversation. When people see me, they think I am Arab because of my beard. But then when I speak Spanish or tell them my name is Vicente, they say, you are Latino, and I say yes, and that is a beautiful way for me to start sharing about Islam. For me, it is my opinion, when Latinos or African Americans adopt some Islamic names it is beautiful, it is ok to do it, and it is encouraging, but I think it Arabizes that person in a sense. Although it has nothing to do of being Arabic, it is thought that way and closes doors. You know we are here to build bridges, and there is not, and if I was to go to a place where the majority of the people are Latinos, and they ask me what is your name, and I say my name is Abdullah, they would automatically think that I am Arab, and they would not talk to me, and when I told them that my name is Vicente, that opens doors.[36]

Jaime mentioned that even though he did not change his name, other Muslims tried to give him a new name, and he used the Islamic names for a short period of time.[37] He claimed,

---

33. Zebiri, *British Muslim Converts*, 101–13.
34. Zebiri, *British Muslim Converts*, 106–7.
35. Cuartas/Vicente 2012:10.
36. Cuartas/Vicente 2012:10.
37. Cuartas/Jaime 2012:9.

> I did not change my name, that name is a process that took, it is like two names. The first Islamic name someone gave me means the light of Islam, and I never stuck to any of the names. Because I did not want it to, everyone knows me as Jaime and did not want my conversion to be something, like off the boat. People say I do not need to change my clothes, just because I changed my beliefs. You know unless I am walking naked. You know if I am not violating the rules. Yeah, I accepted the name, but I do not use it. And afterward I took a different Islamic name, and I stuck to that name, I still remember a little of it, but now I do not use any of them.[38]

Something similar happened to Lucía. She retained her previous name, but her husband gave her an Islamic name that meant "life." She mentioned that the new name was important for her husband but not for her.[39] She affirmed that "even though my husband's family is Yemeni, and his family is very strict he himself is not very strict. So, in his Arabic culture not in Islam, they are not even supposed to know your name. They do not call you by your name but by the name of the first child of his mother."[40]

María did not change her name legally. She prefers to use a nickname. She stated, "for the prophet of Islam, the Prophet Mohammad taught us that one should change its name if the name has a negative meaning. And my name does not."[41] Contrary to Lucía, she did not mention any conflict with her husband regarding her name.

The following are the comments of one of the imams with regard to the meaning of names:

> A person who has converted to Islam does not need to change their name unless their name symbolizes the worship of someone or something other than *Allah* [Arabic word for God]. Therefore, if the original name does not comprise or imply something forbidden in Islam, then Muslim converts are allowed to retain it their previous names. However, some say it is preferable to change one's name to an Islamic name. It will also distinguish him or her from the non-Muslims. But it is not mandatory.[42]

---

38. Cuartas/Jaime 2012:9.
39. Cuartas/Lucía 2012:7.
40. Cuartas/Lucía 2012:7.
41. Cuartas/María 2012:8.
42. Cuartas/Imam 2 2012:3.

Here, one can recognize the negotiations that take place at different levels between imams, converts, and their Muslim spouses. Even though some Muslims encourage new converts to change their names, the responses of the converts are diverse. Such is the case of Lucía, whose Muslim husband gave her a different name. According to the imam's comments, the name can become a marker to differentiate a Muslim from a non-Muslim. However, it is worth noting that Vicente's approach was different; he wanted to retain his Latino name to be able to reflect his Latino culture. The varied choices and tensions between ethnicity and religion are also observed here.

Dress and Physical Features

Regarding the dress and physical features, the responses of the converts are varied. María wears the *hijab* only occasionally and dresses modestly. María does not wear the *hijab* often because she does not consider it essential to her faith. She stated, "I use it just when I pray or on certain occasions that I find appropriate. But I do not understand the use of the *hijab* as mandatory." She respects the choices of other Muslim women and added, "if you think that makes better Muslims, by all means, use it. And nobody has the right to prohibit use. But, the fact you have turned to the conclusion that it is vital for you, a vital part of faith, does not mean that that entitles you to put it on another person, other women." When I asked her about the use of the *niqab* [face veil], she replied, "it is absurd. We are talking about the face veil. It is absurd."[43]

On the other hand, Camila experienced difficulties making the necessary dress changes, but she does see the use of the *hijab* as being an important requirement. She replied, "at my work, I do not wear a *hijab*, so people do not really know I am a Muslim, so I do not really talk about it. My coworkers are non-Muslims. I am sure if I did it would be different because I work with a very high-risk population. I work in South Bronx, and there is not a lot of Muslims, so I do not know what it would be like, but for me, it is not an issue."[44] The continuous tensions about this matter are evident in the following comments:

> I am still struggling, I do not wear *hijab* unless I am around Muslims or if I am in an Islamic compound and you know, I wear it to school now. That was a big step for me. In the beginning, I wore it and you know I would like to leave my house and put it on in the car and then I would like to stop a block away when I was coming home and take it off and kind of like hide it.

43. Cuartas/María 2012:12.
44. Cuartas/Camila 2012:7.

But I was not ready for that, and so I am still going back through this whole process of putting it back on.[45]

The choices about dress are often more difficult for Muslim women than for Muslim men because the use of the *hijab* is an indicator of being a Muslim.[46] However, there are also diverse responses among male Hispanic Muslims. For example, Héctor dresses like a Muslim male, and he decided to grow his beard. Héctor also wears the *taqiyah* (short, rounded skull cap) frequently. Martín, on the other hand, has not changed his dress at all. He continues to dress as a typical Latino man.

Language

In terms of the language, the participants show diverse levels of fluency in Spanish and English. Based on the demographic survey, Simón, Jaime, and Héctor reported a degree of familiarity with speaking and writing in Spanish. It is worth noting that these individuals are second-generation Hispanics. María and Martín are first-generation Hispanics. María reported being fluent in both Spanish and English, whereas Martín is fluent in Spanish but said he had a degree of familiarity to write in English (according to the demographic survey completed by the participants). María preferred to conduct the interview in Spanish rather than English. She is also fluent in Portuguese.

There are some individuals who reported a degree of familiarity with the Arabic language. This is the case for Héctor and Camila. However, the convert who is most fluent in Arabic is Vicente. He mentioned that learning Arabic is very important, particularly to be able to read the Qur'an. He said that he is able to speak and read in Arabic since he lived in Egypt for almost a year.[47]

Vicente and Héctor, in particular, used some Arabic words during the interview. Camila mentioned some of the dynamics at the Islamic center with regard to languages when she stated, "I heard that is a lot of English language going on, sometimes they do announcements in Arabic or the sermon in Arabic, but for the most part I do not think it is a problem with the languages. Even here we have translation in Spanish."[48] Though they

---

45. Cuartas/Camila 2012:8.

46. Hermansen, "Keeping the Faith," did a study on the identity formation of Euro-American female Muslims in the United States. See also Bourque, "How Deborah Became Aisha." She conducted extensive research on the identity formation of female Muslims in Scotland. For diverse studies on female Muslims in deferent countries, see Van Nieuwkerk, "Gender, Conversion, and Islam."

47. Cuartas/Vicente 2012:8.

48. Cuartas/Camila 2012:13.

did not have materials available to them in Spanish, they generally did not express any limitations of understanding.

Learning Arabic is important for Muslims since the Qur'an is recited during *jum'ah* [Friday prayer meetings].[49] Thus, the new Muslims are encouraged by other Muslims and even by imams to learn Arabic, and this can become a marker of religious commitment to Islam. Several Islamic centers are providing the Qur'an in different languages, such as Spanish and English.[50] Martín mentioned that at times there are limitations on his participation because he is not familiar with the Arabic language.[51]

Díaz-Stevens analyzed the immigration experience and the maintenance of language and culture among Hispanics in the United States. In her study, Díaz-Stevens underlined the significance of bilingualism:

> Bilingualism had an important effect on Latinos because it reversed the pattern of linguistic imperialism. Further, the Council's sympathetic view of popular religiosity also served to aid Hispanics in their new identification process, as this was an area of many commonalities calling for ritualization on the one hand and transformation through adaptation and reformulation on the other.[52]

In addition, Díaz-Stevens suggests that we "must consider the role of the Spanish language and bilingualism in relation to both education and religion."[53]

Dietary Restrictions

With regard to the dietary restrictions followed in Islam, there are different responses by the Hispanic Muslim converts. For instance, Héctor decided not to eat pork before he became Muslim. He mentioned that he had given up eating pork in high school. He said, "if Jesus was a Jew and Jews do not eat pork, why do we eat pork?"[54]

Also, some of Héctor's comments with regard to traditional activities in his family reflect the tensions between culture and religion. I asked him to share some of the most significant challenges after becoming a Muslim, and he said,

49. Hodge, "Social Work," 162–73.
50. Cuartas/Imam 3 2012:6.
51. Cuartas/Martín 2012:12.
52. Díaz-Stevens, "Colonization Versus Immigration," 76.
53. Díaz-Stevens, "Colonization Versus Immigration," 75.
54. Cuartas/Héctor 2012:6.

> I think the hardest part was changing some of the traditional things that I used to do with the family. I used to do the *parrandas* [Latino parties] and usually that does not happen without [drinking] alcohol. I never drank before or after the *parrandas* but obviously the family does, so certain type of activities and events I am not going to because of some of the environment that is there. That was a challenge for everybody because you do not want to hurt anybody's feelings, you do not want to make people feel that you are judging them per se but at the same time, you need to respect on both ends. So, getting them to understand it, it was tough.[55]

Camila also mentioned that it was common in her family to eat pork and shared that the Latino tradition of eating pork is one aspect of her culture that is contradictory to the Islamic faith. She stated, "there are things like eating pork, clearly I am not going to do that anymore. I think some people [Muslims] allow that, but for me, it is not possible."[56]

Claudia, Héctor, and Martín also revealed that they often combine Hispanic food with Arabic food, choosing to retain some of the family traditions. In the following excerpt from Claudia's interview, it is evident that she is still following some traditions from her family, especially from her father. But her parents are also respecting some of Claudia's changes regarding diet:

> A lot of the Latino culture is still very strong in our life. I mean, we still get together, you know, when the weather is good on every Sunday at my father's house. I mean every weekend we are with my family for dinner. They come over for dinner. The fare, if my dad is cooking, it is usually Argentine food, especially when it is nice outside, he usually has an *asado* (barbecue, grill) and *molleja* and *bacio* and *encebada* [typical Argentinian barbecue]. He mixed up everything. You know, there he got the Tango [Argentinian music] in the background, and he has the Argentine grill. So, you know that part of the culture is still very much in my life and my kids' life. You know, my kids call my parents '*abuelo*' [grandfather] and '*abuela*' [grandmother].[57]

In some cases, the parents of the converts are also involved in the process of the choices these individuals make. Claudia reported that her parents decided neither to drink alcohol nor to eat pork in front of them.

---

55. Cuartas/Camila 2012:12.
56. Cuartas/Camila 2012:12.
57. Cuartas/Claudia 2012:14.

She said that her parents used to cook *chorizo* (pork sauce) and put it on the same plate, but now they do not cook pork around her at all.[58]

Simón chose to continue eating Latino food, but he replaced the pork for vegetables. He stated, "my grandmother makes *tamales,* and it will have much hot bacon in it but the more I read sort of the history of Spain, and the way that people tried to prove that they were sincere Christians that you know pork were thrown into dishes, it is not really it. I decided to go get *tamales* completely vegetarian, and they are delicious."[59]

Relationships

In terms of relationships with non-Muslims, the choices also varied strongly among the converts. María still has interactions with unrelated men and sees no need for gender separation. She is part of the interfaith dialogue, so she has a high degree of interaction with Muslims and non-Muslims:

> Relationships with men have been no taboo for me. Other than that, I do not know why I have always tended to be more popular with men than with women. And do not say because I am nice or because I have a good personality or because I am so incredibly attractive. I do not consider myself very girly. So maybe that has influenced. My best friend of all life is a man, even until today. So, I do not see the impossibility of friendship or relationship of respect between a man and a woman. I have no such problems shaking hands with a man.[60]

Thus, there is a partial break with the previous community in part due to her active involvement in interfaith dialogue. She had good relationships with non-Muslim relatives back in Panama. She has no problem in relating to non-Muslim friends.

Héctor is still close to his family, but he has created some limitations between himself and women who are not in his immediate family. This is contrary to Maria's response in terms of relationships with the opposite sex. Héctor stated that there were challenges in accepting some of the ways that men and women behave with each other. For example, there is a lot of hugging and kissing in the Latino culture. He added, "that was a big adjustment for everybody. It's not that I love you any less it's just that certain things I can't do anymore in that regard."[61]

58. Cuartas/Claudia 2012:11.
59. Cuartas/Simón 2012:15.
60. Cuartas/María 2012:12.
61. Cuartas/Héctor 2012:15.

He also interacts with the interfaith dialogue and Hispanic community to inform them about Islam, making it possible to interact with non-Muslims. There is much more of a full break from his previous religion in that monotheism is very important to him, rather than contemplating the Trinity.

Héctor has not, however, broken away from his Hispanic heritage because everything he does is related to the Hispanic community. His wife is also a Hispanic Muslim from Puerto Rico. And though there is a partial break due to the Islamic view of gender separation, his parents are still Catholics, and he has regular interactions with his family.

Camila finds much comfort in the gender nuances within Islam. It makes her feel respected. She works outside of the Muslim Hispanic community, and many of her coworkers do not know that she is Muslim.[62] She has some friends who are non-Muslims. Camila appears to be living in two different worlds; she is a Muslim only in the Muslim community. Thus, there is a partial break because she wanted to make sure that she would have other Hispanic Muslims to befriend and talk to before she made the conversion. One of the first things that she did after her conversion to Islam was to find other Hispanic Muslims:

> I started looking for people because I did not know anyone and I wanted to walk into like a mosque, and I do not think I would have even seen a mosque, and so I started looking for like people and like adding random people on Myspace and looking for other Hispanics and Latinas that I could relate to or have gone through this [embracing Islam] and it was like so surprising to see that there were so many other people. I never thought, I never knew that there were Hispanic Muslims.[63]

In Martín's case, his friendships have not changed. Most of his friends are non-Muslims. Martín has not made a break from his Hispanic background. Based on the data, Martín has not made a full break from his previous religion because he is still in a place where he does not know what he believes. Something that helps him to remain in Islam is the fact that he is married to a Hispanic Muslim convert.

Martín mentioned some of the challenges he had with his relatives and friends after his conversion to Islam. His mother did not talk to him for almost two months. He said that it took two years to re-establish his relationship with other members of his family. This situation even affected

---

62. Cuartas/Camila 2012:9.
63. Cuartas/Camila 2012:8.

his relationship with coworkers, who reacted negatively. Also, some of his friends decided to "disappear" for a while.[64]

4.3.3 Institutional Agency and the Development of Collective Identities

The reconstruction of identities of the Hispanic Muslims is also shaped by the level of interactions and socialization with imams, immigrant Muslims, and born-Hispanic Muslims. The levels of socialization are very diverse. One of the main factors is the multiple interactions with imams and other Muslims not only at the Islamic centers but also attending meetings organized by the Muslim Student Association (MSA) and other Islamic organizations such as ISNA (the Islamic Society of North America).[65] According to Nyang, ISNA is currently the largest Islamic organization in the United States.[66] Another Muslim organization that was mentioned by the informants was the Nation of Islam.[67]

The Muslim Student Associations (MSAs) are very active across universities in the United States. Leaders of MSAs frequently organize meetings where they invite students to address different topics. These MSAs play a significant role in transmitting Muslim values and beliefs. Both Héctor and Camila participated in meetings organized by MSAs. In particular, Héctor attended meetings to have discussions with a local college Muslim group and for regular mosque attendance.[68] Martina participated in a local MSA looking for guidance on how to be a Muslim. Claudia had multiple friendships in high school and college in which she very intentionally observed Muslims. Vicente actively attended discussion meetings with local college Muslim groups. Teresa had multiple interactions with coworkers and new Muslim classes.

Camila attended several meetings with members of the Nation of Islam, attended college classes about Islam as a religion, and connected with Hispanic Muslims through social media.[69] Simón, to a lesser degree, took an

---

64. Cuartas/Martín 2012:11.

65. According to Hodge, "Social Work," 167, "The ISNA grew out of the Muslim Student Association (MSA), the largest Muslim student organization in the United States. According to the former president of MSA, more than 500 chapters exist in the United States."

66. Nyang, *Islam in the United States*, 18–19.

67. e.g., Cuartas/Camila 2012:10; Cuartas/Lucía 2012:12.

68. Cuartas/Héctor 2012:6.

69. Cuartas/Camila 2012:4, 6.

Arabic class and joined AmeriCorps, followed by participating in a college program that took him to the Middle East where he constantly interacted with Muslims.[70]

As previously noted, born-Hispanic Muslims and immigrant Muslims play an active role in helping the new converts to embrace and integrate into the new religion. They become role models to be followed by others. The born-Hispanic Muslims, in particular, provide an example to Hispanic Muslim converts, showing that it is possible to navigate the tensions between culture and religion and that it is possible to become a Muslim without losing Hispanic ethnicity.

Here, we can observe the degree of both social and personal interaction in the identity formation of individuals, as suggested by Schwartz.[71] Several individuals highlighted the importance of building community and developing a sense of belonging. As diverse societies have higher levels of interaction with each other, it has been proposed that it is becoming more significant to people that they have a sense of the unique identity of their community. This unique identity serves as a means of managing the different challenges from outside the group and of competing on the global scale.[72]

4.3.4 Values and Beliefs—What Has Really Changed?

Personal values and beliefs are of paramount importance in the process of reconstructing identities. The question of what has really changed helps us to understand how the values and beliefs of individuals are shaped as they switch religions. Also, it facilitates the analysis to understand the values and beliefs that are retained or the new values and beliefs that are adopted by new Muslims. Gordon[73] studied important values in the United States. Haddad and Lummis[74] and Hodge[75] conducted research emphasizing significant Muslim values. Scholars such as Kim,[76] Leon,[77] and Rinderle and Montoya[78] highlighted relevant values among Hispanics.

70. Cuartas/Simón 2012:1–2.
71. Schwartz et al., "Introduction," 2.
72. Kraft, *Searching for Heaven*, 98.
73. Gordon, *Assimilation in American Life*.
74. Haddad and Lummis, *Islamic Values*.
75. Hodge, "Social Work," 162–73.
76. Kim et al., "Latino/a Values Scale," 71–91.
77. Leon, "Latino Cultural Values," 13–25.
78. Rinderle and Montoya, "Hispanic/Latino Identity Labels," 144–64.

Hispanic Muslims emphasized diverse values in their narratives. Some individuals highlighted the significance of family, community, and respect. For example, María mentioned that the "sense of family and community" were very important for her.[79] Héctor underlined the importance of family and said that this value is very compatible between Hispanics and Muslims.[80] Camila also mentioned the "sense of community" and said that "everyone [is] equal and no one [is] better than the other person."[81] Vicente stated that "the devotion and dedication to your family are very important and appealed to me because being Latino, you already have strong family values."[82] Claudia also said that respecting your elders and your family is very important.[83]

With regard to the importance of building a sense of community with other female Muslims, Lucía stated,

> I love getting together with all the sisters. You know, we all get together—we all bring our kids. It's nice—it is nice to have Islamic values, and it is very strict. If you follow them, you have to be a certain kind of person. You see, in the Catholic faith—I can go get drunk and then go to church. I can do that, but that does not work with Islam. So, the type of people we hang out [with]—these types of people are family. We all consider ourselves sisters, it is Sunni—once you are Muslim, you are sisters, and it is a deeper connection.[84]

Martina said that it is nice in a general social setting to have people [Muslims] who can echo back or support your belief—people who will stop whatever they are doing to pray with you. This significantly helps reinforce those practices and beliefs in Islam and keep them strong.[85]

Vicente indicated that he stopped doing things that he was not supposed to do. He said "I stopped going to parties and I started doing other things. I started practicing Islam and adding values of how to treat women. Like being Latino, it is okay to hug and kiss, but being a Muslim, it is not okay, because you have that value for respect for women, and all that."[86]

79. Cuartas/María 2012:8.
80. Cuartas/Héctor 2012:16.
81. Cuartas/Camila 2012:6.
82. Cuartas/Vicente 2012:7.
83. Cuartas/Claudia 2012:7–8.
84. Cuartas/Lucía 2012:3–4.
85. Cuartas/Martina 2012:11.
86. Cuartas/Vicente 2012:9.

Héctor underlined the importance of treating guests well and respecting your elders.[87]

Martín did not mention specifically the value of family in his narrative. He said that his "values never changed." He said that now he understands the meaning of life.[88] He also mentioned the negative reactions of his family and friends after he embraced Islam.[89]

Family, community, hospitality, and respect for elders are Muslim values highlighted in studies by Hodge[90] and Haddad and Lummis.[91] In terms of the American values, two of the values mentioned by new Muslims are individualism and compassion (service). Another value that was noted was the opportunity for entrepreneurship. Gordon[92] emphasized the following values in the United States: individualism, respect for life, rationality, family, hard work, independence, and entrepreneurial spirit and innovation.

Family and respect are shared values among Americans, Muslims, and Hispanics.[93] Family, community, hospitality, and respect for elders are shared values between Muslims and Hispanics.[94]

Some converts have partially moved more toward individualism. Individualism, hard work, and compassion are salient values in America's culture.[95] Such is the case of Jaime, who has chosen to remain separated from the local Islamic community and is largely focusing on Islam more privately than publicly. One of the reasons for this has to do with his job:

> I am a contractor. I do not own my own business. I do not work in a private company that I just go to. I am working, I work for the [American] government, and sometimes they are afraid. You just need one person just to be nutty, just all afraid and just complain. So sometimes there is that fear of being seeing at the workspace and creating a problem. There is also the question, how much time are they taking away from your work?[96]

87. Cuartas/Héctor 2012:15.
88. Cuartas/Martín 2012:16.
89. Cuartas/Martín 2012:10.
90. Hodge, "Social Work," 162–73.
91. Haddad and Lummis, *Islamic Values*, 67–97.
92. Gordon, *Assimilation in American Life*.
93 ; Rinderle and Montoya, "Hispanic/Latino Identity Labels," 144–64. See also Gordon, *Assimilation in American Life*; Haddad and Lummis, *Islamic Values*.
94. Haddad and Lummis, *Islamic Values*; Rinderle and Montoya, "Hispanic/Latino Identity Labels," 144–64.
95. Gordon, *Assimilation in American Life*; Haddad and Lummis, *Islamic Values*; Wang, *Uncertain Future*.
96. Cuartas/Jaime 2012:10.

Jaime also mentioned that for many years he was his own Muslim community.⁹⁷ There is no evidence from the data about explicit disappointments of Jaime with Islam, but he mentioned that he was more involved at the beginning of his conversion and currently he is not practicing Islam as before:

> At the beginning, I wanted to practice everything I learn, and praise be to God, I have a teacher who was very open-minded, and just, you know you just can have very good principles. Principles take the good and reject the bad. And he explained a story of one of the companions of the prophet. That if you try to practice all the religion, the religion will break you. You cannot do it. And then you reminded me, the religion took several years, it can take over two decades to reveal. It was not revealed, and everyone started practicing. So, at first, I did a lot of things, and then I calmed down. And now I would say, it is me coming back to a steadier pace.⁹⁸

Martín shared some of his challenges he experienced practicing Islam in the United States. He claimed, "I was trying to do it [practice Islam] 100 percent, but living in this country it is impossible. If you go deep, you cannot walk in the streets in this country."⁹⁹ The reasons for these choices still need to be further explored.

Simón is the only participant in this study who self-identified first as an American, then as a Muslim. He is a second-generation Hispanic, and his mother is Mexican-American from San Antonio, Texas.¹⁰⁰ His wife is an American Muslim convert.

His desire for serving others is noted in the following comment: "when I got out of high school, I did not immediately go to college, I took a year off to serve with AmeriCorps organization, which is a service program that it is similar to Peace Corps. I did it for a year."¹⁰¹ Volunteering and serving the

---

97. Cuartas/Jaime 2012:13.
98. Cuartas/Jaime 2012:10.
99. Cuartas/Martín 2012:16.

100. Simón will be technically considered 2.5 generation since his mother was born in the United States. For more details about 2.5 generation see Ramakrishnan, "Second-Generation Immigrants?"

101. Cuartas/Simón 2012:1; AmeriCorps is a civil society program supported by the US federal government, foundations, corporations, and other donors engaging adults in intensive community service work with the goal of "helping others and meeting critical needs in the community." For more information about AmeriCorps and Peace Corps, see http://www.nationalservice.gov/programs/americorps and http://www.peacecorps.gov/

community are values that are highly emphasized in the United States.[102] Generational aspects will be further discussed in the following chapter. María and Martín are first-generation Hispanics, while Héctor and Camila are second-generation Hispanics, both born in the United States.

4.3.5 Religious Beliefs

Religious beliefs in general play a significant role in people's lives.[103] Ozorak suggests that the "individual's beliefs remain anchored in the parents' beliefs, and that change is tempered by the conservatism of those beliefs and by the strength with which parents adhere to them."[104] However, one important question that needs to be considered is: What happens when individuals switch to another religion? What really changes in terms of religious beliefs during the post-affiliation stage?

The participants expressed several aspects in terms of their beliefs. They also emphasized different teachings from the Qur'an. For example, in María's case, one of the aspects that she mentioned regarding the teachings of Islam was that there is no original sin, but that "everyone is responsible for their own actions. That the actions of the parents do not fall, or they will not be judged on the children."[105]

María also mentioned another aspect in terms of her beliefs: "I found it amazing that the sense of responsibility for the world, that sense of responsibility for the world that Islam teaches, went with what my father had taught us: to care for the rest of the world. He always thought that what we were doing can influence others. And, I was also impressed by the sense of God's mercy."[106]

Héctor mentioned the importance of realizing that there is "one God and from the direct connection to him that you have, you do not need any

---

102. Gordon, *Assimilation in American Life*, 46–48.

103. Gooren, *Religious Conversion and Disaffiliation*, 93–112; Norris, "Converting to What?," 171–81; See also Rambo, *Understanding Religious Conversion*.

104. Ozorak, "Social and Cognitive Influences," 449.

105. Cuartas/María 2010:12.

106. Cuartas/María 2012:12; According to the Qur'an, "there is no notion of an inherited 'original sin,' committed by the progenitors of the human race, for which all humanity suffers. The sin of Adam and Eve is just that—their own personal sin" (Esposito, *Islam: The Straight Path*, 30). For more details about the theological perspective of Islam about original sin, see Esposito, *Islam: The Straight Path*, 27–31. For a comprehensive explanation of the major beliefs in Islam, see Esposito, *Islam: The Straight Path*.

intermediaries."¹⁰⁷ In addition, he questioned the concept of the Trinity.¹⁰⁸ He was attracted by "the strict monotheism of Islam and the social racial justice that Islam strongly supports."¹⁰⁹

Camila emphasized the sense of community, the lack of hierarchy, and teachings from the Qur'an: "like everyone being equal and no one being better than the other persons, the fact that there are verses in the Qur'an talking about racism that no one is better than any other person in that way, social justice which is being a fair person, an honest person, a kind person, that all really, it touches me, so that influenced me a lot."¹¹⁰

Similar to Hector's experience, Martín also had some issues with the Trinity. He shared, "I realized that Jesus was just another prophet from God. That was the main deal that I studied all my life. I could never understand the Trinity when I learned it in Islam. I really knew nothing about Islam. When they told me that, I always was thinking about that. It did not make any sense."¹¹¹

Nevertheless, something different that Martín emphasized was the fact that "Islam was just a way to live, a way of living. Islam is not like just going to the church or whatever it was like your actions. You live Islam through your actions."¹¹²

4.3.6 Women and Islam

Haddad conducted a study on the conversion experiences of women to Islam in the United States. She also described some similar findings in her study regarding theological issues and beliefs:

> A large number of the women converts discussed, to varying degrees, the theological superiority of Islam over Christianity as an important reason for their conversion. Problems with Christian theology they identified included the perennial doctrines that have set the two faiths apart: the concepts of incarnation and Trinity, the divinity of Jesus, crucifixion, and the doctrine of original sin. Many said that they had been troubled by confusing and complicated theological notions in Christianity.¹¹³

107. Cuartas/Héctor: 2012:10–11.
108. Cuartas/Héctor: 2012:2.
109. Cuartas/Héctor: 2012:2.
110. Cuartas/Camila 2012:10.
111. Cuartas/Martín 2012:10.
112. Cuartas/Martín 2012:13.
113. Haddad, "Quest for Peace in Submission," 29–30.

María said that Islam teaches about the sense of family and responsibility for the world, which is everything that her father taught her. For María, there is no original sin. For Héctor, the belief in one God was very important to him as a belief and that man has direct access to him. That is something that has not changed. In Camila's case, the teaching of Islam about the importance of community was an important aspect, along with treating everyone as equals and giving to charity and learning how to be a good person. Martín emphasized the fact that Islam is not about going to church and that it was more about a way of life.

As previously described in chapter 3, there is evidence for the integration of the new religion's values and beliefs in the narratives of the converts. Vicente underlined the monotheistic nature of Islam.[114] Claudia had some issues with the Trinity.[115] Teresa noted that Islam is only a religion.[116] Here one can notice the diverse responses of the converts regarding their beliefs and the tensions they experienced with some theological aspects, such as the Trinity and the nature of sin.

4.3.7 Marriage and the Transmission of Values

Marriage is also a very significant choice in terms of identity construction. Intermarriage can be used as a marker of "integration" or "structural assimilation."[117] According to research on intermarriage, low intermarriage rates usually imply lower tensions and adjustments and high retention of ethnic values.

On the contrary, high intermarriage rates generally show higher tensions and adjustments, and less retention of ethnic values.[118] Thus, the dynamics in marriage shape the way in which Muslim parents transmit their religious and cultural values to their children.

Vicente and Camila are married to Hispanic Muslim converts. Héctor and Catalina are married to born-Hispanic Muslims, and they grew up with strong Hispanic values at home thanks to their parents. Lucía, Martina, María, and Claudia are married to born-immigrant Muslims from Middle Eastern countries (e.g., Yemen and Palestine). By contrast, Simón and Jaime are married to American Muslim converts.

---

114. Cuartas/Vicente 2012:7.
115. Cuartas/Claudia 2012:8.
116. Cuartas/Teresa 2012:17.
117. Gordon, *Assimilation in American Life*, 205–6. See also Song, "What Happens after Segmented Assimilation?"
118. Gordon, *Assimilation in American Life*, 1197.

The dynamics of parental intermarriage and the experiences of intermarriage among the Hispanic Muslims are significant because they help us to understand the transmission of values by parents.[119] Out of the four selected cases, Camila is the only individual whose parents are not from the same country of origin. Camila's father is from Puerto Rico, and her mother is from Switzerland (intermarriage), but María's parents are from Panama, Héctor's are from Puerto Rico, and Martín's are from Bolivia. To be married to a person of the same ethnicity facilitates the transmission of values to their children.[120]

One of the born-Hispanic Muslims I interviewed shared that his experience as a father was one of the factors that shaped the relationships with his friends. He shared, "I stay close with them [non-Muslim friends] over the years. I have put more of distance between them and me, just because at times it interferes with my religion. They may want to do things that I cannot or should not do. So, I keep a little bit more of a distance. And now being a father, I retract more to being home than being out with my non-Muslim friends."[121]

He also shared the diverse choices he needed to make raising Muslim children, as well as some of his major concerns:

> To be a father, gives an appreciation for what my parents went through. That was big. Understanding that being a parent, they [people] do not give you a handbook, you are the same person you were before, now you have to learn overnight. And then trying to figure out what is the best way to raise them. What are the decisions you have to make to put a stable home environment, to give them the education choices, I mean, to loving and enriching environment that I should provide? I mean, I constantly think about what I can do to be a good parent. How can I give them Islam the way I love Islam? How can I show them that? And I am always worried that they would leave the religion, or not practice it. And that is a fear of mine. I constantly think of how I can show them, and have them love it, the way I love it.[122]

Another born-Hispanic Muslim commented about his experience in raising his children as Muslims in the United States:

---

119. Leon, "Latino Cultural Values," 13–25.

120. Kim et al., "Latino/a Values Scale," 71–91; Leon, "Latino Cultural Values," 13–25; Rinderle and Montoya, "Hispanic/Latino Identity Labels," 144–64.

121. Cuartas/BHMM1 2012:6; Here, BHMM means Born Hispanic Male Muslim. I also use BHFM meaning Born Hispanic female Muslim.

122. Cuartas/BHMM 1 2012:11.

> Well my kids are young and right now I am just teaching them certain rituals, such as eating with the right hand, which is a very difficult thing for them to do. They do not do it all the time, but they are still kids. My oldest son is three years old, so I do not think he is ready for it yet. There is not much we can do. We just try to let them listen to the Arabic Qur'an, so they can at least feel familiar with it. Not as much as we should.[123]

A born-Hispanic Muslim mother emphasized the importance for her to focus on raising her children:

> Because the role of my life right now as mother and a home-schooler, I am active in two Muslim home-schooling groups which I believe [it is important in Islam]. And personally I have come to these terms that my work that I do is in my home with my children. I view it as a form of being active in Islam because if I do not raise them right, I fail the next generation. I am taking my energy from outside things, and I focused on my home for now when they are young. When that time changes and it will, my energy will change for I was teacher, and their time when my energy was outside. But I really honestly believe that if I do not do this part right, I failed my job.[124]

She also shared that there are few Hispanic Muslim couples. Her husband is a Hispanic Muslim who accepted Islam after marriage:

> To find a Latino growing up Muslim, that marries another Latino, to have children to be a second or third generation, I am the only one that I know of to go that far. I know that now, I am starting to see a couple of Latinas married to Latinos. They may not even be of the same country, but at least they are Latinos, they speak Spanish, and they can communicate. But at least they are Latinos, and there are still similarities within the culture. There are similarities that span different Latin American cultures. So that is newer, but for me it is even rarer that I do not see it very often because I think even for my parents at that time, there were many like them, but my father was very active in the community, and he worked a lot giving information about Islam to Latinos, and I grew up in that environment also.[125]

While some of the female Hispanic Muslims experience diverse levels of cultural tensions after marriage (as for example, Lucía, Claudia, and María),

---

123. Cuartas/BHMM2 2012:8.
124. Cuartas/BHFM1 2012:12.
125. Cuartas/BHFM1 2012:4.

there is evidence of some retention of Hispanic values in all of them. For example, Claudia is married to a Palestinian Muslim. She has been able to retain her Hispanic values. This is in part due to the strong transmission of ethnic values by her parents. Ethnic values were very important for her and especially the relationship with her father. Even her Palestinian Muslim husband ended up accepting some Hispanic customs such as hugging and kissing.

Most of the converts made comments about the importance of family and community to develop a sense of belonging.[126] These values are more appreciated particularly among Hispanic immigrants who came to the United States, leaving behind relatives and friends. This has been reported by several studies on immigration and religions in the United States.[127]

Imams and Islamic community leaders emphasized these shared values of family and community with other ethnic groups in their teachings and also in the contents of the websites of the Islamic centers where these individuals generally participated.[128] This has become an important strategy to attract ethnic minorities such as African-Americans and Hispanics.

It is important to mention that unlike other ethnic groups, most of the Hispanic Muslim converts prefer to attend and participate in specific Islamic centers rather than going to several places. Of course, this becomes a challenge for those who want to follow the five daily prayers. Some converts mentioned the challenges they experienced in practicing Islam in the United States were due to that lack of collaboration from their supervisors to allow them to pray at their jobs.

4.3.8 Tensions between Culture and Religion

As I mentioned in the previous chapter, Hispanic Muslims experience diverse tensions between culture and religion. María and Héctor have experienced low tensions between culture and religion. For example, María expressed that Islam has had a lot of influence on Hispanic culture because of the occupation of Spain,[129] so she finds no real tensions. This is a discourse that is emphasized by some imams.[130] It seems that anything that she does not necessarily believe in (such as the *hijab*, and male and female relationships), she does not abide by. Héctor acknowledges some differences

---

126. e.g., Cuartas/Héctor 2012:6; Cuartas/Catalina 2012:7.

127. See, for example, Kim et al., "Latino/a Values Scale," 71–91; Leon, "Latino Cultural Values," 13–25.

128. e.g., Cuartas/Imam 4 2012; Cuartas/Imam 5:2012.

129. Cuartas/María 2012:13.

130. Cuartas/Imam 1 2012, Cuartas/Imam 4 2012.

between culture and Islam, but he has been willing to reconcile the differences. He is very concerned about being Hispanic and helping Hispanics, so perhaps he uses Islam as a sort of enhancement to his life.

Camila's experience is different. When she is with Muslims, she behaves and dresses like a Muslim. When she is not around Muslims, most people do not know she is a Muslim. There is a high level of tension for her because she is still navigating through what she sees as her responsibility to Islam.

Martín's case is unusual. Martín acts in accordance with American culture. As this is the case, he finds it a lot easier not to practice his religion the way that he should if he were strictly adhering to the Qur'an. He justifies his responses, arguing that it is difficult to practice Islam in the United States as things are different here. As described before, his children do not attend a Muslim school and instead attend a Catholic school. Martín has assimilated more into American culture.

Lucía has learned to retain some traditions from the Latino culture. She is still cooking Latino food but cooks according to the dietary restrictions of Islam. She still listens to Latino music. She mentioned that she cannot dance to salsa [Colombian music], but she still listens to it. She still likes certain outfits; though she cannot wear them outside, she can wear them in her house.[131]

One of the female born-Hispanic Muslims commented on her interactions with female Latinas who are non-Muslims:

> A lot of times because I have the advantage that a lot of Latinas do not have being Muslim, is that I know who I am, and I am very comfortable with that, and I know my religion. So, they do not know that I am not like them until they got to know me, and they get very surprised. I know their culture far better than they know mine. So, I can play the game when I need to play the game. So most of the time, getting into a funny spot where I do not understand, but most of the time I understand the rules of the mystery. I understand the rules in different settings, so I do not attract attention.[132]

Most of these individuals were generally attracted to what they perceived as the complementary values expressed between Hispanic culture and Islamic culture. One of the significant patterns among the converts is the idea of decision-making. Essentially, converts want to be accepted into

---

131. Cuartas/Lucía 2012:10.
132. Cuartas/BHFM1 2012: 11–12.

the new religion and are challenged to navigate the idea of connecting their past selves with the present.

4.3.9 Self-Identification of the New Muslims

Here, the interplay of ethnicity, culture, and religion is paramount. These processes are complex because ethnic identity is shaped as converts embrace the new religion and partially assimilate—to varying extents—into American culture.[133] Self-identification has been used by several scholars as an indicator of identity.[134]

There is a variety of ways in which the new Muslims self-identify. For example, María and Camila identified themselves as Muslim Latinas. Héctor emphasized that he is a Muslim from Puerto Rico, while Martín preferred to be identified as a Hispanic Muslim. On the contrary, Simón (from previous chapters) identified himself as an American Muslim. Teresa and Lucia (from previous chapters) identified themselves as Hispanic and Latina Muslims, respectively.[135]

In general, the Hispanic Muslims used the following words when they shared their self-identification: Hispanic/Latino (ethnicity) white (race); Puerto Rican/Nicaraguan/Mexican-American (nationalities); female Hispanic (gender). In his study of Muslims in Britain, Song reported one of the experiences of the converts:

> In addition to the multiplicity and fluidity of identifications Paul articulated, there was often a blurring around the use of racial (white), ethnic (Chinese) and national (Irish or British)

---

133. For studies on ethnicity see Comas-Díaz, "Hispanics, Latinos, or Americanos," 115; Gracia, *Hispanic Latino Identity*; Portes and MacLeod, "What Shall I Call Myself?," 523–47; Yang, *Chinese Christians in America*.

134. Cristian, *Who are We?*; Hashmi, "From Ethnicity to Religion."

135. Prevalent discourses on Hispanic/Latino/a identity have been largely focused on Catholic background (De La Torre and Espinosa, *Rethinking Latino(a) Religion and Identity*; Gracia, *Hispanic Latino Identity*; Gracia, *Latinos in America*; Martínez-Vázquez, "Alianza Islámica"; Stevens-Arroyo and Cadena, *Old Masks, New Faces*.) For research on identity among Hispanics, see Abalos, *Latinos in the United States*; Avalos, *Introduction*; Aponte and De La Torre, *Handbook of Latina/o Theologies*; Comas-Díaz, "Hispanics, Latinos, or Americanos"; De La Torre and Espinosa, *Rethinking Latino(a) Religion and Identity*; González *Harvest of Empire*; González, "Mañana"; Gracia, *Hispanic Latino Identity*; Gracia, *Latinos in America*; Medina, "Hispanic/Latino Identity"; Medina, "Women." For research done on the Hispanic identity formation in the second generation, see Portes and MacLeod, "What Shall I Call Myself?" The Pew Research Center, in 2014, conducted an extensive research on the shifting of religious identity of Latinos in the United States.

categories. Even though Paul did not feel straightforwardly Irish or European, he felt much more European, or Western, culturally, than he did Chinese, given his upbringing in Ireland and England. For Paul, being both Chinese and English did not in any way preclude his sense of belonging in white mainstream Britain as experienced, for instance, by some second-generation groups in the United States.[136]

4.3.10 Contrasting Self-Identification with Biography

Here, I will contrast the self-identification of the converts with their biography to evaluate the level of consistency or contradiction. The variety of choices shows the complex dynamics between ethnicity, culture, gender, and religion. Even though I have identified some markers to facilitate the analysis, it is a very difficult task to identify which identity is predominant. Ethnic (Hispanic), cultural (American), and religious (Muslim) identities intersect each other in different ways, and they do not remain static.

When considering many of María's beliefs, such as the wearing of the *hijab* and the separation between men and women, she does not always appear to be Muslim.[137] Because of the culture she grew up in, she has no problem saying what it is that she wants. In general, one can say that there are some contradictions in her primary self-identification as a Muslim.

Héctor is Muslim first in that he is willing to change his lifestyle to suit his religion, but everything in his life is geared around being Puerto Rican. His wife is Puerto Rican. His children are Puerto Rican, and he is highly motivated to work with Hispanics in helping to not only see to their needs but to also help educate them about Islam.[138]

Camila is a special case. I think that she would not have converted unless she had found other Hispanics who were also Muslim because she admits that having other Hispanic Muslims in her life is important to her. She went out of her way to travel to a mosque that had more Hispanic Muslims rather than attend the mosque that was closest to her.[139] She also believes that wearing the *hijab* is a requirement but freely admits she does not wear it in her everyday life unless she is around other Muslims.

Martín is very honest about the fact that he does not put being Muslim first, even though he demands that people consider him a revert rather than

---

136. Song, "What Happens after Segmented Assimilation?," 1203.
137. Cuartas/María 2012:9.
138. Cuartas/Héctor 2012:2.
139. Cuartas/Camila 2012:9.

a convert.[140] He has made no real changes in his life other than saying that he is a Muslim. Where I would disagree with him is that I think that, even though he is an immigrant from Bolivia, he is much more American than he is Muslim. I believe this because, to Martín, it is more important to be "spiritual" than to focus on what is required of him by his religion. He generally does not fully participate in Islam.

4.3.11 Contextual Factors and Present State of the New Hispanic Muslims

As it has been stated in previous chapters, context plays a significant role in all the stages of the process of affiliation and conversion. The social, cultural, and religious factors are paramount as individuals reconstruct their identities.[141]

María's social life is wrapped around Islam and the interfaith and feminist dialogue that she engages in. She thoroughly enjoys standing up for what she believes in and likes feeling she has a choice and the ability to help changes come into being. She is married to a Muslim (born in an unknown country from the Middle East). She is the interfaith director in her Islamic center and helps teach classes for new Muslim converts.

Culturally, being Hispanic is very important to her because it seems that it helps her engage more in the interfaith dialogue. Her religious conversion is heavily influenced by her Hispanic culture. She has kept all of her cultural values but has ultimately changed her religion. This contrasts with how she self-identifies in her demographic survey, which says that she is Muslim first. Religiously, she feels very strongly about what she believes to be cultural differences in the religion and what she feels is actually part of the religion. She refuses to wear the *hijab* and truly dislikes the *niqab* (a veil which covers the face and head). She does not believe in gender separation because she herself gets along well with men and has a male best friend.

Héctor is very involved with his Muslim community in social justice issues. He is also a leader in his Islamic center that is in charge of the outreach for the youth. He is beginning to enter into the stage of doing *dawah* (but he has already been engaged in it before), and he desires to join the interfaith dialogue. Culturally, he is very much Hispanic, and he thoroughly enjoys doing activities that are geared toward educating the Hispanic community. He is married to a Puerto Rican wife. He teaches his children about

---

140. Cuartas/Martín 2012:8.

141. Rambo, *Understanding Religious Conversion*; Kraft, *Searching for Heaven*; Yang, *Chinese Christians in America*.

being Muslim, and so it is important that he has a strong handle on the contents of his religion. At first, he believed that Islam was a sect of Christianity.

Camila is an atypical case because she came to Islam as an atheist and not a Christian. She is invested in social justice issues but is not always around the Muslim community. Her job is outside of the community, so she does not wear the *hijab* when she is away from her community. Consequently, most people do not know that she is a Muslim. Culturally, the Islamic center she attends has Hispanic Muslims, and she herself is married to a Hispanic Muslim. Religiously, it seems that Camila is still navigating her way through her religion and the things that are required of her.

Martín is hardly a participant in the Islamic community, but he is married to a Muslim woman. Culturally, his wife is Hispanic (also from Bolivia). Religiously, he does not read the Qur'an, nor does he attend mosque, so he does not interact with other Muslims. For him, it is much more about mentally professing and making a personal commitment to God, so he considers himself an active Muslim.

4.4 SELECTED THEORIES

I will concentrate now on the descriptions of some of the theories that I will use to understand the process of reconstruction of identities by the Hispanic Muslims, as well as the interplay of cultural, ethnic, and religious identities. These theories include assimilation and integration.[142]

4.4.1 Assimilation Theory

After the 1950s, assimilation became the scholarly canon as well as the ideological norm for American society.[143] Assimilation takes place when

---

142. For more details about assimilation, see Yang, "Religious Conversion and Identity Construction"; Yang, *Chinese Christians in America*. For more details about isolation/marginalization, see Bagby, *American Mosque 2011*. For more details about segmented assimilation, see Portes and Zhou, "New Second Generation"; Schneider and Crul, "New Insights." For integration theory, see Laurence and Vaïsse, *Integrating Islam*; El Kacimi, "Identity and Social Integration." For adhesive identities, see Kim and Hurh, "Beyond Assimilation and Pluralism"; Yang, *Chinese Christians in America*. For symbolic interactionism, see Ameli, *Globalization and British-Muslim Identity*; Beyer, *Religion and Globalization*; Greil and Davidman, "Religion and Identity"; Kraft, *Searching for Heaven*. Adhesive identities and symbolic interactionism will be discussed in the next chapter.

143. Alba and Nee, "Rethinking Assimilation Theory," 826–74; See also Park, *Race and Culture*; Warner and Srole, *Social Systems*.

individuals adopt the cultural norms of the dominant or host culture over their original culture.[144] Gordon made a significant distinction of various assimilation theories between Anglo-conformity, the melting pot, and cultural pluralism:

> 'Anglo-conformity' theory demanded the complete renunciation of the immigrant's ancestral culture in favor of the behavior and values of the Anglo-Saxon core group; the 'melting pot' idea envisaged a biological merger of the Anglo-Saxon peoples with other immigrant groups and a blending of their respective cultures into a new indigenous American type; and 'cultural pluralism' postulated the preservation of the communal life and significant portions of the culture of the later immigrant groups within the context of American citizenship and political and economic integration into American society.[145]

Gordon followed Robert Park and suggested seven stages in the assimilation process: 1) civic assimilation (lack of conflict regarding values and power); 2) behavior receptional assimilation (absence of discrimination); 3) attitude receptional assimilation (the immigrant acts out the attitudes of the new culture to avoid prejudice); 4) identificational assimilation (sense of citizenry or peoplehood based on the dominant group; the immigrant identifies with the host culture and rejects the culture of national origin); 5) marital assimilation (marrying into the host culture); 6) structural assimilation (membership in host society institutions; contacts with the host society); and 7) cultural or behavioral assimilation (the person reflects the cultural patterns of the dominant culture; immigrants changed their values and beliefs to mirror the cultural norms of the host society).[146]

Structural and cultural assimilation in particular are significant for my study because these indicators facilitate the analysis to understand the degree to which the converts assimilated into American society. Park and Gordon supposed the inevitability of the eventual "disappearance of

---

144. For more details about assimilation, see Gordon, *Assimilation in American Life*; Yang, *Chinese Christians in America*; Yang,"Chinese Conversion to Evangelical Christianity"; Yang, "Religious Conversion and Identity Construction." Acculturation (anthropologists), or cultural assimilation (sociologists), explains the process of cultural and psychological change that results following meeting between cultures. The effects of acculturation can be perceived at several levels in both interacting cultures. For more details about assimilation, see Gordon, *Assimilation in American Life*; Kaba, "Religion, Immigration and Assimilation."

145. Gordon, *Assimilation in American Life*, 85.

146. Gordon, *Assimilation in American Life*, 70–71; Anthropologists used the term "acculturation" to refer to cultural assimilation, which is more often used by sociologists.

the ethnic group as a separate entity and the evaporation of its distinctive values."[147] Generally, the classic conceptualization of the theory of assimilation "foresees the progressive weakening and ultimate disappearance of the primordial traits and bonds of ethnicity as succeeding generations adopt the general society's unitary system of cultural values and become absorbed into economic, social, and political networks that are blind to ethnicity."[148]

Nevertheless, this classic assimilation theory has been highly criticized since the 1960s. According to Yang,

> Strictly speaking, the classic conceptualization of assimilation expects complete disappearance of ethnic distinctiveness. It presumes the existence of an American core society and core culture to which immigrants are expected to assimilate. In contemporary American society, however, the core has been eclipsed and pluralism has become more acceptable.[149]

As an alternative, the ethnic pluralism model rose and became the prevailing model in theory and politics.

4.4.2 Integration Theory

Integration occurs when individuals are able to adopt the cultural norms of the dominant or host culture while preserving their culture of origin. El Kacimi conducted a study of identity and social integration among Muslim immigrants in the United States. El Kacimi focused his research on cultural assimilation and cultural integration. He analyzed the construction of identities of the Muslim immigrants.[150] Some of the most important findings in his study are the following:

> Muslim immigrants highly identified themselves as Muslim, with the large majority having the skills to navigate both the Arabic and the American society worlds. About one-third of the

---

147. Gordon, *Assimilation in American Life*, 81; "Assimilation is a state of a high degree of acculturation into the host milieu and a high degree of de-culturalization of the original culture. It is a state that reflects a maximum convergence of strangers' internal problems with those of the natives and a minimum maintenance of the original cultural habits" (Gudykunst and Kim, cited in El Kacimi, "Identity and Social Integration," 11).

148. Morawska, "Sociology and Historiography of Immigration," 189.

149. Yang, *Chinese Christians in America*, 17.

150. For new insights into assimilation and integration theory, see Schneider and Crul, "New Insights." For details about selective integration, see Ozyurt, "Selective Integration." He did extensive research on selective integration among Muslim immigrant women in the United States.

participants expressed some form of cultural dissonance with American society and its values. Muslim immigrants' greatest concern is for their children to learn the Arabic language and maintain their cultural heritage. The participants have a strong desire for their children to maintain their primary language and maintain their Muslim identity. This desire to maintain ties to their cultural heritage is balanced by an understanding of the need to learn the English language for survival and advancement within the host society.[151]

Yang identifies three different options that are pursued as people develop their immigrant convert identities. Fragmentary integration describes when someone adopts some values or lifestyles from others but continues to maintain one dominant identity. Fusive integration blends several cultures and softens distinct characteristics. He claims that someone with fusive integration never fits in, seeming too Chinese to Americans and too American to Chinese. Finally, adhesive integration is when people add multiple identities without necessarily losing one, allowing for positive interaction with people in a variety of different social settings.[152]

4.4.3 Link to My Research and Limitations of Selected Theories

Assimilation and integration theories have been used by several scholars such as El Kacimi, Ozyurt, and Yang. These scholars have studied the diverse dynamics of identity construction among immigrants. Yang emphasized the relationship between assimilation and pluralism. However, there is limited research that shows how the responses to assimilation and integration shape the reconstruction of identities as individuals affiliate with a new religion.

One of the main problems is that both concepts, assimilation and integration, are limited because it is difficult to measure specific indicators of them to facilitate the analysis of data. Another limitation of these theories is that the concepts generally imply that there is full assimilation or integration. The data has shown that there are negotiations, choices, and tensions involved as individuals reconstruct their identities, and for some of them, there is a selective assimilation or integration.

Therefore, it is more helpful to concentrate on the different types of assimilation and integration in order to better understand the process of how individuals adopt new values from the host society.[153] Here, I will focus on

---

151. El Kacimi, "Identity and Social Integration," v.
152. Yang, *Chinese Christians in America*, 183–85.
153. For an extended analysis of some of the limitations of assimilation and

the stages of assimilation proposed by Gordon and the types of integration suggested by Yang. Focusing on the types of assimilation and integration can be helpful to better understand the different experiences of the converts as they try to integrate at diverse levels: culturally, socially, and religiously. Also, it can facilitate the study of the dynamic interplay between identity, religion, and ethnicity.

An important question informing my research is to analyze the extent to which the responses of the new converts to assimilation and integration shape the level of participation and commitment in Islam. This question will be further explored in the next chapter.

4.5 EXPLANATION OF THE RESULTS IN LIGHT OF THEORIES

Frequently immigrants—particularly Hispanic Muslim immigrants—do not fully assimilate or integrate; rather their assimilation or integration is partial or selective. In terms of identity construction, individuals can construct not only one but multiple identities due to the fluid dynamics between ethnicity, culture, and religion. These result in tensions and choices that new converts need to make particularly during the post-affiliation stage. Hispanic Muslim converts are not exceptional.[154]

As described earlier, Gordon proposed seven stages in the process of assimilation that can be helpful to analyze the different aspects that are involved when individuals assimilate to the host culture.[155] For this study in particular, structural and cultural assimilation are significant because these facilitate the analysis to understand the degree of assimilation of the converts.[156]

Structural assimilation is related to the membership in host society institutions. In the cultural assimilation stage (acculturation), the individual reflects the cultural patterns of the dominant culture. Here, individuals

---

integration, see Alba and Nee, "Rethinking Assimilation Theory"; Schneider and Crul, "New Insights"; Yang, *Chinese Christians in America*, 17–18.

154. Yang, *Chinese Christians in America*, also reported in his study the tensions that Chinese immigrants often experienced as they converted to Christianity in the United States. Thus, it is important to understand the nuances that take place in these processes.

155. Gordon, *Assimilation in American Life*, 70–71.

156. For more details about assimilation, see Gordon, *Assimilation in American Life*; Yang, *Chinese Christians in America*; Yang, "Chinese Conversion to Evangelical Christianity"; Yang, "Religious Conversion and Identity Construction."

usually change their values and beliefs, reflecting the cultural norms of the host society.[157]

Even though the stages are helpful to understand the complex process of assimilation by immigrants, one of the limitations is that Gordon's model largely assumes that "cultural assimilation" will precede or concur with "structural assimilation."[158] However, some new immigrant groups and their second-generation children who attain structural assimilation in their socioeconomic life nonetheless resist cultural assimilation in their religious practices. This is the case for Héctor and Camila, who are second-generation Hispanic Muslims. By contrast, Martín is more assimilated into American culture, adopting new values such as individualism while barely participating with the Islamic community.

Another theory that has been suggested by several scholars is the process of selective assimilation that emphasizes ethnic retention.[159] As explained earlier, this is the case for María, Héctor, and Camila. However, it is observed that these individuals not only experienced the retention of ethnic values such as the importance of family and community but also some beliefs from their previous religion. In addition, informants reported that prayer and fasting were very significant practices for them, and these are shared and common practices in Catholicism and Protestantism. Rituals and practices will be further discussed in the subsequent chapter.

There is not only evidence for selective assimilation but also for selective integration as Hispanic Muslims try to integrate at different levels: religiously (as new Muslims), culturally (as Americans), and ethnically (as Hispanics in the United States). As a result of these complex and difficult processes, individuals can experience anomie, disappointment, and a desire for experiencing something better, as reported by Kraft.[160]

As described earlier, Yang identifies three types of integration: fragmentary integration, fusive integration, and adhesive integration.[161] These types of integration, in light of the self-identification of the converts, can be very helpful to understand the integration of several identities, as suggested by Kraft and Yang. Furthermore, Yang argued that adhesive integration is the best way to develop an immigrant identity.

---

157. Gordon, *Assimilation in American Life*, 70–71.

158. Gordon, *Assimilation in American Life*, 70–71.

159. Schneider and Crul, "New Insights," 1143–48; Song, "What Happens after Segmented Assimilation?," 1194–1213; Vermeulen, "Segmented Assimilation," 1214–30.

160. Kraft, *Searching for Heaven*, 110.

161. Yang, *Chinese Christians in America*, 183–85.

Thus, Yang's identification of several types of integration is helpful because it recognizes the tensions, challenges, and interactions between ethnicity, religion, and culture as individuals increase their levels of participation in and commitment to the new religion. In addition, this model also focuses on the experiences of immigrants.

In my study, fragmentary integration was more common among individuals who identified first as Hispanic or Latino. For example, Martín, Teresa, and Lucía adopted some values from Islam but continued to maintain one dominant identity as Hispanics.

In the case of Teresa, she made a clear distinction between Islam (religion) and Hispanic culture. Teresa ultimately maintained her existing personality, as most changes in her life were experienced before her conversion, and she considers Islam to be just a religion. This allows her to practice what she likes of Islam and discard the things that she does not like. She has a certain attitude about the kind of changes that she is willing to make. She does not want to wear the *hijab*, and so she does not.[162] It could be that she is still building her identity; consequently, her experience is a good test case.

Fusive integration is predominant among individuals who identify first as Muslims. Here, the religious identity comes ahead of the ethnic identity. Some examples include Camila and Catalina. However, in other cases, the opposite occurs where the ethnic identity is more salient than the religious identity, as is the case for Claudia and Vicente.

Finally, examples of adhesive integration include the following informants: María, Héctor, and Martina. Here, there is an integration of ethnic and religious identities. Depending on the experiences of the converts, one of these identities can facilitate the process of integrating the others.

In other cases, it is possible that there is only one identity that is dominant. For instance, María is someone experiencing adhesive integration. She is part of the interfaith dialogue and so has to take on a lot of identities that allow her to blend in cohesively, but ultimately, she still maintains a core personality suited to all the different interactions that she manages to have in various types of social settings. To a degree, this integration can be fusive as well because there are times when her ethnic identity is ahead of her religious identity as a Muslim. These examples show the complexities and intersections of diverse identities.

From the perspective of immigration integration, women present an interesting dilemma: they can simultaneously act as "facilitators of change" and as "sustainers of tradition." Migrant women can be perceived as "barriers

---

162. Cuartas/Teresa 2012:23.

to assimilation" because they are intergenerational transmitters of cultural practices, religious values, customs, and mother-tongues.[163]

Yang reported in his research that most people were integrating their Chinese and American identities: their Christian identity became adhesive, which helped to bind the other two together.[164] By holding multiple identities, adhesive identities can also be beneficial for the new converts as they can expand their interactions and contacts with other people:

> People who have adhesive identities can function well in various cultural settings. Depending on circumstances, they can freely choose to act like Americans among Americans and like Chinese among Chinese, or they can act like Chinese among Americans and like Americans among Chinese. Many leaders at the Chinese church enjoy adhesive identities. One example is Kevin Cheung, who was born in the 1940s in Shanghai of a Cantonese family, graduated from high school in Hong Kong, came to the United States to attend college, received a doctorate in engineering, and works in the aerospace industry. He speaks fluent English, Mandarin, and Cantonese and is a well-respected lay leader among Mandarin-, Cantonese-, and English-speaking congregants.[165]

4.6 CONCLUSION

The data has shown the links between religion, culture, ethnicity, and identity. It documents the importance of both individual and group levels, the changes that occurred in terms of values and beliefs, as well as the different choices and tensions that take place as individuals reconstruct their identities. Another important link is the self-identification of the converts and the different types of integration.

As a result of the reconstruction of the Hispanic Muslim identities, there is a dynamic interplay between ethnicity, culture, and religion in which social relationships are also altered. For some individuals, this means almost a total break with the previous community and in some cases with their own relatives, extended family, and friends. For others, the break is

---

163. Anthias and Yuval-Davis, "Contextualizing Feminism," 62–75; Espiritu, *Homebound*; Ozyurt, "Selective Integration," 1617–37; For a comprehensive study on the transmission of female Muslim identity, see Hermansen, "Keeping the Faith."
164. Yang, *Chinese Christians in America*, 183.
165. Yang, *Chinese Christians in America*, 185.

partial, and they manage to maintain relationships with the previous community, extended family, and even non-Muslim friends.

There are three levels of integration here: religious (Muslim community), cultural (United States society), and ethnic (with other Hispanics in the United States). Specific markers have been used to facilitate the analysis of these three categories of integration.

Some of the converts who integrate more with the Muslim community chose to attend particular Islamic centers that emphasized community, hospitality, and welcoming diverse ethnicities. They become involved in practices such as Friday prayers.

The new Hispanic Muslims, who integrate more selectively into mainstream US society, usually perceive no significant tensions between culture and religion, therefore their view of Islam is more holistic as a way of life. These individuals are usually bilingual (Spanish and English) and some of them, such as Héctor and Vicente, have also learned Arabic.

Individuals who assimilate more selectively into mainstream US society generally experience greater tensions between culture and religion. Their view of Islam is more limited because they make a distinction between culture and religion. Some individuals even comment that "Islam is just a religion." Yet, there is significant retention of ethnic values such as the importance of family and community, which are shared values with Muslims. Even American culture emphasizes the importance of family to a certain extent.[166]

The rejection or retention of values and beliefs is a difficult process because sometimes the converts are not fully aware of the changes that are occurring. Some new values and beliefs emerge in the process of reconstructing their Hispanic Muslim identities. However, they can be more conscious about making choices regarding changes such as name, dress, and preferred language.

Regarding the integration of Hispanic Muslims with other Hispanics, the data show that some individuals are very motivated by *dawah* (e.g., Vicente and Héctor). Individuals who are involved with interfaith dialogue, including María and Héctor, have no problem relating to non-Muslims. Most of them have maintained relationships with their relatives. However, it has been difficult for some of them (e.g., Martín).

In general, female Hispanic Muslims are confronted with higher tensions as they need to decide about post-affiliation changes in terms of dress, marriage, and gender relationships. This does not mean that male Hispanic Muslims do not experience challenges and tensions, for example in maintaining relationships with non-Muslim friends and limitations to practice

---

166. Gordon, *Assimilation in American Life*, 31–32.

Islam due to their jobs. The data show that both male and female Hispanic Muslims are confronted with tensions, challenges, and choices.

Studies on intermarriage suggest that the possibility of ethnic retention is lowered.[167] However, the data in this study has shown that it is possible for female Hispanic Muslims to have a high level of ethnic retention. Some of the reasons why this is possible are because of the strong ties to their families (e.g., Claudia) and the fact that some of them are married to Hispanic Muslims (Catalina and Camila).

The higher the levels of religious and social integration of the new Muslims, the higher the possibilities are for developing collective identities as the new Muslims interact with imams, immigrant Muslims, Islamic community leaders, born-Hispanic Muslims, and Muslim spouses. In addition, some individuals choose to become very active in Islamic organizations. This has been the case for María, Héctor, Martina, and Vicente.

As I have argued, there is an active agency on the part of the converts, not only in the conversion process but also as they reconstruct their identities. They are challenged to respond to the changes, tensions, and negotiations. The experiences are diverse and difficult as they try to fit into American culture and the new religious community. In addition, their social identity is altered in the process, shaping the way in which they relate to family, non-Muslim friends, the Muslim community, and the wider society.

Theories such as assimilation and integration are helpful to understand the possibilities of the construction of multiple identities in a pluralistic and globalized world. However, these theories by themselves are limited to understanding the complex choices experienced by new Muslims in the United States. To facilitate this analysis, I propose the use of assimilation stages suggested by Gordon and Yang into types of integration (fragmentary, fusive, and adhesive). One important question that emerged from these theories is the relationship between the responses of the converts to assimilation and integration and the shaping of the new identities of the converts.

In addition, it is important to identify and analyze the intersections between culture, ethnicity, gender, and religion. An important question to consider is: What is the relationship between the responses of the converts to assimilation and integration and the levels of commitment and contributions to local Islam? This question will be addressed in the following chapter.

The data shows that there is not only "ethnic retention" as reported by previous researchers,[168] but there is also the retention of some previous

---

167. Gordon, *Assimilation in American Life*, 8; Song, "What Happens after Segmented Assimilation?," 1197.

168. Song, "What Happens after Segmented Assimilation?," 1194–95; Yang, *Chinese*

religious practices and beliefs, meaning there is not a full break with the previous religion. There are shared values (e.g., family and respect) among Americans, Muslims, and Hispanics that are also retained.

The emphasis on community, solidarity, and hospitality are shared values by both Muslims and Hispanics. In turn, the retention of ethnic values is shaped by different factors including the experiences of the individuals with parents, the type of marriage of the parents (same ethnicity or intermarriage), and dynamics of the converts with their spouses (same ethnicity or intermarriage) whether or not individuals marry immigrant Muslims or Muslim converts.

Rituals and practices in Islam such as prayer, fasting, and almsgiving are known to some degree by the new Muslims because they are common in other religions (e.g., Catholicism and Protestantism). This shows us the new Muslims feel more comfortable with practices that they already know from their previous religious background. Therefore, it is vital to consider the diverse levels of choices of the new Hispanic Muslims with regard to participation and commitment in a minority Muslim context as it is the case in the United States. These aspects will be the main focus of the analysis in the following chapter.

Christians in America, 17–20.

Chapter 5

Being a Hispanic Muslim in the United States

Patterns of Religious Commitment and Practice

5.1 INTRODUCTION

The argument presented in this thesis is that there is a high level of agency among the converts. Even the converts who may be less active appear to make important choices at different post-affiliation stages of conversion, thus reshaping their identity as Muslims in the United States. Previous chapters have highlighted the important role the converts play in making pre-affiliation choices (ch. 2); the different revealing emphases the converts lay in their narratives of conversion (ch. 3); and the choices that converts make as they reconstruct their new identities while they experience tensions and different changes (ch. 4), which arguably lead to the diverse choices that Hispanic Muslims make concerning religious commitment and practice.

Consequently, this chapter will concentrate on the different levels of religious commitment and practice which is the central research question of this thesis: *To what extent do Hispanic Muslim converts play a role in making different choices regarding religious commitment and practice?* This chapter focuses on the patterns in different dimensions of religious commitment, particularly looking at religious practices (rituals and devotionals) shown by both the less active and more active converts.

The aim of this chapter is to analyze the diverse choices that converts make regarding religious commitment and practice in their chosen locations. I will also examine and challenge the position of scholars who make a distinction between low and high levels of religious commitment.[1]

Part of the problem is that the high and low levels of commitment suggest that individuals with low commitment are perhaps less committed in *all* the dimensions of religious commitment and vice versa, that individuals with high commitment are more committed in all the dimensions of religiosity.

In addition, these studies suggest that religious activity is largely an indicator of greater religious commitment among individuals. To what extent is high religious activity among Hispanic Muslim converts an indicator of more religious commitment or piety? What are the nuances among the Hispanic Muslim converts in terms of religious commitment and practice especially looking at the ritualistic and devotional dimensions?

Another problem is related to the conceptualization of religious commitment. The conceptualization of religiosity is reflected in the indicators that have been used to measure religious commitment. Considering these problems, I intend to address the following questions: Is it possible for individuals labeled as "low committed" or "moderately committed" to show reasonable or high commitment in some of the dimensions of religiosity? Do converts who are more active and are categorized as having high religious commitment show more commitment in the ritualistic and devotional dimensions of commitment? These dynamics and nuances will be analyzed in this chapter.

I will accomplish this aim in three sections. In the first section of this chapter, I will review the literature on religious commitment to highlight current definitions, methods, and debates to conceptualize and problematize religious commitment among Hispanic Muslims in the United States.

In the second section, I will use the "high and low" levels of commitment included in different studies of religious commitment, using suggested indicators to measure religious commitment to show their limitations regarding the dynamics in several dimensions of religiosity among the "less active" Hispanic Muslim converts. A distinction will be made between religious activity and religious commitment. Here, I will assess the position of scholars who make a distinction between low and high levels of religious commitment by analyzing the patterns of religious commitment and practice looking at both the "more active" and the "less active" converts,

---

1. Barker and Currie, "Do Converts?," 305–13; See also, Pew Research Center, "Muslim Americans: Middle Class"; Pew Research Center, "Muslim Americans: No Sign of Growth."

following a multi-dimensional approach[2] and also including contextualized emerging indicators from my own data.

I will pay special attention to patterns regarding the religious practices (rituals and devotionals) of the Hispanic Muslim converts, also highlighting significant similarities and differences between male and female Hispanic Muslim converts. In the final section, I will discuss the results in light of theories including socialization and social networks, as well as other studies done on religious commitment.

5.2 THE NATURE OF RELIGIOUS COMMITMENT

There is significant debate among scholars about definitions, the conceptualization, operationalization of religious commitment, and the selection of suitable indicators to measure religiosity. Consequently, I first seek to bring clarity to these terms.

5.2.1 Definitions of Religious Commitment

The definition of commitment itself and the nature of commitment are problematic. There is a lack of clear definition, particularly in sociological studies. What does religious commitment mean? Psychological and sociopsychological scholars have attempted to propose some definitions. However, few studies provide a clear definition of religious commitment.

There are different definitions of religious commitment (religiosity) proposed by several scholars. For example, Worthington defines religious commitment as "the degree to which a person adheres to his or her religious values, beliefs, and practices and uses them in daily living."[3] The supposition is that a highly religious person will evaluate the world through religious schemas and thus will integrate his or her religion into much of his or her life.[4]

Other scholars, including Bréchon and Voas, use the term "individual religiosity" to refer to an individual's degree of religious commitment, or the quality of being religious, not—as often in common usage—the display of excessive or affected piety. Religiosity is bound up with attitudes, behavior,

---

2. Bader et al., *American Piety in the 21st Century*, 1–54; See also Glock and Stark, *Religion and Society in Tension*.
3. Worthington et al., "Religious Commitment Inventory," 84.
4. Worthington et al., "Religious Commitment Inventory," 84–85.

and values, while religion is arguably more like ethnicity, something that for most people is transmitted to them rather than chosen by them.[5]

Stark and Glock emphasize the challenges of defining the term "religious." It can be understood in different ways by different people. According to Stark and Glock, the term "religious" can mean the following: "church membership, belief in religious doctrines, ethical way of life, attendance at worship services, and many other acts, outlooks and conditions to denote piety and commitment to religion."[6]

Here, religious commitment is understood as a multi-dimensional and dynamic phenomenon that includes religious activity (participation), beliefs, practices (rituals and devotionals), and daily life experiences that are shaped by multiple contextual factors.[7] In addition, the degree of religiosity of individuals may vary throughout different times.[8]

5.2.2 Distinction between Religious Activity, Recruitment, Conversion, and Commitment

Religious activity (attendance and participation) is one indicator of religious commitment. Religious activity is not equated to religious commitment. Thus, participation may or may not indicate religious commitment, particularly in Islam, which is a very rich religion in terms of rituals (e.g., every Muslim should pray five times a day). Religions emphasize different rituals and practices among their followers.

One of the most important contributions of Gooren's typology of religious activity is the distinction between affiliation, conversion, and confession. Affiliation is a formal membership in a religious group, without

---

5. Bréchon, "Cross-National Comparisons," 463–89; Voas, "Surveys of Behaviours, Beliefs and Affiliation," 145.

6. Stark and Glock, *American Piety*, 11; commitment is highlighted by Rambo in his definition of "intensification," which is the revitalized commitment to a faith with which the convert has had previous affiliation, whether formal or informal. It occurs when nominal members of a religious institution make their commitment a central focus in their lives, or when people deepen their involvement in a community of faith through profound religious experience and/or life transitions like marriage, childbirth, and approaching death (Rambo, *Understanding Religious Conversion*, 13). The five most common elements of the commitment stage are decision-making, rituals, surrender, testimony manifested in language transformation and biographical reconstruction, and motivational reformulation (Rambo, *Understanding Religious Conversion*, 124).

7. Worthington, "Understanding the Values of Religious Clients," 166–74. See also Stark and Glock, *American Piety*.

8. For another definition of religious commitment see Stark and Glock, *American Piety*, 13–14.

change of identity. According to Gooren's typology, an example of this is a member or baptized member.[9]

Conversion in the limited sense of the conversion career approach is defined by Gooren as a "radical" change of religious identity, followed by a commitment to a (new) religious group.[10] Some of the terms used in churches are "convert," "full member," and "baptized member." Confession is a core member identity with a high level of participation inside the (new) religious community and a strong evangelism on the outside. Here, I prefer to use the term "high commitment" instead of "confession" to emphasize the different levels of commitment of the converts. The terms that have been generally used are "leader," "core member," "deacon," and "missionary."[11]

This distinction made by Gooren's study is very helpful for researchers who examine religious commitment, because he highlights important aspects in both conversion and confession. In the conversion stage, both change and a certain level of commitment are emphasized, whereas in the confession stage there is an expectation of a higher level of commitment and strong evangelism. These aspects can inform the selection of indicators to measure the level of religiosity by individuals looking at specific religions. According to Gooren, recruitment by a church does not equate to conversion of the individual.[12]

Barker and Currie argued that "conversion and commitment have often been incorrectly equated in the social science literature. The question is asked whether those who have converted to a particular religious perspective are more committed than those who have been brought up in that tradition. The latter are referred to as 'alternators.'"[13]

5.2.3 Conceptualization of Religiosity

Numerous studies have been designed and employed for examining whether religious involvement is a unidimensional or a multidimensional construct. Some scholars, including Clayton, Clayton and Gladden, and Fullerton and Hunsberger, have largely supported a unidimensional conceptualization of religiosity.[14] However, the multidimensional nature of religion has been the

9. Gooren, "Conversion Narratives," 50.
10. Gooren, *Religious Conversion and Disaffiliation*, 3.
11. Gooren, "Conversion Narratives," 133.
12. Gooren, "Conversion Narratives," 40.
13. Barker and Currie, "Do Converts?," 1.
14. See Clayton, "5-D or 1?"; Clayton and Gladden, "Five Dimensions of Religiosity"; Fullerton and Hunsberger, "Unidimensional Measure of Christian Orthodoxy."

subject of much research and debate in the sociology of religion.[15] Consequently, "most researchers have concluded that religion cannot be regarded as a single, all-encompassing phenomenon."[16]

Scholars such as Bader at al., Stark and Glock, and Hassan have conceptualized religious commitment (religiosity) as a multidimensional phenomenon.[17] In this regard, Stark and Glock propose several dimensions to understand different patterns of religiousness among individuals: religious belief, religious practice (rituals and devotionals), religious experience, and religious knowledge.

Later, Bader et al. conducted a comprehensive study of religiosity in the United States. This group of scholars linked up with the pioneering surveys conducted by Stark and Glock in the 1960s.[18] This study focused on religious affiliation and religious beliefs looking at the complexities of religiosity among individuals from diverse religions including evangelical Protestantism, mainline Protestantism, Catholicism, Judaism, Buddhism, Hinduism, Islam, and unaffiliated religions. They state: "Nearly 400 items in the Baylor Religion Survey cover several matters of religious beliefs and practices, including consumerism, and nonstandard beliefs such as astrology, and practices including meditation, and New Age therapies."[19]

Hassan's 2007 analysis of Muslim piety in a Muslim-minority context was based on Stark and Glock's 1968 conceptualization of religious piety. Hassan's 2007 study concentrated on born Muslims, not converts, from Muslim-majority countries such as Indonesia, Pakistan, Egypt, Malaysia, Iran, Turkey, and Kazakhstan, and his study was largely quantitative.

There is, therefore, a need to conduct qualitative studies to examine the patterns of religious commitment among Hispanic Muslims in the United States, which presents an interesting contrasting context of a Muslim-minority country. It is necessary to propose new categories in these dimensions of religiosity to have a better understanding of the dynamics of religious commitment among converts in Muslim-minority countries. These categories should include, for example, the previous religious background of the converts, and individual perspectives of the converts about

---

15. See Ammerman, *Sacred Stories, Spiritual Tribes*; Audi, *Rationality and Religious Commitment*; Voas, "Surveys of Behaviours, Beliefs and Affiliation."

16. De Jong et al., "Dimensions of Religiosity Reconsidered," 866.

17. See Bader et al., *American Piety in the 21st Century*; Stark and Glock, *American Piety*; Hassan, "On Being Religious."

18. Bader et al., *American Piety in the 21st Century*, 5.

19. Bader et al., *American Piety in the 21st Century*, 5.

commitment. These aspects have been mainly overlooked in the literature of religious commitment.

5.2.4 Limitations of Glock and Stark's 1968 Dimensions

Worthington et al. identified two major problems of Glock and Stark's Dimensions of Religious Commitment inventory and others such as King and Hunt's 1969 Basic Religious Scales.[20] The primary problems are that they (a) "were developed for use with individuals within the Judaic and Christian traditions and (b) focus in large part on the degree to which a person believes in and adheres to traditional doctrines."[21] For this reason, I will add new indicators and dimensions in light of my own data.

5.2.5 Operationalization of Religious Commitment

Several scales have been proposed to measure religious commitment. Most of the studies are quantitative and have been conducted by psychologists.[22] One of the approaches to analyze religious commitment is to focus on the identification and validation of different markers of religious commitment. "The validation and verification of the multidimensionality of religion have been achieved largely through studies of inter-correlations of scales which seek to represent different dimensions."[23]

5.2.6 Debates among Muslim Scholars

There have been substantial discussions lately among Muslims about "the nature as well as the contents of religious commitment (religiosity) that a Muslim must display and adhere in order to be a Muslim or true believer."[24]

20. For a summary, see Hill and Hood, *Measures of Religiosity*.
21. Worthington et al., "Religious Commitment Inventory," 85; For additional comments with regard to some limitations of Glock and Stark's proposed dimensions, see also Krauss et al., "Muslim Religiosity-Personality Measurement Inventory," 137–38.
22. See Altemeyer, *Enemies of Freedom*; Pfeifer and Waelty, "Psychopathology and Religious Commitment"; Sethi and Seligman, "Optimism and Fundamentalism."
23. Hassan, "On Being Religious," 440; See King and Hunt, "Measuring the Religious Variable: Amended Findings"; For a comprehensive analysis of scales that have been used by several scholars to measure religious commitment, see Hill and Hood, *Measures of Religiosity*, 205–15. For a discussion on the advances in the conceptualization and measurement of religion and spirituality, see Hill and Pargament, "Advances."
24. Hassan, "On Being Religious," 437.

According to Hassan, "One of the key claims in this debate is that to be a Muslim, there must be evidence of religious piety at the behavioral, ethical, and cognitive levels. Islamic philosophy and theology contain a large body of expository literature dealing with this issue."[25] There are different perspectives between Muslim leaders (imams) and followers. Even among Muslim followers, there are arguably different perspectives between born Muslims and converts.

According to Hassan, there are limited studies that explore the nature and contents of Muslim piety, sociologically. Here, special attention will be given to the different perspectives of Hispanic Muslim converts regarding the meaning of a good or committed Muslim.

5.3 HIGH AND LOW LEVELS OF RELIGIOUS COMMITMENT

I will describe some indicators that have been used by several scholars, including Alston, Barker and Currie, and the Pew Research Center.[26] Later, I will explain the indicators that I will use and how to measure them. I will focus on the twelve selected cases that represent different genders, stages, generations, religious activity, and religious commitment. I will show different patterns regarding religious activity and commitment, looking especially at the ritualistic and devotional dimensions of religiosity.

I will analyze the selected cases based on the index of religious commitment used by different scholars in their study among American Muslims.[27] Then I will use these levels of religiosity to show the nuances and patterns among both those who are "less active" and "more active." Here, religious activity is one of the indicators of commitment. It will be measured by the weekly religious activity of the converts at the Islamic centers.

5.3.1 Indicators Used to Measure Religious Commitment

Scholars have used different indicators to measure religious commitment. For example, Alston, in his study among Jews, Catholics, and Protestants in the United States, proposed the following measures of religiosity: subjective

---

25. Hassan, "On Being Religious," 437; See also Esposito, "Islam"; Rahman, *Major Themes of the Qur'an*.
26. See Alston, "Three Measures"; Barker and Currie, "Do Converts?"; and Pew Research Center, "Shifting Religious Identity."
27. Pew Research Center, "Muslim Americans: Middle Class"; Pew Research Center, "Muslim Americans: No Sign of Growth."

(self-perceived strength of religious affiliation), behavioral (church attendance), and quasi-institutional (extent of respect given to religious leaders).[28] The categories used in the analysis by Alston are strong, not very strong, and somewhat strong.[29]

Barker and Currie studied the differences regarding religious commitment between "converts" and "alternators." According to Barker and Currie, "alternators" are those who have been brought up in that tradition.[30] These scholars also make the distinction between low and high commitments.

Barker and Currie proposed six indicators to measure religious commitment: 1) importance of religion to the respondent (alternators scored slightly higher than converts); 2) church attendance (converts scored marginally higher; 3) church involvement (alternators scored higher than converts. More converts found themselves in learning roles, while more alternators found themselves in serving roles); 4) devotional commitment expressed in private prayer and Bible reading (no significant differences were found); 5) willingness to recruit others (no significant differences were found); 6) financial giving to the church (both were equally likely to be regular financial contributors to the church).[31]

Barker and Currie expanded the conceptualization of commitment proposed by Alston and other scholars, adding more indicators in their analysis. One of the important contributions of their study is the distinction between attendance and religious involvement. In assessing religious involvement, they highlight two important roles of the informants: serving roles and learning roles.

Another important finding is that "alternators scored higher than converts in measures of church involvement. No church involvement, other than attendance, was reported by 40 percent of the converts as opposed to 13 percent of the alternators."[32]

I will include the devotional commitment in the next section that will focus on different dimensions of religious commitment to better understand the nuances among less active and more active converts. Some of my informants mentioned the significance of *zakat* (almsgiving) as a religious practice in Islam. The patterns regarding almsgiving will be included later in this section.

28. Alston, "Three Measures," 166.
29. Alston, "Three Measures," 168.
30. Barker and Currie, "Do Converts?," 305.
31. Barker and Currie, "Do Converts?," 309.
32. Barker and Currie, "Do Converts?," 310.

5.3.2 Index of Religious Commitment

Scholars who are part of the Pew Research Center (PRC) have proposed an Index of Religious Commitment based primarily on three indicators: a) importance of religion in their lives (very important, somewhat important, and not too/at all important); b) mosque service attendance (weekly or more; monthly/yearly; and seldom/never); and c) daily prayer *(salah* prayers for Muslims—all five *salah* daily; some *salah* daily; less often; and never pray).[33] For the frequency of prayer, the PRC used the following categories: at least once/day, weekly/monthly, seldom/never, and don't know.[34]

The PRC also conducted a study among Hispanic Protestants and Catholics in the United States. The focus of the study was on the shifting religious identity of Hispanic participants. Additional indicators of religious commitment were proposed by researchers, but they were not included to measure the index of religious commitment of Hispanic Catholics and Protestants. The following are additional indicators used by PRC: engagement in congregational life (personal involvement in the church); volunteering (civic engagement in, for example, churches, neighborhoods, and schools); reading Scripture outside of worship services; participation in Bible study or prayer groups; sharing the faith; praying to saints and giving confession (among Roman Catholics).[35]

5.3.3 How are These Studies Informing My Research?

Some of the above indicators included in the recent study conducted by the PRC can be helpful to measure religious commitment among Hispanic Muslims, particularly reading Scripture outside of worship services in the case of Islam (reading the Qur'an), and participation in group discussions with other Muslims or prayer groups. These indicators will be included in the examination of religious devotions.

5.3.4 How Will I Measure the Proposed Indicators?

I will use the following categories here: frequency of attendance at mosque, frequency of daily prayers, and the importance of religion in daily life. Rather than asking respondents to describe the importance of their religion

---

33. See Pew Research Center, "Shifting Religious Identity."
34. See Pew Research Center, "Shifting Religious Identity."
35. Pew Research Center, "Shifting Religious Identity," 54–58.

subjectively, I will analyze the following indicators from the data, paying special attention to post-affiliation changes to assess the importance of religion in daily life: change of name, dress and outward appearance, prohibitions of pork and alcohol consumption, changes in friendships, and vocations.

Regarding the importance of the frequency of the observance of religious rituals, Hassan states,

> Islam is a ritual-rich religion. Muslims are required to perform specific rituals as an expression of their faith. Rituals such as *salât* (daily prayers) and *wudü* (the cleansing of hands, face and feet prior to performing the prayers) have always been and remain significant in promoting a sense of religious community among Muslims. The frequency of observance of religious rituals is a useful and meaningful indicator of an individual's religiousness or religiosity.[36]

Attendance at the mosque will be measured according to the hours spent weekly. Performance of the five daily prayers (*salah*) will be measured according to the number and duration of the convert's daily prayers. Participation in Friday prayer meetings will be analyzed by frequency of attendance.

The categories that I will use to classify the convert's levels of commitment are high, moderate, and low. Scholars from the PRC have used high, medium, and low. My purpose is to label informants with the indicators that PRC scholars have used to highlight the limitations of distinctions between low and high commitments. Before analyzing indicators of religious commitment, however, I will describe the religious affiliation of the Hispanic Muslim informants.

5.3.5 Religious Affiliation of the Hispanic Muslim Converts

The majority of Muslims in the United States are Sunni (65 percent). Nevertheless, there is a minority of Shia Muslims (11 percent). There is also an increasing number of Muslims in the United States that are "unaffiliated" (15 percent).[37] These Muslims describe themselves as "just a Muslim."[38] These

---

36. Hassan, "On Being Religious," 441–42.
37. Pew Research Center, "Muslim Americans: No Sign of Growth," 23.
38. Pew Research Center, "Muslim Americans: No Sign of Growth," 23.

variances are also reflected in the composition and politics of mosques and Islamic centers in the United States.[39]

Religious affiliation among the Hispanic Muslim informants is slightly diverse. Most of the informants (ten out of twelve) identified themselves as Sunni Muslims. However, two of the female Hispanic Muslim converts identified themselves just as Muslims, arguing that they do not subscribe to either Sunni or Shia Islam (Martina and María). This is consistent with trends observed by scholars among Muslims in the United States.

Only two of the male Hispanic converts mentioned their preference for following a specific school of thought within Islam. One of the converts follows the Shafi'i school of law.[40] Another Hispanic Muslim convert mentioned the Hanafi school of law.[41]

Camila reported that she studied Sufism for a while.[42] Héctor has been partially influenced by Alianza Islámica (a Hispanic Muslim organization) because his wife's family was very involved in this organization.[43] Lucía said that she mainly considers herself a Sunni Muslim because she does not like

---

39. Esposito, *Islam: The Straight Path*, 76; Pew Research Center, "Muslim Americans: No Sign of Growth," 23; "Muslims who have no specific affiliation make up a much larger share of the US-born Muslim population than of the immigrant population. About one-in-four native-born Muslims (24 percent) have no specific affiliation, compared with just 10 percent of Muslims born in other countries" (Pew Research Center, "Muslim Americans," 23). For an extensive study of the mosques in the United States, see Bagby, *American Mosque 2011*. For important characteristics of American Muslims, see also An-Na'im, *What Is an American Muslim?*; Bilgrami, "What is a Muslim?"; Gallup Center for Muslim Studies, "Muslim Americans."

40. The Shafi'i is one of the schools of Islamic law in Sunni Islam. It was founded by the Arab scholar Al-Shafi'i in the early ninth century. The Shafi'i school was, in the early history of Islam, the most followed ideology for Sharia. Nevertheless, with the Ottoman Empire's expansion, it was replaced with the Hanafi School in many parts of the Muslim world. For more details about the Shafi'i School of thought, see Dickson, "Tablighi Jama'at in Southwestern Ontario"; Esposito, *Islam: The Straight Path*; Rahim, *Principles of Muhammadan Jurisprudence*.

41. See Dickson, "Tablighi Jama'at in Southwestern Ontario"; Esposito, *Islam: The Straight Path*. The Hanafi School is one of the oldest and perhaps the largest in parts of the world. One of the characteristics of this school is that there is a strong emphasis on the role of reason. There are movements within this school such as *Deobandis* and the *Tablighi Jamaat* which are largely concentrated in South Asia and in most parts of India.

42. See Lecesse, "Islam, Sufism, and the Postmodern"; Zebiri, "'Holy Foolishness'"; Sufism is a mystical form of Islam that focuses more on the spiritual aspects of the religion of Islam. For more details about Sufism, see Lecesse, "Islam, Sufism, and the Postmodern"; Zebiri, "'Holy Foolishness.'"

43. Alianza Islámica was founded in Harlem, New York in 1975 by a group of Puerto Rican Muslim converts. For more information about Alainza Islámica, see Martínez-Vázquez, "Alainza Islámica."

the practices of Shia Muslims.[44] She stated that, "In the *Qur'an* it is said you have to be perfect so in order to perfect you have to follow exactly what is in it. And to be perfect, you need to be Sunni. That is just my personal opinion. It is not that I do not consider them brothers and sisters in Islam, but I just chose to practice Sunnism. And the kids are learning Sunnism as well."[45]

It is important to note that the question of religious affiliation caused the greatest hesitation among those interviewed. Some of the reasons for this include the following: negative stereotypes of Muslims in the United States, Islamophobia, minority status of Hispanic Muslim converts, and the overall social turmoil in different countries in the Middle East.[46]

Another important aspect here is the participation of the converts at specific Islamic centers. Among the twelve selected cases, nine informants reported that they participate primarily at one of the Islamic centers rather than going to different mosques (María, Héctor, Vicente, Teresa, Simón, Claudia, Martina, Camila, and Lucía). However, three of the informants usually attend different Islamic centers (Jaime, Catalina, and Martín). See Appendix 6 for general information about the converts.

Some of the Islamic centers where these informants attend highly emphasize the importance of community and belonging, so this characteristic is very attractive to the converts (María and Claudia). The variation of the frequency of attendance and participation among the informants will be analyzed later.

5.3.6 Indicators of Religious Commitment among Hispanic Muslim Converts

Attendance at the Islamic Centers

Regarding attendance of Hispanic Muslims at Islamic centers, two aspects will be included in the analysis: frequency and duration of weekly visits to the Islamic centers (with the frequency of attendance being the more important factor). Five converts reported weekly attendance at the Islamic centers (María, Héctor, Vicente, Teresa, and Simón). Six Hispanic Muslims reported that they do not attend Islamic centers weekly (Claudia, Jaime, Martina, Catalina, Camila, and Lucía). Only one of the male Hispanic Muslims (Martín) mentioned that he is not currently attending an Islamic center.[47]

---

44. Cuartas/Lucía 2012:9.
45. Cuartas/Lucía 2012:6.
46. Jung, "Islamophobia?," 113–26. See also Helbling, *Islamophobia in the West*.
47. There is another factor here. Except Jaime, they are all women. Female

Among the informants who attend Islamic centers on a weekly basis, there are some patterns regarding the time these informants spend there. Two of the converts (María and Héctor) spend more time, averaging forty hours weekly. Vicente and Teresa's attendance is moderate, averaging four hours weekly. Simón spends two hours weekly at the Islamic center. The average weekly time at the Islamic centers by the converts who do not attend weekly ranged from one hour (Jaime and Claudia) to forty or forty-five minutes (Martina, Catalina, Camila, and Lucía).

Martín is not currently attending a local mosque, although in the past he attended one occasionally. He explained his nonattendance as owing to the demanding nature of his job and the fact that it is difficult to practice Islam in the predominantly non-Muslim United States. Martín's rationale for not participating at a local mosque underscores the need for further study to better understand additional reasons for this pattern of behavior.

One of the reasons for such a high attendance shown by María and Héctor is the fact that both work full-time at the Islamic centers, serving in different leadership capacities. María works as a chaplain and Héctor serves as a youth outreach director. Vicente is also highly involved at the Islamic center, teaching martial arts and otherwise engaging the community.

In summary, five Hispanic Muslim converts attend Islamic centers weekly. The weekly attendance ranges from less than one hour to forty hours. Six of the converts do not attend Islamic centers weekly, and they spend one hour or less at the mosque. Consequently, their participation in different activities is limited.

Daily Prayers

The analysis undertaken here will focus primarily on the frequency of daily prayers and the hours spent in prayer weekly (both privately and publicly) by the converts. Of greater importance in this study will be the frequency of the daily prayers by the informants, since the weekly time of prayer reported by the informants includes both community prayers at the mosque and private prayers. Later in the analysis, I will use the following categories: more commitment to daily prayers and less commitment to daily prayers.

Frequency of Prayers

There are three patterns regarding the frequency of prayer by the informants: five *salah* prayers daily, two to three *salah* daily, and no *salah*. Five of the Hispanic Muslim converts pray all five *salah* prayers daily (María,

---

participation at the mosque is often not emphasized in Islam. It is primarily for the men.

Héctor, Vicente, Teresa, and Simón). Three informants pray two to three *salah* prayers daily in the mosque (Claudia, Jaime, and Martina). Three female participants pray less often at the local mosque (Catalina, Camila, and Lucía). Martín does not currently pray at the mosque.

It is important to highlight the fact that some informants, including Jaime, Claudia, Catalina, Camila, and Martín, reported that prayer life is significant to them. These informants pray more regularly at home and less often at the mosque. This aspect of private prayer will be further analyzed later in this chapter.

Time Spent in Community Prayers

The average time spent weekly including both community prayers at the mosque and private prayers varies among the Hispanic Muslim converts. Among the five informants who pray all five *salah* daily, there are some who spend more time weekly in public prayer and others who spend less time. Simón spends more time weekly in prayer (twelve hours), while three other informants spend seven hours (María, Héctor, and Vicente). Teresa reported three and a half hours in prayer during the week.

Among the six informants who pray two to three *salah* prayers daily, two informants (Catalina and Camila) spend seven hours in prayer weekly. However, they mentioned that they are praying more at home. Two female Hispanic Muslims (Martina and Claudia) spend an average of three and a half hours in weekly prayer. Two informants (Jaime and Lucía) spend thirty minutes in weekly prayer. Although Martín is not participating at the local mosque, he reported spending time praying privately.

Another pattern that has emerged from the data is the distinction between community and private prayers. Most of the informants (seven out of twelve) are particularly focused on praying at home with their families. These informants include Claudia, Jaime, Martina, Catalina, Camila, Lucía, and Martín.

Some female Hispanic Muslim converts who are married and have children (e.g., Claudia, Catalina, and Lucía) reported limitations to participating frequently in different activities at the mosque. Their prayers are more private and generally more informal than community prayers at the mosque. Other informants, including María, Héctor, Vicente, Teresa, and Simón, are more focused on community prayers at the mosque. These differences in informants' choices between public and private practices will be further discussed in the following section.

Participation at Friday Prayer Meetings

Out of the five selected male Hispanic Muslim converts, three of them (Simón, Vicente, and Héctor) attend Friday prayer meetings weekly, whereas two do not (Jaime and Martín). The difference between Jaime and Martín is that Jaime attends Friday prayer meetings occasionally, whereas Martín does not attend them at all. Like Martín, Jaime also reports difficulties in practicing Islam in the United States. Jaime works for an American company that is related to the government, and he reported not wanting to risk his job as his reason for not participating more frequently in community prayers on Fridays. Further analysis will be included in the next section.

Participation at Friday prayer meetings is a significant indicator of religious commitment, particularly for Muslim men because they are required to attend Friday prayers at the mosque. This indicator was mentioned by a group of female Muslim converts in the focus group interviews. However, because Muslim women are generally more involved in religious practices in some Islamic centers, the attendance of Muslim women is likely higher than expected. This is in spite of the fact that some of the female informants reported various limitations because they have several children for whom to care.

Based on the frequency and average hours spent weekly at Islamic centers, the participants are labeled as follows: the more active converts are María, Héctor, Vicente Teresa, and Simón, while the less active converts are Claudia, Jaime, Martina, Catalina, Camila, Lucía, and Martín. It is significant to note here that there are nuanced differences within both the more active and the less active informants. These nuances will be analyzed later in this chapter. Martín is "inactive" regarding his attendance at the mosque.

Importance of Religion in Daily Life

I will now concentrate on important indicators to measure the importance of religion in daily life. Some of these aspects have been briefly examined in chapter 4. Nevertheless, I am expanding the analysis in this section to focus mainly on religious commitment and practices, looking at the different patterns among the twelve selected cases. The following are the indicators that I will analyze regarding the importance of religion in the daily life of the Hispanic Muslim converts: change of name, dress and outward appearance, prohibition of pork and alcohol consumption, changes in friendships, and vocations.[48] Out of the twelve selected cases, there are seven Hispanic Muslim women and five Hispanic Muslim men.

---

48. Haddad and Lummis, *Islamic Values*, 106–7. See also Zebiri, *British Muslim Converts*.

Change of Name

Regarding the change of name, all twelve of the informants reported that they retained their original names. Some of the informants mentioned different reactions from Muslims and motivations for keeping their names. For example, Jaime and Lucía mentioned that other Muslims try to give them new names. Lucía's husband also encouraged her to change her name. However, she did not pay much attention to him and instead chose to keep her original name. Vicente decided to keep his name to reflect his Ecuadorian heritage, and he is highly motivated to share his Muslim faith with other Hispanics who are not Muslims.

Dress and Outward Appearance

Wearing the *hijab* is an important aspect of religious identity and one of the indicators that have been used to measure religious commitment among Muslim women.[49] There are different patterns among Hispanic Muslim women about wearing the *hijab*. Out of the seven Hispanic Muslim women, four of them (María, Teresa, Martina, and Camila) do not wear the *hijab* frequently. Only three female informants (Lucía, Catalina, and Claudia) wear the *hijab* regularly.

Hispanic Muslim women have different motivations for wearing the *hijab* regularly. For instance, Lucía considers it important to follow the rules in Islam. She has been following Islam for two years and is married to a Muslim man from Yemen. Catalina finds comfort in wearing the *hijab*, and it is important for her to look like a Muslim because she feels respected. Claudia's experience is different because she wanted full approval from her father before making any dress changes. Once she got support from her father, she became very strict in dressing modestly.

The four female informants who do not wear the *hijab* reported different reasons. María believes that wearing the *hijab* is neither compulsory nor essential to her faith. Camila and Teresa both reported that they wear the *hijab* at the mosque but not at work. Camila has experienced pressure to make the necessary dress changes. Nonetheless, she believes that wearing the *hijab* is an important requirement.

Camila highlighted the fact that her coworkers are not Muslims and they do not know that she is a Muslim, so she is very private with her Muslim faith at work. She only wears the *hijab* when she is at the mosque or around other Muslims.

---

49. Haddad and Lummis, *Islamic Values*; Zebiri, *British Muslim Converts*.

Martina wears the *hijab* occasionally, primarily for prayer both at the mosque and in private.[50] Martina makes her changes based on her level of understanding from studying Islam, and she is in the process of getting more knowledge about wearing the *hijab*. This is interesting because Martina is very involved in advocacy projects beyond local Islamic centers, and she is more involved with Islamic institutions. She has shown a tendency to study the Qur'an and take time to reflect before making changes regarding practices.

Regarding dress and outward appearance among male Muslim converts, there are several patterns. Out of the five Muslim men selected here, two had significant changes (Héctor and Vicente). Two of the male informants did not show any changes in terms of dress or outward appearance (Simón and Martín). One of the informants had a change of attitude regarding external changes (Jaime).

Among the Hispanic Muslim men who made changes, Héctor and Vicente are practicing Muslims and very involved in leadership at their local Islamic centers. Both wear the *taqiyah* (cap) and have grown out their beards. Their outward appearance is that of a typical Muslim male. On the contrary, Simón and Martín did not change their outward appearance. They neither grow their beards nor wear the *taqiyah*. Lastly, Jaime reported that at the beginning he made some changes, but currently he has slowed down on making changes. He is more focused on his faith and beliefs than practicing the rituals at the mosque. I believe there are additional motivations for this attitude of limited changes that need further exploration.

Dietary Restrictions

Analyzing the twelve selected cases, there are several patterns regarding dietary restrictions, particularly concerning pork and alcohol consumption. All the informants reported that they are not currently drinking alcohol. All the informants have restrictions regarding eating pork. Overall, all twelve informants largely abide by the dietary restrictions recommended in Islam.

Nonetheless, there are some nuances among the participants regarding the intensity of the decision to make dietary changes and not to drink alcohol. For example, Claudia gave up pork to abide by the dietary restrictions, but she still barbecues following the Argentinian style that she learned from her father. Lucía still cooks Hispanic foods but only according to the dietary restrictions of Islam. Simón chose to become a vegetarian two years before his conversion to Islam. Thus, he did not have any difficulty observing the dietary restrictions.

50. Cuartas/Martina 2012:9.

Teresa and her family had some issues with alcoholism before she embraced Islam, but she nonetheless stopped drinking alcohol following her conversion. Conversely, Catalina liked neither pork nor alcohol prior to conversion, so it was easy for her to follow the dietary restrictions after she converted to Islam. As observed earlier, the converts mainly follow Islamic dietary restrictions, but the level of intensity of their changes varies by individual.

Changes Regarding Friendships

One important aspect to examine here is the post-affiliation changes that Hispanic Muslim converts make regarding friendships. What are the choices converts make regarding friendships particularly with non-Muslim friends? What are the changes that occur regarding interactions with the opposite gender?

There are several patterns among the informants. The majority of the informants (eight out of the twelve) made some changes regarding perspectives about relationships with the opposite gender: Héctor, Vicente, Teresa, Simón, Claudia, Martina, Camila, and Lucía. Four of the informants did not make significant changes regarding their previous friendships: Catalina, María, Jaime, and Martín. The friendships were also shaped by the negative reactions of some friends when the participants (Vicente, María, Catalina, and Martín) decided to embrace Islam.

The intensity of the changes varies among the informants. For example, Simón prizes close relationships, so he has intentionally built a strong social network of male Muslim friends. He has also continued to build friendships with people from multiple religions.

Teresa made moderate changes. She found the relationships between men and women in Islam to be interesting and helpful in her transition to Islam. She still has non-Muslim friends that she met before her conversion to Islam, but most of her friends are Muslims.

Vicente and Héctor mentioned that they gained a new perspective regarding how to treat women and how to conduct themselves better with the opposite gender, preferring now to have more interactions with Muslim men. Gender separation is something that is emphasized in Islam, and there is a strong emphasis on morality and conduct.[51]

Regarding previous friendships with non-Muslims, most of the Hispanic Muslim converts maintained contact with their non-Muslim friends, except for Lucía who chose to separate from her non-Muslim friends because of lifestyle differences. In addition, she sees no need to have interactions

---

51. See Haddad and Lummis, *Islamic Values*.

with Muslim men who are not her husband. She has much interaction online with Muslim women.

Among the participants who did not make significant changes, María continues to interact with men and with non-Muslims, particularly in interfaith dialogue. Most of her close friends in her life have been men. María states the following:

> I grew up with three brothers. So, relationships with men has been no taboo for me. Other than that, I do not know why I have always tended to be more popular with men than with women. And do not say it because I am a nice person or because I have a good personality or because I am so incredibly attractive. Maybe because I do not like sports. I do not consider myself very girly. So maybe that has influenced. No? Other than that, my best friend of all life is a man, even until today. So, I do not see the impossibility of friendship or relationship of respect between a man and a woman. The fact that I have no such problems shaking hands with a man.[52]

Jaime's personality allows him to be content with few friends. Catalina, similarly, did not make significant changes. She does not feel a need to have many friendships, nonetheless she considers that it is a good thing to have friends. However, Catalina finds much comfort and respect in the gender distinctions within Islam. It makes her feel respected. She, her husband, and their children are the only Muslims in her family. Martín's friendships have not changed much. Most of his friends are not Muslims, and he is not concerned.

Current Occupations of the Converts

The current occupations of the converts are an important indicator of religious commitment. This reflects the importance of religion in the lives of individuals.[53] Among the twelve selected informants, four of the informants (María, Héctor, Vicente, and Martina) currently work full-time at Islamic centers or Islamic institutions. Three of the converts (Simón, Claudia, and Jaime) have occupations related to information technology and software developing. Three of the Hispanic Muslim converts work in different fields. One of the female converts (Camila) works in a private business as a health educator and Zumba instructor. Another female informant (Teresa) works as a financial broker for an American company. Martín is currently working as a lead repair technician for an American company. Finally, two of the

52. Cuartas/María 2012:12.
53. Lin and Dumin, "Access to Occupations," 365–85; Hodge, "Social Work," 162–73.

Hispanic Muslim women (Lucía and Catalina) are presently housewives, largely focused on raising their children.

It is important to note the ways in which the current occupations of the informants help to shape their religious activity. This is reflected not only in the extended hours that some Hispanics spend at the Islamic centers, but also in their active involvement as part of their present vocations (for instance, María, Héctor, and to some extent, Vicente).

Occupations of the Converts Before Islam

Now, I will analyze the occupations of the informants before they decided to follow Islam. Most of the informants (Martina, Catalina, Simón, Vicente, Camila, and Héctor) were college students. One of the male informants (Jaime) was in his senior year of high school. Two of the female participants (María and Teresa) worked as administrators in an unknown field. Two of them (Lucía and Martín) worked in jobs related to the auto industry. Another female informant (Claudia) worked as an information technology recruiter.

To summarize the changes regarding the occupations of the informants, most of the converts (ten out of twelve) had some changes regarding their occupations. Only two out of the twelve informants (Claudia and Martín) did not have major changes regarding their occupations. Claudia has been working in different capacities in the areas of information technology, and Martín has worked in the autobody industry for many years.

Summary of the Daily Life Changes

Based on the findings, Muslim converts experienced different changes after their conversion to Islam. The informants have shown that religion is important for them, but they express this in different ways. Nevertheless, the major differences among the Hispanic Muslim converts are the motivations and choices that female converts make regarding when to wear the *hijab* and the attendance of Friday prayers by male converts. There are also some perspective differences regarding relationships with the opposite gender.

Generally, there are similarities between male and female converts regarding maintaining their original names, preserving contact with non-Muslim friends, following dietary restrictions, and making changes regarding their occupations.

However, there is a strong contrast between genders regarding the changes in their religious activity. In general, female Hispanic converts experience more changes than male converts, particularly about dress and outward appearance. The frequency of wearing the *hijab* is higher among the less active converts. Conversely, the more active female converts wear the *hijab* only occasionally.

The opposite trend occurs among the male Hispanic Muslim converts. The use of the *taqiyah* (cap) and changes regarding outward appearance (e.g., growing a beard) is more prevalent among the more active male converts. The less active male converts did not make significant changes to their outward appearances. Following, I will compare and contrast the more and less active converts by analyzing religious activity (frequency of daily prayers and attendance at the mosque) among the converts, looking at important similarities and differences regarding gender as well.

5.3.7 Comparison and Contrast between the More Active Converts and the Less Active Converts

Mosque Attendance and Frequency of Daily Prayers

Considering the frequency of mosque attendance and daily prayers by the Hispanic Muslim converts, the informants are categorized here as more active or less active. Five informants (three male and two female) are labeled as "more active" converts: María, Héctor, Vicente, Teresa, and Simón. Seven informants (five female and two male) are categorized here as less active converts: Claudia, Jaime, Martina, Catalina, Camila, Lucía, and Martín, who are not currently attending the local mosque.

Regarding gender, there are some significant differences in terms of religious activity. I will begin here with the more active informants. The more active male converts pray all five *salah* daily (Héctor, Vicente, and Simón). The more active female converts also pray all five *salah* daily (María and Teresa). Thus, there are no significant gender differences among the more active informants in terms of the frequency of daily prayers.

The less active male converts, Jaime and Martín, are more focused on private prayers outside the local mosque. One similarity between the less active male informants is that neither of them attends Friday prayers. However, Jaime reported that he prays less often (two to three *salah* prayers daily) at the mosque, whereas Martín does not pray at all at the mosque.

Most of the less active female converts (Catalina, Camila, and Lucía) pray less often at the mosque. Two of the "less active" female converts pray two to three *salah* prayers daily in the mosque (Claudia and Martina). One similarity among the less active converts including Catalina, Camila, Jaime, and Martín, is that these informants are generally more observant of private prayers (*dua* prayers), which are mainly more informal than public prayers.

This indicator of private prayers is based on the responses of the informants regarding the weekly time they spent in prayer, Following, I will compare the daily changes of the more active and less active converts, also looking at differences in terms of gender.

Religious Activity in Relation to Post-Affiliation Changes

The more active converts are María, Héctor, Vicente, Teresa, and Simón (three Muslim men and two Muslim women). Here, I will compare the different patterns of daily changes, paying special attention to gender.

There are some similar patterns among the more active male converts. None of the more active male informants changed their names. All three of the more active male converts participate weekly in the Friday prayers at the mosque. Overall, the more active converts follow the dietary restrictions recommended by Islam. In addition, these informants have not made changes regarding friendships with non-Muslims. All the active male converts changed their occupations.

The difference among the more active male converts is that two of the informants (Héctor and Vicente) have made changes related to dress and outward appearance. Both wear the *taqiyah* and grew their beards. On the contrary, Simón did not make changes, and his outward appearance remains the same.

There are also some similarities among the more active female informants. None of the more active female informants changed their name. María and Teresa wear the *hijab* only occasionally. Both also experienced changes regarding their occupations.

The main difference among the more active female converts is in terms of the changes made regarding friendships. María did not make changes in her friendships, whereas Teresa made some changes.

Of the less active converts (Claudia, Jaime, Martina, Catalina, Camila, Lucía, and Martín—five women and two men), none changed their names. Regarding wearing the *hijab*, there are different patterns. Three of the less active Muslim women wear the *hijab* regularly (Claudia, Catalina, and Lucía). Two of the female converts (Martina and Camila) wear the *hijab* only occasionally. It is important to highlight that the only informants who wear the *hijab* regularly among the female Hispanic Muslim converts are the less active informants. As already observed, Muslim women are usually confronted with more daily life choices than Muslim men.

Both of the less active male informants made no changes regarding dress and outward appearance. However, there are some differences among the less active male converts. While Martín did not change his external appearance because of his conversion, Jaime's experience has been slightly different. As I mentioned earlier, Jaime made some changes after he decided to follow Islam, but lately, he has chosen not to make significant changes.

Another distinction among the less active and the more active male informants is that the less active male Muslim converts (Jaime and Martín) do not participate weekly in the Friday prayers at the mosque. This is contrary to the more active male converts who actively participate in the Friday prayer meetings (Héctor, Vicente, and Simón). In general, all of the less active converts followed the dietary restrictions recommended by Islam.

Regarding the changes made in terms of friendships by the less active converts, the only active convert who did not make any changes was María. The other active Muslim converts made some changes regarding friendships. In general, the less active converts experienced more daily life changes in comparison with the more active converts. In addition, the intensity of the changes was considerably higher among the less active informants.

Levels of Commitment among Hispanic Muslim Converts

I will now concentrate on the levels of commitment used by the PRC to analyze the limitations and challenges. The challenge is that these studies largely focus on the description and data of the highly-committed Muslims, mostly ignoring the nuances among the low and moderately committed Muslims.[54] Even though these studies provide a brief description of the low-committed Muslims, the focus of the analysis is on the informants who are labeled as highly committed.

Based on the three indicators, a highly committed Muslim is a respondent who attends a mosque at least once a week, prays all five *salah* every day, and says religion is very important in their lives.[55] Less-committed Muslims include those individuals who attend mosque and pray only for Eid (or less often) and generally regard religion as not very important in their lives.[56]

High and Low Levels of Religious Commitment of the Informants

The following are descriptions of the three levels of religious commitment within this study: a high-committed Hispanic Muslim convert is a respondent who attends a mosque at least once a week, prays all five *salah* every day, and has made some changes regarding religion in everyday life.

---

54. Barker and Currie, "Do Converts?," 305–13; Pew Research Center, "Muslim Americans: No Sign of Growth."

55. Pew Research Center, "Muslim Americans: No Sign of Growth," 27.

56. Pew Research Center, "Muslim Americans: No Sign of Growth," 27.

A medium-committed (moderate) convert is a respondent who attends a mosque at least once a month, prays some (two to three) of the *salah*, and has made few changes regarding religion in everyday life. Finally, a low-committed Hispanic Muslim convert is a respondent who attends a mosque rarely or not at all, prays the *salah* rarely, and has made minimum changes regarding religion in everyday life. The major differences are in terms of the intensity of the changes that converts make, which make it difficult to use these levels of commitment.

Based on these descriptions, using the three indicators, the selected Hispanic Muslim converts are labeled accordingly. The following converts have high religious commitment: María, Héctor, Vicente, Teresa, and Simón. Converts with moderate religious commitment include Claudia, Jaime, and Martina. And the following converts have a low religious commitment: Catalina, Camila, Lucía, and Martín.

Here, I make a distinction between commitment and religious activity. The proposed categories that I will use here are "more active," "moderately active," and "less active." This will facilitate the analysis of the nuances and patterns in different dimensions of religious commitment (rituals and devotions).

Next, the ritualistic and devotional dimensions of commitment among the more active and less active converts will be examined. The purpose is to extend the analysis beyond the indicators used by the PRC to better understand the patterns and nuances among the high- and low-committed Hispanic Muslim converts.

5.3.8 Ritualistic and Devotional Dimensions of Religious Commitment among Hispanic Muslim Converts

To better understand the nuances of religious commitment among the less active and more active converts, it is important to look at additional indicators. Here, I will focus largely on the ritualistic and devotional dimensions of religious commitment suggested by two studies by Glock and Stark.[57]

Dimensions and Indicators in Light of the Data

One of the important aspects of the multidimensional conceptualization developed by Stark and Glock is that it recognizes the "distinctions in the way religion may be expressed, as well as the degree of intensity with which it may

---

57. See Glock and Stark, *Religion and Society in Tension*.

be practiced."[58] Looking at the nuances and patterns facilitates the analysis among both the more active and the less active Hispanic Muslim converts.

Scholars[59] who have analyzed the dimensions of religiousness have paid limited attention to important contextual factors, including individual and socioinstitutional factors. Individual factors such as the current occupations of the converts, and individual perspectives about the meaning of a so-called good or committed Muslim, need more consideration. Socioinstitutional factors, including the nuances of religious socialization among the converts, deserve more examination. Here, it is important to analyze the interactions and contacts of the Hispanic Muslim converts with spouses, Muslim friends, and other Muslims as they perform the different rituals at the Islamic centers (e.g., Friday prayers, fasting during Ramadan, and almsgiving).

One of the limitations about the distinction between "low or high" commitment is that it distracts one from fully appreciating a) the role played by those classified as "low" or "moderate" religious commitment, and b) the nuances and patterns of religious commitment in different dimensions (particularly ritualistic and devotional) among the less active converts. Here, I will mainly follow Stark and Glock's 1968 approach by including both "rituals" and "devotionals" as part of religious practice.

The Ritualistic Dimension

Religious rituals are an essential part of formal religion. These rituals comprise acts of religious practice such as worship, devotion, and "the things people do to carry out their religious commitment."[60] Born Muslims and converts in the United States base their religious practices on similar requirements gathered from both Scripture and tradition.

Even though Muslims in the United States are diverse—representing different races, cultures, and varied interpretations of Islam—they largely have similar expectations about prayers, fasting, almsgiving, and other prescribed acts of worship.[61] As Hodge notes, "It is largely agreed that the practices and the beliefs that underlie the five pillars of faith which are derived from the *shari'a* Islamic law, constitute a shared core of a wider reality."[62]

58. Hassan, "On Being Religious," 439.
59. Bader et al., *American Piety in the 21ˢᵗ Century*; Hassan, "On Being Religious," 437–78; Stark and Glock, *American Piety*.
60. Stark and Glock, *American Piety*, 15.
61. Siddiqi, "Practicing Islam," 159.
62. Hodge, "Social Work," 164.

The Five Pillars of Islam are the declaration of faith (*Shahadah*), prayer (*salat*), charity or almsgiving (*zakat*), fasting (*saum*), and the pilgrimage to Mecca (*hajj*). According to Esposito,

> The belief that Islamic law was a comprehensive social blueprint was reflected in the organization and content of law. Legal rights and duties are divided into two major categories: 1) duties to God (ritual observances), such as prayer, almsgiving, and fasting; and 2) duties to others (social transitions), which include penal, commercial, and family laws. The heart of the former is the so-called Five Pillars of Islam; that of the latter is the family law.[63]

The first pillar is the *Shahadah*, which is the profession of Muslim faith: "There is no god but God and Muhammad is His Messenger."[64] *Shahadah* is the essential doctrine in the Islamic faith.[65] "The praxis orientation of Islam is witnessed by the remaining four pillars or duties."[66]

The second pillar is the performance of ritual prayers, *salat*, in which the individual faces Mecca, the holy city and center of Islam. Prayer is understood to be a holistic practice that includes not only the body but also the mind and emotions. Daily prayers are both an individual and a communal obligation for Muslims.[67] Prayers are performed five times throughout the day and reinforce the concept that daily life and faith are continuously intertwined.[68] An important rite that is often performed by Muslims before the daily prayers is ablution, which symbolizes purity.[69]

---

63. Esposito, "Religious Life," 106.
64. Esposito, "Religious Life," 107–9.
65. El Azayem and Hedayat-Diba, "Psychological Aspects of Islam," 42; I have already discussed some aspects regarding the *Shahadah* in chapter 3. The major focus here is on private prayers, almsgiving, and fasting.
66. Esposito, "Religious Life," 107.
67. Esposito, "Religious Life," 107–9.
68. El Azayem and Hedayat-Diba, "Psychological Aspects of Islam," 45; According to El Azayem and Hedayat-Diba, "the recitation of the Koran during prayer, either silently or aloud, represents a continuous chain of teaching, listening, and memorizing Koranic sayings, and a reminder that the Muslim's daily life and faith are continuously intertwined" (El Azayem and Hedayat-Diba, "Psychological Aspects of Islam," 45). For more details about daily prayers in Islam, see Esposito, *Islam: The Straight Path*; Siddiqi, "Practicing Islam."
69. Ablution is very important among Muslims. El Azayem and Hedayat-Diba, "Psychological Aspects, of Islam," 42–43 emphasize that "unless one has performed the rite of ablution, one may not touch the Koran or perform prayer. The Koran dictates: 'O ye who believe! When ye prepare for prayer, wash your faces, and your hands (and arms) to the elbows; rub your heads (with water); and wash your feet to the ankles. If ye are in a state of ceremonial impurity, bathe your whole body. But if ye are ill, or on

The third pillar is charity or almsgiving (*zakat*). A percentage, usually 2.5 percent, of accumulated wealth and assets are given to the community to alleviate economic hardships and promote the general welfare. While in some countries it is mandatory as a form of tax to the destitute, *zakat* is largely a voluntary activity.[70]

As an act of worship and service to others, the *zakat* leads to a sense of thanksgiving to God for his goodness and a sense of community identity and responsibility.[71] The performance of the *zakat* is both an individual and a communal obligation for Muslims (as are the daily prayers).

The fourth pillar is fasting (*sawm*), which is performed every year during the month of Ramadan from dawn to sunset. Ramadan is the ninth month in the Islamic calendar. The breaking of the fast by Muslims is usually followed by a time of celebration in community. As El Azayem and Hedayat-Diba note, "During daylight, they are to abstain from food, drink, sex, and smoking. The sick and the elderly, as well as pregnant or nursing women, are exempted from fasting."[72]

The fifth pillar is the pilgrimage to Mecca (*hajj*). Every Muslim not prevented by financial or physical impediments is expected, at least once in their lifetime, to take a pilgrimage to the *Kaba*, the cube-shaped "House of God" built by Abraham and his son Ishmael, where God first entered into a covenant with Ishmael, and by extension, the Muslim community.[73] Muslims of different ethnicities and from various countries gather to "perform the rite of pilgrimage in groups, during which they ask God to forgive their sins and grant them His blessings."[74]

I have already examined the daily prayers (more formal and usually done in community) in the previous section. The purpose here is to look at the nuances in terms of religious practice. For this reason, I will focus on the ritual observances, particularly looking at almsgiving and fasting rituals. I will also include some observations about private prayers and the pilgrimage to Mecca (*hajj*). Private prayers are generally more informal and

---

a journey, or one of you cometh from offices of nature, or ye have been in contact with women, and ye find no water, then take for yourselves clean sand or earth, and rub therewith your faces and hands. God doth not wish to place you in a difficulty, but make you clean, and to complete His favor to you, that ye may be grateful'" (5; 6). Youssef Ali (1983) translation.

70. El Azayem and Hedayat-Diba, "Psychological Aspects of Islam," 46.
71. Esposito, "Religious Life," 32–33.
72. El Azayem and Hedayat-Diba, "Psychological Aspects of Islam," 45.
73. Esposito, "Religious Life," 111.
74. El Azayem and Hedayat-Diba, "Psychological Aspects of Islam," 46.

spontaneous. The pilgrimage to Mecca is an indicator of religious commitment among Muslims.[75]

Charity or Almsgiving (Zakat)

Among the more active Muslim converts, all five informants mentioned the importance of the observance of almsgiving (María, Héctor, Vicente, Teresa, and Simón). Among the more active converts, Teresa was the informant who most emphasized the significance of *zakat* during the interview. She stated, "I love to give back, it is very important. I really love the idea of charity as one of the pillars."[76]

The patterns regarding the importance of charity among the less active Muslims are different. Most of the less active converts (four out of seven) mentioned the importance of charity as an important ritual to observe. Claudia, Jaime, Martina, and Camila highlighted the importance of *zakat* as an important ritual.

Nonetheless, three of the informants (Claudia, Jaime, and Martina) mentioned almsgiving as one the most common religious rituals that they practice. Three of the less active converts (Catalina, Lucía, and Martín) consider that *zakat* is less important. Among the less active Hispanic Muslim converts, Camila was the informant who most emphasized the significance of almsgiving.

In summary, the importance of the observance of almsgiving varies among the informants. Overall, the significance of charity is more prevalent among the more active converts. Nevertheless, the majority of the less active converts also believe that charity is an important ritual. In terms of gender, the observance of charity is important for both female and male Hispanic Muslim converts.[77]

Observance of Fasting During Ramadan (Sawm)

Regarding fasting during Ramadan, there are different patterns among the informants. Among the more active Muslims, all five informants mentioned the importance of fasting during Ramadan. María, Héctor, Vicente, Teresa, and Simón generally fast every year. Teresa shared that, "The fasting is so important because it teaches you everything."[78]

75. Esposito, "Religious Life," 51–52. See also Hodge, "Social Work"; Siddiqi, "Practicing Islam."

76. Cuartas/Teresa 2012: 20.

77. For an extensive study on gender and conversion in the West, see van Nieuwkerk, *Women Embracing Islam*.

78. Cuartas/Teresa 2012:20.

Among the less active Muslims, there are some differences regarding the observance of fasting during the month of Ramadan. Four out of the seven less active converts (Claudia, Martina, Catalina, and Lucía) fast during Ramadan. Three of the less active informants (Jaime, Camila, and Martín) fast, but less often.

Claudia and Martina spend time at the local mosque but attend less often during Ramadan. Catalina and Lucía highlighted the importance of observing the fast annually during Ramadan. On the contrary, Jaime, Camila, and Martín spend most of the time during Ramadan with their spouses and other Muslim friends at home.

The different experiences regarding the observance of the fast during Ramadan are expressed in the following comments made by two of the less active female informants. Catalina mentioned that she performs the ritual of fasting once a year during Ramadan, and she spends time together with her family.[79] On the contrary, Camila reported that she struggles to follow some of the required rituals in Islam, including fasting during Ramadan. Camila stated,

> In terms of practicing all the required rituals, I am still struggling. You know stopping five times a day is not the easiest thing either. Not something that I am used to the discipline of doing something and at the present moment you are not accountable, and I believe that eventually, I will be. But it is still hard to do things you are not immediately accountable for, so it takes time to get used to that. For example, Ramadan, it took me three years to finally be able to fast the whole month, and now I do it but that took a lot of time.[80]

In summary, most of the more active and the less active converts fast during the month of Ramadan. One of the significant differences among the informants is the challenges that some of the less active converts experienced as they decided to follow all the required rituals. Another difference is in terms of the frequency of fasting during Ramadan. In general, the observance of fasting during the month of Ramadan is more common among the more active converts. Nevertheless, most of the less active converts also fast during the month of Ramadan.

Overall, there are some strong differences between male and female converts. The observance of fasting during the month of Ramadan is more prevalent among female Muslim converts. Among the Muslim women who

---

79. Cuartas/Catalina 2012:12.
80. Cuartas/Camila 2012:8.

are committed to fasting, even the less active female converts fast during the month of Ramadan.

Pilgrimage to Mecca (Hajj)

Regarding the pilgrimage to Mecca, none of the more active converts have performed the ritual of *hajj* (María, Héctor, Vicente, Teresa, and Jaime). However, Vicente mentioned his desire to perform *hajj* as soon as he gathers the financial means to do so.[81] Simón mentioned that he has not done the pilgrimage to Mecca, but he decided to learn more about Islam after watching a video about the experience of Muslims from different countries celebrating the pilgrimage to Mecca.[82]

On the contrary, the pattern regarding the pilgrimage to Mecca among the less active Hispanic Muslims is very different. Out of the seven less active converts, two of the female informants went to Mecca to perform the pilgrimage. They make observations about their different experiences of *hajj*.

Claudia stated, "Yes, I have done *hajj*. I did it with my husband the year before we got pregnant with our first child."[83] Claudia and her husband from Palestine spent almost three weeks traveling to experience *hajj*. They went to Mecca and Medina.

Catalina commented the following about her experience of *hajj*: "I went to Mecca in 2009 to perform *hajj* with my husband for the first time. It was an amazing experience. It was almost surreal. It was like you pray toward Mecca five times a day every day. It is all very surreal."[84]

As it has been observed, only two informants out of the twelve selected cases have done the pilgrimage to Mecca. Both are less active female converts. Even though the pilgrimage to Mecca is not mandatory for all Muslims, this ritual is very important not only for the opportunity to visit the holy place for Muslims but also as an act of worship.[85]

Summary of Findings Regarding the Ritualistic Dimension

In summary, there are some nuances among the converts in terms of the ritualistic dimension. The importance of charity is more prevalent among the more active converts, but most of the less active converts also consider that charity is a significant ritual. In terms of gender differences, there are

81. Cuartas/Vicente 2012:12–13.
82. Cuartas/Simón 2012:13.
83. Cuartas/Claudia 2012:17.
84. Cuartas/Catalina 2012:8.
85. Siddiqi, "Practicing Islam," 169.

no significant differences between male and female converts regarding the observance of charity.

The observance of fasting during Ramadan is higher among the more active informants. Yet, most of the less active converts also fast during Ramadan. There are robust differences between male and female converts. Perhaps one of the most important differences between male and female converts is in regard to the pilgrimage to Mecca. None of the five more active informants have performed the ritual of *hajj*. On the contrary, two of the less active female informants went to Mecca and did the *hajj*. Thus, in this study, the pilgrimage to Mecca is more prevalent among female Hispanic Muslim converts.

5.3.9 The Devotional Dimension

This dimension is similar to the ritualistic dimension. Both the ritualistic and devotional dimensions are part of the religious practice of the converts. According to Hassan, "rituals are highly formalized aspects of religious expression and commitment. Participation may or may not indicate religious commitment or piety among Muslims. This, however, does not apply to acts of devotion, which are private, and often spontaneous. For these reasons, devotionalism is a good and meaningful indicator of religious commitment."[86]

I will include here two indicators to analyze the religious devotion of Hispanic Muslim converts: private prayers (outside the services at the mosque) and reading the Qur'an to make daily decisions. Regarding the reading of the Qur'an, I will look at the weekly time spent in general as well as the consultation of the Qur'an to make daily decisions.

Private Prayers

There are several patterns concerning the private prayers of the informants.[87] In general, all the more active converts (María, Teresa, Héctor, Vicente, and Simón) are more focused on daily prayers at the mosque. Among the more active, Simón is the one who mentioned that he spends some time in private prayers, but mainly he prays at the mosque.

---

86. Hassan, "On Being Religious," 442. For more details about these indicators for religious devotions (private prayers and reading the Bible or the Qur'an), see also Barker and Currie, "Do Converts?"; Pew Research Center, "Shifting Religious Identity"; Siddiqi, "Practicing Islam."

87. Private prayers are usually called *du'a* prayers, which are often more informal prayers. See Siddiqi, "Practicing Islam."

On the contrary, the less active informants are mainly more focused on private prayers. Most of the less active converts (five out of seven) pray privately more often, while two of them pray at home less often (Lucía and Martín). Claudia, Martina, Jaime, Catalina, and Camila reported that they spend time in prayer with their families at home.

In addition, Catalina and Claudia reported that they often include their children in the prayer time at home. They both highlighted the importance of raising their children as good Muslims. Modeling prayer to their children is important for these Hispanic Muslim mothers.

In summary, private prayers at home are more common among the less active converts. Regarding gender differences, generally, the less active female converts have the tendency to pray more often privately than males who are less active Muslim converts. Private prayers with spouses and children are more likely to occur among the female Hispanic converts. Both male and female Hispanic converts who are more active pray at the mosque with greater frequency.

Reading the Qur'an at the Mosque and Privately

There are several patterns among the informants regarding the reading of the Qur'an. Some of the Hispanic Muslim converts read the Qur'an more often than others. The time spent by the Hispanic Muslim converts in reading the Qur'an weekly varies. This time includes both reciting the Qur'an at the mosque and reading it privately.

Among the more active converts, all the informants read the Qur'an often. However, the time spent reading the Qur'an varies. For example, three of the more active informants (Vicente, Teresa, and Simón) spend between two and four hours reading the Qur'an in English or Spanish. Nevertheless, María and Héctor, who are considered the most active Muslims among the informants, spend less time reading the Qur'an (one hour weekly). Among the more active converts, Vicente and Teresa spend more time reading the Qur'an.

Four of the seven less active informants (Claudia, Martina, Camila, and Lucía) read the Qur'an often. Three of the less active Hispanic Muslim converts (Catalina, Jaime, and Martín) mentioned that they do not read the Qur'an frequently. Catalina mentioned that she reads or consults the Qur'an only when she feels the need for it or when she is looking for a specific answer.[88]

Claudia mentioned that she usually spends one hour reading the Qur'an. Martina and Camila spent an average of only fifteen minutes weekly

---

88. Cuartas/Catalina 2012:12–13.

reading the Qur'an. Martina usually reads the Qur'an less often. Overall, Catalina, Jaime, and Martín are the less committed informants regarding reading the Qur'an.

One of the significant findings here is that Lucía spends more time reading and consulting the Qur'an among the selected cases. She reads an average of seven hours weekly, usually reading the Qur'an in ninety days around the time of Ramadan.[89] Lucía is a less active Hispanic Muslim convert, and yet she is highly committed to reading the Qur'an, especially during the month of Ramadan.

Overall, reading and reciting the Qur'an publicly at the local mosque is more common among both male and female informants who are more active. In general, female Hispanic Muslim converts spend more time weekly reading the Qur'an than male informants. Usually, the more active converts spend more time reading the Qur'an than the less active informants. Nevertheless, even some of the less committed converts—such as Lucía—are highly committed to reading the Qur'an.

Consulting the Qur'an to Make Daily Decisions

There are some patterns regarding consulting the Qur'an to make daily decisions by the informants. Most of the converts (eight out of twelve: Simón, María, Héctor, Jaime, Teresa, Catalina, Camila, and Martín) consult the Qur'an privately less often. Among the five more active converts, Vicente is the only informant who consults the Qur'an more often to make daily decisions. María, Héctor, Teresa, and Simón do consult the Qur'an, but less often.

Among the seven less active converts, four informants (Jaime, Catalina, Camila, and Martín) consult the Qur'an less often, and three of them, including Claudia, Martina, and Lucía, consult the Qur'an outside the religious services at the mosque more often.

Usually, Muslims in the United States have access to the Qur'an in different languages, including Arabic, English, and Spanish. However, one of the motivations to consult the Qur'an is related to the level of proficiency of Arabic language. Vicente is the only Hispanic Muslim convert who is fluent in Arabic. He usually reads the Qur'an in Arabic.

Five informants have some level of familiarity with Arabic: Héctor, Simón, Martina, Claudia, and Camila. Six informants (María, Teresa, Jaime, Catalina, Lucía, and Martín) know neither how to read nor speak Arabic. Thus, the ability to read or speak in Arabic is a good indicator to include in this analysis.

---

89. Cuartas/Lucía 2012:15.

In summary, consulting the Qur'an to make daily decisions is more prevalent among the less active informants. Regarding gender differences and religious commitment, consulting the Qur'an to make daily decisions is more common among the female informants who are less active. Reciting the Qur'an during daily prayers at the mosque is more prevalent among male converts who are more active.

Summary of the Findings Regarding the Devotional Dimension

To summarize, there are different patterns observed among the informants regarding their religious practices, including the ritualistic and devotional dimensions of religiosity. The more active converts have a greater focus on the daily prayers at the mosque, whereas private prayers at home are more common among the less active converts. In terms of gender differences, the less active female converts largely pray more often in private than do male informants. Female Hispanic Muslim converts also spend more time weekly reading the Qur'an than male converts.

The reading and recitation of the Qur'an at the local mosque is more common among both male and female informants who are generally more active. Yet, some of the less active converts are highly committed to reading the Qur'an (e.g., Lucía).

Consulting the Qur'an to make daily decisions is more common among the less active informants. Concerning gender differences, the consultation of the Qur'an to make daily decisions is more common among the female informants than male converts.

5.3.10 Religious Commitment in Relation to the Perspectives of the Converts Regarding the Meaning of a Committed Muslim

There are different perspectives and emphases among the Hispanic Muslim converts regarding the meaning of a committed Muslim within the context of the United States. Being religious or having high religiosity can mean different things to different converts. In general, the informants highlight diverse dimensions of religiosity.

For some Hispanic Muslim converts, being a "committed" Muslim entails not only religious practice but also the importance of having a moral commitment and developing a good character that is reflected in daily life experiences and one's responses to others. Character was mentioned by two informants (Teresa and Jaime). For others, the main emphasis was on the religious rituals (Vicente, Catalina, and Lucía). On the contrary, Jaime and

Martín emphasized the religious belief and the personal relationship with God rather than the religious rituals that are required of Muslims.

The question of characteristics that mark a good, committed Muslim was not asked of all the informants, namely, María, Héctor, Simón, Claudia, Camila, and Martín. However, most of the informants (seven out of twelve: Vicente, Teresa, Jaime, Martina, Catalina, Lucía, and Martín)—being of both genders and different religious commitment levels—answered the following question: *What is the meaning of a "committed Muslim?"* To facilitate the analysis here, I will look at the different dimensions of religiosity[90] highlighted by the Hispanic Muslim converts.

Highly Committed Muslims

Two out of five informants who have high religious commitment shared their insights regarding the meaning of being a committed Muslim. There are different dimensions that they emphasized in their responses. The male Muslim convert mentioned the importance of religious practices, whereas the female Muslim informant highlighted the significance of having integrity and character.

The following examples illustrate the different perspectives of these committed converts. Vicente reported that a committed Muslim is "the one who completes all the obligatory pillars, the one who follows the commands of the Qur'an, and the traditions of the prophets upon him. [It is] the one who does not step over the bounds of its liberties of God. So basically, it is one who abides by the Laws."[91] Teresa stated the following:

> Overall, it is someone who is a good human being. I mean that can be . . . they do not have to be Muslim. That can be anybody, but you are asking me what a committed Muslim is. I mean it just is hard to describe it. It is so many things, you know. But I cannot judge anybody. So, it is hard to say who is a good Muslim and who is not, because you just never know. Of a good

---

90. Stark and Glock, *American Piety* identified five core dimensions of religiousness: 1) Belief (ideological); 2) Religious Practice (including rituals and devotions); 3) Experiential (feelings, perceptions, emotions); 4) Knowledge (expectation that religious persons will possess some minimum of information about the basic tenets of their faith, rites, Scriptures, and traditions); 5) Consequences (consequential)—the effects of religious belief, practice, experience, and knowledge in persons' day-to-day lives. In this study, the knowledge and the consequences dimensions will not be included since I did not include specific questions in the interviews regarding knowledge. The consequences dimension will be included in the final chapter as part of the analysis of the contributions to local Islam by Hispanic Muslim converts.

91. Cuartas/Vicente 2012:15.

committed Muslim... I mean, it is someone who basically does everything. I think as long as you try to become a committed Muslim, then it is fine.[92]

Moderately Committed Muslims

Two out of three informants who have moderate religious commitment answered the question regarding the meaning of a committed Muslim. Here, we also have male and female informants. The male informant underlined the importance of character, but he also mentioned the tensions between being good to others and practicing the rituals. He believes that character is more important than rituals. The female convert emphasized the importance of the experiential dimension by "having a close relationship with God and submission to him."[93]

Jaime said,

> That person [a committed Muslim] does not need to pray very often, if at all. Preferably, they would be the ideal person. An ideal person is a person with a good character that is the basis of faith. You know that they are not averse to others. Someone who may do the wrong thing, but is not averse to others, and is willing to help others, to me is good. But someone who does, who prays, but it is adverse, like for example, thinks they are better than someone else, or someone who prays but when they hear a different way of praying, or when they hear about something else, they just, they get angry, and they start... that can turn you off, at a certain level, at a level that is very ambiguous. Sorry if it is not very clear.[94]

One similarity among the moderately committed converts is that both said that God is the one who knows best and defines it.

Lower Committed Muslims

Three out of four informants who have a low commitment answered the question about the meaning of a committed Muslim. There are contrary perspectives among the least committed informants. Two of the females converts (Catalina and Camila) emphasized the ritualistic dimension of commitment, whereas the male convert (Martín) highlighted the

---

92. Cuartas/Teresa 2012:18–19.
93. Cuartas/Teresa 2012:18–19.
94. Cuartas/Jaime 2012:20.

experiential dimension (e.g., feelings, perceptions, and emotions) rather than the ritualistic dimension.

These contrary perspectives are illustrated in the following comments: Catalina shared that, "A good, committed Muslim believes in God, and makes his or her prayers. These are the most important things for me."[95] And Martín said, "I am glad that Islam is not about going to the mosque, and that it was more about having a way to live."[96]

It is important to notice here that more active Hispanic Muslim converts are not necessarily highly committed in all the different aspects of practice and rituals within Islam. The same is true with the less active converts. It cannot be assumed that these individuals will have a low commitment in all dimensions of religious commitment. Following, the main findings considering some theories and research done by other scholars will be described. See Appendix 7 for a summary of the findings.

5.4 DISCUSSION OF THE FINDINGS CONSIDERING THEORIES AND STUDIES DONE ON RELIGIOUS COMMITMENT

5.4.1 Religious Socialization and Social Networks

The theory of socialization has been largely used in the studies of the sociology of religion.[97] Studies done by several scholars have demonstrated the importance of patterns, friends, and peers regarding the process of religious socialization.[98]

Nevertheless, one of the problems is that most of the studies done on religious commitment have mainly focused on the influence of different agents of socialization in the lives of the converts.[99] Thus, the responses of the converts to religious socialization have been largely overlooked. The diverse choices that converts make need to be considered in the analysis of religious practice and commitment because they can help shape their involvement in different religious rituals and devotions that are essential in

---

95. Cuartas/Catalina 2012:11.

96. Cuartas/Martín 2012:13.

97. Bartkowski, "Religious Socialization among American Youth," 511–25; Cornwall, "Influence of Three Agents," 207–31; Snow and Machalek, "Sociology of Conversion," 167–90.

98. Cornwall, "Influence of Three Agents," 207–31; Kraus et al., "Religious Socialization," 499–518.

99. Cornwall, "Influence of Three Agents," 207–31; Himmelfarb, "Agents of Religious Socialization," 477–94.

the new religion. To operationalize religious socialization, I will rely mainly on Fichter, as well as Schlenker.[100] To better understand the responses of Hispanic Muslim converts in this study, it is necessary to include different perspectives about religious socialization.

Fichter proposes two different perspectives to describe the dynamic process of socialization, one that is more objective and another that is more subjective. Objectively, the process of socialization can be understood as society acting upon the individual, whereas the subjective perspective understands socialization as a process of the individual responding to the society.[101] Thus, these perspectives can facilitate the process of understanding the choices that converts make as they practice Islam in the United States.

Based on these two perspectives suggested by Fichter, religious socialization can be described as a dynamic process not only of transmitting religious meanings, values, and expressions, both institutionally and individually (objective perspective), but also comprising the construction of the individual's religiosity in the process of engaging the new religious community.[102]

Another important aspect is the role of primary agents of religious socialization. Several scholars have studied the influence of family members, religious community, and peers regarding religious socialization.[103]

Schlenker highlights the following different audiences that can influence individuals in different contexts: a) the inner self of internalized values, standards, and knowledge that individuals use for self-evaluation; b) interactions with different people; and c) the audience that he describes as "reference other," which includes parents, best friends, close relatives, spouses, admired leaders, and reference groups.[104] These are individuals who can influence the converts by their examples, attitudes, and opinions. Some of them have the potential to become important role models for the converts.[105]

Here, I will pay special attention to the "reference other" proposed by Schlenker. I will analyze the patterns of religious socialization among the converts, looking at both the influence of different agents as well as the responses of the informants.

100. See Fichter, *Sociology*; Schlenker, "Identity and Self-Identification"; Schlenker, "Self-Identification."

101. Fichter, *Sociology*, 29–30.

102. Fichter, *Sociology*, 29–30.

103. Anthony et al., "Religious Practice and Religious Socialization," 100–28; Cornwall, "Influence of Three Agents," 207–31.

104. Schlenker, "Self-Identification," 28.

105. Schlenker, "Self-Identification," 28.

Considering these studies, the following questions emerged in my study: Who are the most significant agents of religious socialization among both the more active and the less active converts? How do the responses of the "less active" Hispanic Muslim converts to religious socialization shape their religious practices? Are there new expressions of religious practice among the more active and less active converts? The subsequent sections include different patterns regarding religious socialization among the informants in order to answer these questions.

Muslim Spouses

Religious activity and involvement of the spouses of Hispanic Muslim converts can shape the religious commitment of these individuals.[106] In Islam, Muslim women are required to marry Muslim men. This is not the case for Muslim men, since they usually have the option to marry Jewish, Christian, or Muslim women.[107] Thus, there is an expectation among immigrant Muslims that female Muslim converts are to marry Muslim men. Even among female Muslim converts, these expectations can be an important marker of commitment to Islam.

There are several patterns regarding marriage among the informants. All the selected informants are married to Muslim spouses. Among the seven selected female Hispanic Muslims, there are five (Lucía, Martina, Claudia, Teresa, and María) who are married to immigrant Muslims. Lucía, Martina, Claudia, and María's husbands are from Middle Eastern countries. Lucía's husband is from Yemen, while Claudia's husband is from Palestine. Martina and María's husbands are from unspecified Middle Eastern countries. In addition, Teresa is the only female Hispanic convert who is married to an immigrant Muslim from South Asia (Pakistan). Two of the female participants are married to Hispanics (Catalina and Camila). Catalina is the only female Muslim convert who is married to a born-Hispanic Muslim. Her husband is from Brooklyn, New York, with a Puerto Rican background. Camila's husband is a Hispanic Muslim convert from Uruguay.

Among the five selected male Hispanic converts, there is one informant who is married to an American Muslim convert (Jaime). There are two converts who are married to Hispanic Muslim female converts (Vicente and Martín). Héctor is the only Hispanic Muslim convert who is married to a born-Hispanic Muslim from Puerto Rico. In addition, Simón is the only convert who is married to a Muslim woman whose parents are immigrants from

---

106. Mahoney, "Religion in Families," 805–27; Shatzmiller, "Marriage, Family, and the Faith," 235–66.

107. Haddad and Lummis, *Islamic Values*, 144–51. See also Smith, *Islam in America*.

the Middle East (unknown country). Based on the interview, it is difficult to know whether she was born in the United States or in the Middle East.

Vicente's wife is of Puerto Rican origin and very committed to Islam. Martín's wife is from Bolivia, and like her husband, she does not attend the mosque frequently. Héctor's wife is very involved at the Islamic center and is working alongside her husband, serving the youth in different capacities. She is also working with Hispanic Muslim women converts.

Support or Lack of Support from Parents and Relatives

The responses and attitudes of the parents and relatives during post-affiliation also shape the religious commitment of the converts. This is true, particularly among female Hispanic Muslim converts. Culturally, it is very important for Hispanic daughters to have support from their parents, especially from their fathers.[108] This was the case of Claudia and María, for example. Both reported the importance of their fathers' understanding before making significant choices (for example, Claudia's decision to wear the *hijab*).

Among the selected informants, Vicente perhaps has the most support from his parents, siblings, and relatives. His parents and siblings are also Muslims, and he has played a significant role in the conversion process of his parents and siblings to Islam. This is an important aspect because he has the chance to practice some rituals and important celebrations with them.

Interactions and Contacts with Other Muslims

Interactions of the Muslim converts with other Muslims are important.[109] There are several patterns regarding relationships with others in daily life. Three female informants (Lucía, Claudia, and Camila) are mainly focused on interacting only with Muslims. Six informants (three men and three women: Martina, María, Teresa, Héctor, Vicente, and Simón) are very open to interacting with both Muslims and non-Muslims.

However, there are different contexts for these interactions. Martina, María, Héctor, and Vicente are largely involved in the Muslim community and participate actively in Islamic centers that support interfaith dialogue. Teresa is involved in business activities, so she is very interested in expanding her interactions with non-Muslims. This is beneficial for her in terms of business opportunities, and she is very intentional about expanding her

---

108. Gracia, *Hispanic Latino Identity*, 50–60; King, "Influence of Religion," 382–95.

109. Cornwall, "Influence of Three Agents," 207–31; Eve, "Integrating Via Networks," 1231–48; Kraft, "Faith Is Lived Out in Community," 954–82.

network of contacts. In Simon's case, it is part of his personality since he is very relational. He has friends from different religious backgrounds as well.

There are three converts (Jaime, Catalina, and Martín) who by choice have limited interactions with other Muslims, and their interactions with non-Muslims vary. The most important interaction for Jaime is with his Muslim wife. He works most of the time among non-Muslims. Catalina interacts mostly with her Muslim husband, and she spends more of her time at home with her children. She has limited interactions with non-Muslims.

It is important to note that Martín is the only informant who reported that most of his friends are not Muslims. He has not changed this dynamic. His interactions with other Muslims are also very limited due mainly to his low attendance at the mosque and his occupation. However, I believe that there are additional reasons in Martín's case that need further consideration.

Generally, Hispanic Muslim women have more relationships with other Muslims than do Hispanic Muslim men. One of the reasons is because most of the women attend different meetings and activities outside their regular services at the mosque. They are also involved in activities with their children at Muslim schools (Claudia, Camila, Catalina, and Lucía). Martina and María are very active with Islamic institutions. However, the degree of these relationships varies among the Muslim converts.

It is worth highlighting that all twelve converts mentioned that they have some degree of interaction with other Muslims via Facebook. Among these informants, Claudia, Martina, and Lucía emphasized in their narratives the use of the Internet and social media networks to connect with Hispanic Muslims. This practice is especially true for Lucia because she mentioned that she intentionally contacted other female Hispanic Muslims via the Internet during post-affiliation.

These interactions with other Hispanic Muslims and Muslim converts via Facebook (outside of the main scope in this chapter) are important because they help individuals to build relationships with other Muslims but also redefine the common nature and understanding of community that has been largely based on face-to-face communication.

Summary of the Cases That Do Not Fit

These theories of socialization and social networks largely suggest that individuals are influenced by others. However, the influence of "reference others" including spouses, parents, Muslim leaders, and friends, does not necessarily mean that the converts do not play a role in making choices that can shape their religious beliefs and practices.

The responses of the less active converts to religious socialization, including those by Jaime, Catalina, Camila, Lucía, and Martín, are important because these responses shape their religious involvement and religious practices, focusing more on private religiosity than on public rituals. These individuals have limited and selective interactions with some friends. They are all married to Muslim spouses, but they are also influenced by their "inner self" perspectives that help them to construct their own understanding of the meaning of a committed Muslim.[110]

5.4.2 Similarities and Differences with Other Studies Done on Religious Commitment

I will describe here some of the most significant findings of studies, including those of the PRC and Barker and Currie, for comparison with the findings of my study among Hispanic Muslims in the United States.[111]

As I described earlier, Barker and Currie claim that "alternators scored higher than converts in measures of church involvement."[112] Barker and Currie state that one of the reasons for this trend is because alternators "have had a lengthier and more consistent exposure to the functioning of the local church along with socialization to involvement in church-related activities. Additionally, the stronger ties within groups may have provided easier access for alternators to elected positions in the church."[113]

According to Barker and Currie's findings, "greater visibility should not be equated with greater commitment."[114] One of the limitations of this study is that these scholars do not include gender differences in the analysis of their findings.

In my study among Hispanic Muslims, there are different patterns and contrary findings. First, I will begin with the more active converts. Then, I will look at the moderately active and less active informants.

More Active Converts

Among the more active converts, María, Héctor, and Vicente have been following Islam for the longest time (eighteen, seventeen, and eleven years,

---

110. Schlenker, "Self-Identification," 21–62.

111. See Barker and Currie, "Do Converts?"; Pew Research Center, "Muslim Americans: No Sign of Growth"; Pew Research Center, "Muslim Americans: Middle Class."

112. Barker and Currie, "Do Converts?," 310.

113. Barker and Currie, "Do Converts?," 310–11.

114. Barker and Currie, "Do Converts?," 309.

respectively). These three informants are very active at the Islamic centers, having an extended social tie to the Muslim community. Thus, it is not surprising that they have high religious activity and involvement.

Teresa and Simón, on the other hand, have been following Islam for a relatively short time (only three and five years, respectively) in comparison with María, Héctor, and Vicente. However, they still have high religious activity and involvement at the mosque. They both have high levels of socialization and ties with the Muslim community. Both also have high exposure to the structure and functioning of the Islamic center, particularly Teresa, who used to work at one of the Islamic centers.

Moderately Active

Among the "moderately active" converts, Jaime and Claudia have been following Islam for twelve and eleven years, respectively. Martina has been a Muslim for only seven years, and she is more involved with Islamic organizations than at the local mosque.

The responses to socialization vary among these informants. Jaime was very selective, and even though he had contacts with Muslims, his socialization was very limited. This is partially due to his personality and difficulty making friends. The ties within the Muslim community are also very limited. His marriage to a Muslim woman is helping him to become more open to connecting with other Muslims.

Less Active Converts

Among the less active converts, Lucía has shorter and less exposure to the functioning of the local mosque. She has been following Islam only for two years, but she is highly committed to the reading of the Qur'an and to private prayers. Martín is a surprising case among the less active converts because he has been following Islam for a longer time (nine years), and yet he is the least committed Muslim among all the selected cases.

Based on these findings, it is important to note that one's length of time as a Muslim does not necessarily mean that the individual is going to have more commitment. There are different factors that play a role in the current involvement of the converts, particularly the way in which they respond to socialization and the ties that they maintain with other Muslims.

Now, I will look at the main findings of the PRC. Among the Muslim American informants included in this study, only 29 percent have high levels of religious commitment, and 22 percent of the informants have low levels of religious commitment. However, nearly half of the participants (49 percent) have moderate religious commitment. Thus, 71 percent of

American Muslims have moderate and low levels of commitment, but the main analysis of the study concentrates on individuals with high religious commitment.

Overall, men and women have roughly similar levels of religious commitment, and there are no differences in religious commitment across age groups.[115] The majority of American Muslims (65 percent) identified with Sunni Islam and only 11 percent identified with the Shia tradition.[116]

Based on the findings in my study among Hispanic Muslim converts, it is difficult to generalize the religious commitment of the participants due to the nuances and different patterns regarding the ritualistic and devotional dimensions of religious commitment. However, there are some aspects to highlight here.

In general, there are no significant differences between Hispanic Muslim men and women in terms of religious activity. One of the similarities among the less active men and women converts in terms of the ritualistic commitment is that these individuals largely pray less often at mosques. Regarding the observance of charity, there are no significant differences between Hispanic Muslim men and women.

Overall, the ritual of fasting is more prevalent among Hispanic Muslim women. The same pattern is observed regarding the pilgrimage to Mecca. Overall, the religious commitment among Hispanic Muslim men and women roughly varies in different rituals, particularly among less active converts.

In terms of the devotional dimension, the more active converts are more focused on praying at the mosque. The less active women pray privately more often than men. Hispanic Muslim women consult the Qur'an more often to make daily decisions than men. This is also more common among the less active participants.

In general, Muslim men attend mosque more regularly than Muslim women.[117] According to this survey, Muslim men attend mosque more frequently than Muslim women (57 percent versus 37 percent, respectively). This is not surprising since there is a "common understanding among Muslims that attendance at weekly religious services is mandatory for Muslim men but optional for women."[118]

This dynamic is not the case in my study; there are similarities regarding the attendance at the mosque by both Muslim men and women. In general, the more active converts attend the mosque more often, but this

---

115. Pew Research Center, "Muslim Americans: No Sign of Growth," 27.
116. Pew Research Center, "Muslim Americans: No Sign of Growth," 23.
117. Pew Research Center, "Muslim Americans: No Sign of Growth," 26.
118. Pew Research Center, "Muslim Americans: No Sign of Growth," 26.

does not mean that women do not attend religious services. Some of them also attend mosque frequently. This can be explained in part by the fact that Hispanic Muslim women have more freedom to attend religious activities at the mosque, particularly the Islamic centers that are largely focused on community and are open to the active participation of Muslim women.

Regarding the involvement of American Muslims in social or religious activities at a mosque, Muslim women are just as likely as men to report involvement (34 percent of Muslim men versus 36 percent of Muslim women). In my study, Hispanic Muslim men are slightly more involved than women at the mosque, but Hispanic Muslim women are more involved with their religious communities outside the mosque.

I will conclude this chapter by including final comments regarding the assessment of high and low levels of commitment, conclusions drawn from theories, and findings regarding gender differences.

5.5 CONCLUSION

5.5.1 Assessment of High and Low Levels of Religious Commitment

This study is perhaps the first attempt to qualitatively analyze the religious commitment among Hispanic Muslim converts in the context of the United States. The main approach used here has been assessing the high and low levels of commitment proposed by several scholars.[119] I have identified the most important patterns among both the less active and more active converts.

As has been observed, there are some problems and limitations regarding the use of high and low levels of religious commitment recommended by some scholars.[120] The analysis of the data is largely focused on highly committed informants. These levels are mainly based on three indicators. The indicators used in these studies to measure the religious commitment of Muslims in the United States are mainly based on the responses to the informants (closed-ended questions). It is difficult to analyze the patterns and the nuances, particularly among individuals who are labeled as low to moderately committed. These levels arguably suggest that low-committed informants have low or less commitment in all (or most) of the dimensions of religious commitment.

---

119. Barker and Currie, "Do Converts?"; Pew Research Center, "Muslim Americans: No Sign of Growth"; Pew Research Center, "Muslim Americans: Middle Class."

120. Barker and Currie, "Do Converts?"; Pew Research Center, "Muslim Americans: No Sign of Growth"; Pew Research Center, "Muslim Americans: Middle Class."

The data demonstrate that this trend is not the case among Hispanic Muslim converts. The findings have shown that the more active Hispanic Muslim converts are not necessarily high committed in all the different aspects of practice and rituals in Islam. The same is true with the less active converts. It cannot be assumed that these individuals will have a low commitment in all the dimensions of religious commitment.

The empirical evidence reveals that even individuals who are considered less or moderately active have some degree of commitment, particularly regarding the ritualistic and devotional dimensions of religious commitment. The indicators used by previous studies of American Muslims are rather limited. Including additional indicators of religious commitment alongside the ritualistic and devotional dimensions of religious commitment proposed by Stark and Glock is helpful to facilitate the analysis of the nuances and patterns among both the less active and more active Hispanic Muslim converts.

The empirical evidence suggests that individuals can have high levels of commitment in some dimensions and not necessarily high commitment in other dimensions. In addition, high religious activity does not necessarily correlate to high religious commitment. The commitment shown by individuals in one of the dimensions of religiosity may vary through the times, and it is shaped by several contextual factors. Thus, it is important to make a distinction between religious activity and religious commitment in several dimensions of religiosity.

An important aspect that has been missing in these studies is the limited attention to the responses and choices that individuals make in the process of becoming practicing Muslims. As has been observed, even the less active and moderate converts make choices regarding the rituals and devotions that in turn help these individuals to develop an understanding regarding the meaning of a committed Muslim in their own contexts.

This distinction between low or high commitment distracts one from fully appreciating the role played by those classified as low in religious commitment. High and low levels of commitment that are largely based on limited indicators reflect a more unidimensional conceptualization of religious commitment, contrary to a multidimensional conceptualization of commitment that has been supported by different scholars. Thus, the approach of relying primarily on these levels of commitment can hide significant nuances and dynamics among the converts labeled as low committed. This is significant, particularly in the context of a non-Muslim country (or minority Muslim country). There is evidence in this study that supports the fact that religious commitment is a multidimensional and fluid phenomenon.

It is worth mentioning here that low and high levels of commitment are helpful to have general information regarding the religious activity of the converts as well as the frequency of daily prayer. Important questions have emerged from these studies. For example, what are the differences between the high and low committed Muslims? These indicators of religiosity can be used in addition to other indicators that are identified, particularly among different Muslim converts in the United States. Thus, there is a need for more studies among Muslim converts using different indicators, levels of commitment, and several dimensions of religious commitment.

Overall, the multidimensional approach proposed by Bader et al. and Stark and Glock[121] has proven to be helpful to understand the nuances of religiosity among Hispanic Muslim converts because it facilitates the analysis to appreciate the dynamics, particularly among the less active converts.

5.5.2 Conclusions Drawn from Socialization and Social Networks Theories

Religious socialization among Hispanic Muslims is shaped by dynamic interactions and contacts with Muslim spouses, support or lack of support from parents, siblings, close relatives, and Muslim friends, and the ability to meet with other Muslims at the Islamic centers.

Building relationships with others is important because it shows the different levels of interactions of the converts with non-Muslim friends and with other Muslims in their communities. These interactions with others facilitate not only the involvement of the converts in different activities but also stimulate the religious commitment and practice of the informants. Relationships with others are significant, particularly in Islam where life in community is strongly emphasized.[122]

Overall, the theories of socialization and social networks are helpful to understand the role of different agents in religious socialization. Hispanic Muslim converts are influenced by several agents depending on their own contexts. Social networks are important for some individuals depending on the level of "structural availability."[123] The more intentional that individuals are in interacting with others as they embrace the new community, the more opportunities there are for them to be influenced by others. This is evident

---

121. See Bader et al., *American Piety in the 21ˢᵗ Century*; Stark and Glock, *American Piety*.

122. Kraft, *Searching for Heaven*, 19–23. See also Zebiri, *British Muslim Converts*.

123. Rambo, *Understanding Religious Conversion*, 60–61. See also Kraft, *Searching for Heaven*.

particularly among the more active and moderately active converts (e.g., María, Héctor, Vicente, and Martina).

Nevertheless, the effect of "reference others" does not necessarily mean that the converts do not play a role in making choices that shape their religious beliefs and practices. The less active converts (Jaime, Catalina, Camila, Lucía, and Martín) made significant choices that shaped their religious involvement and religious practices, focusing on more private religiosity rather than public rituals.[124] These individuals have limited and selective interactions with some non-Muslim friends, they are all married to Muslim spouses, but they are also influenced by "inner self" perspectives that help them to construct their understanding of the meaning of a committed Muslim.[125]

Beyond Socialization and Social Networks Theories

It is important to look beyond religious socialization and social networks by also examining the choices that individuals make regarding socialization. Another important aspect to consider is the different perspectives that Hispanic Muslims have regarding the meaning of a committed Muslim. These perspectives are informed and constructed as the participants interact with imams, community leaders, spouses, and other Muslims, including born Muslims and converts. The context of Islam as a minority religion within the United States also plays an important role regarding the nuances of religious commitment and practices, particularly among Muslim converts.

5.5.3 Findings Regarding Gender Differences

An important finding in this study among Hispanic Muslim converts is regarding gender differences in terms of religious commitment within different dimensions of religious practice. To facilitate the comparison and contrast between Hispanic Muslim men and Hispanic Muslim women, I will concentrate on the religious activity of the participants. Considering the data, there are no significant differences between Hispanic Muslim men and women in terms of religious activity. The most significant differences are among the less active converts.

One of the similarities among the less active men and women is that they generally pray less often at the mosque. Concerning the observance

---

124. For a discussion regarding different dynamics of spirituality, see Ammerman's "Spiritual but Not Religious?" For an insightful analysis of religion and spirituality, see Hill et al., "Conceptualizing Religion and Spirituality"; Roof, "Religion and Spirituality."

125. Schlenker, "Self-Identification," 21–62.

of charity, there are no substantial differences between men and women. In general, the ritual of fasting is more common among Hispanic Muslim women. A similar pattern was observed in terms of the pilgrimage to Mecca. Generally, the religious commitment among Hispanic Muslim men and women varies within different rituals, particularly among the less active converts.

Regarding the devotional dimension, the more active converts are more focused on praying at the mosque. The less active Hispanic Muslim women pray privately more often than men do. Hispanic Muslim women consult the Qur'an to make daily decisions more often than men do.

In general, the more active converts attend mosque with greater frequency, but this does not mean that women do not attend religious services. Some of them also frequently attend mosque. One explanation is that Hispanic Muslim women have more freedom in the United States to attend religious activities at the mosque in comparison with Middle Eastern countries.

Concerning the involvement of Hispanic Muslim converts in social or religious activities at a mosque, Hispanic Muslim men are slightly more involved than women, but Hispanic Muslim women are frequently more involved in activities outside the mosque. Some examples of this include prayer groups, small group discussions, and different activities with other Muslim mothers who have children at school.

5.5.4 What Is Next?

The choices of Hispanic Muslim converts, as well as the nuanced dimensions of religious commitment among the more active, moderately active, and less active, are important because they help us to distinguish between and analyze the beliefs and practices that are emphasized by these individuals. In the final chapter, I will summarize the main findings of this research, including some implications and contributions of the study. Then, I will describe some limitations. I will conclude this final chapter with a discussion of prospects for further research and closing remarks.

Chapter 6

Concluding Thoughts

6.1 INTRODUCTION

The first section of this chapter will summarize the main findings of this research. As mentioned in chapter 1, the aim of this research is to describe and examine how the converts make choices which play roles in the post-affiliation stage. These choices regularly have strategic elements. The central research question of this study is: To what extent do Hispanic Muslim converts play a role in making different choices regarding religious commitment and practice?

The main argument presented in this study is that both the more active and the less active converts play a significant role in making choices during the pre-affiliation and post-affiliation stages. These choices can be strategic in nature as individuals commit themselves to the practices of Islam in the United States which is a Muslim-minority country.

This section also revisits the research questions and demonstrates how they have been achieved and answered satisfactorily. In light of the most significant findings of this research, potential implications and contributions to religious conversion studies are considered in the following section.

One of the most influential contributions of this study is the expansion of religious conversion studies by proposing new patterns, nuances, and relationships between multiple factors that have been largely ignored in former research. The limitations of the research are discussed in section 3, though such limitations are not certainly damaging in their consequences. The identification of these limitations provides a valuable guide for future research on religious conversion and illuminates the possible direction that future studies can take. The prospects for future research are therefore discussed in section 4. The last section includes the final remarks concerning the study.

6.2 SUMMARY OF THE MAIN FINDINGS

In discussing the main findings of this research, it is important to revisit the aim of the thesis, the main arguments, and the research questions that have been addressed. As stated in chapter 1, the main aim of this thesis is to show that Hispanic converts to Islam make decisions and play a role in the post-affiliation stage and that these decisions often have strategic elements. The rationale for this research stems from the desire to understand the dynamics and challenges among Hispanics who follow Islam in the United States.

The main argument of the study is that not only do both the more active and the less active converts play a central role in making choices during the pre-affiliation and post-affiliation stages, but that these choices can often be strategic in nature as they practice Islam in a non-Muslim country. Hence, there is a high level of agency among the converts. The different choices that converts make are shaped by multiple factors. There are choices at different levels: before conversion, choices regarding the words they use in their conversion narratives, changes that occur during post-affiliation, identity reconstruction, and choices concerning religious commitment and practice.

The central question of this research is: *To what extent do Hispanic Muslim converts make different choices regarding religious commitment and practice in the United States?* To answer this significant question, it was necessary to address the following questions: *What role do Hispanic Muslim converts play in different conversion motifs? What are the most significant contextual factors?* These questions were addressed in chapter 2.

As argued in chapter 2, there is an individual agency of and an active role played by the converts in making strategic choices in the process leading up to a conversion. One of the most important findings in this chapter was that even the individuals with a less active role made intentional choices. Evidence based on the data showed that the role of the converts in making choices is complex and there is a dynamic interplay of multiple factors that shaped the process leading up to conversion. Thus, there is not a single overarching factor that influences this process.

Considering the collected data, various personal, social, and religious factors shaped the processes preceding conversion. Cultural factors play a more substantial role in individuals with a less active role. Also, there is a dynamic interplay between the role of the converts, the contextual factors, and the conversion motifs. According to the data, converts who are more active might be more influenced by personal and religious factors, while converts with less active roles might be affected more by social and cultural factors. Intellectual or experimental conversion motifs might be more prevalent in individuals with more active agency. In general, affectional conversion motifs might be more common in individuals with less active agency. Family background and structure, previous religious affiliations of the converts, the parental religious commitment, a variety of conversion motifs, and religious structures are important factors in shaping the different choices that Hispanic Muslim converts make.

In chapter 3, the question concerning the words that converts used in different types of conversion narratives and the predominant discourses were addressed. In this chapter, the data have shown that most of the converts continue to display active agency even when retelling their conversion narratives. There is a tendency among the converts to review their past in light of the present. This is important because it expands the examination of the nuances and complexities that arise as converts reconstruct their new identities.

Based on the findings in chapter 3, it has been demonstrated that there are different types of conversion narratives that are fashioned by multiple contextual factors, present circumstances, institutional discourses, and the integration or nonintegration of the newly adopted religious beliefs by the Hispanic Muslim converts. Additionally, there are predominant discourses in their narratives, and converts have diverse purposes for sharing these discourses. One significant theme in the narratives is that both religious and ethnic identities are reflected in their conversion narratives.

As previously discussed in chapter 3, diverse themes emerged from the narratives ranging from religious seeking, discovery, and fulfillment. Additionally, both the background and eventual reconstructed identity of each conversion narrative were different. For instance, some of the converts reconstructed their previous identities by integrating some of the values and beliefs of the new religion. This reconstruction process happened both at the individual and group level. One important observation was that the degree of socialization and participation with other Muslims plays a significant role in this process. The majority of the Hispanic Muslim converts largely participated and made different choices in the process of socialization connecting with Muslim friends, coworkers, and imams.

Additional two significant questions related to the central question are: *What are the factors that shape the evolving Hispanic Muslim identity,* and

What are the most significant changes that occur during post-affiliation? These questions about choices and identity were the main focus of chapter 4.

One of the most relevant findings in this chapter concerning the reconstruction of the Hispanic Muslim identities is that there is a dynamic interplay between ethnicity, culture, and religion that in turn shapes the social relationships of the converts. There are different trends observed based on the analysis of the conversion narratives. For some converts, this means nearly a total break with the former community, occasionally including their relatives, extended family, and friends. Nevertheless, for other converts, this break is partial, and some converts largely manage to preserve relationships with the previous community and extended family. Some of them concentrate more on building relationships with their Muslim friends.

As I have argued in this chapter, the converts have an active role not only in the conversion process but also as they reconstruct their new identities. Hispanic Muslim converts are challenged to respond to the changes, tensions, and negotiations. The dynamics are diverse and difficult as they try to fit into American culture and the new Muslim community. Likewise, their social identity is changed in the process, shaping the way they build relationships with others.

As stated in chapter 4, values and beliefs are important. The rejection or retention of values and beliefs is a problematic process for the converts because these converts are not always fully aware of the changes that they are facing. Consequently, new values and beliefs emerge in this fluid process of reconstructing their Hispanic Muslim identities. Some converts, however, are more intentional about making choices concerning changes such as name, dress, and preferred language as they interact with others.

Pursuing this further, the data have shown the link between religion, culture, ethnicity, and identity. The findings show the significance of both individual and group dynamics, the changes that take place concerning values and beliefs, and the choices and tensions that occurred as the converts reconstructed their identities. Additionally, it is important to examine the link between self-identification of the converts and the different types of integration.

In general, there are three levels of integration here, religious (Muslim community), cultural (United States society), and ethnic (with other Hispanics in the United States). Specific markers were used to facilitate the examination of these three categories of integration. In light of the collected data, I have demonstrated that some of the converts who integrate more with the Muslim community choose to attend particular Islamic centers that emphasize values such as community, hospitality, and ethnic diversity. Thus, these converts become more involved in public practices such as Friday prayers. These observations lead into the summary of the main findings regarding the most important question of this study.

The central question is: *To what extent do Hispanic Muslim converts make different choices regarding religious commitment and practice in the United States?* Thus, chapter 5 examined the nuances of religious commitment and practice among Hispanic Muslim converts. Chapter 5 focused on the patterns in different dimensions of religious commitment, mainly looking at religious practices (rituals and devotionals) shown by both the less active and more active converts. The aim of this chapter was to analyze the different choices that Hispanic Muslim converts make about religious commitment and practice in the United States. In addition, this chapter examined and challenged the position of scholars who make a distinction between low and high levels of religious commitment.[1]

As stated in chapter 5, the responses and choices of Hispanic Muslim converts, as well as the nuances of the different dimensions of religious commitment among both the more active and the less active converts, are significant because they broaden the analysis of the beliefs and practices these Muslim minorities highlight. These choices concerning religious commitment and practice are shaped by multiple factors, including the Muslim-minority context, the levels of socialization of the converts, the different ways converts define religious commitment, and the level of familiarity with previous religious practices.

6.3 IMPLICATIONS AND CONTRIBUTIONS OF THE STUDY

This research has both theoretical and literary implications. The most important theoretical implication of this research is the expanded opportunities for theory building for Rambo's and Gooren's models. As stated in chapter 1, the definition of religious conversion is problematic.

6.3.1 Theoretical Implications

As described in chapter 1, the understanding of conversion in this study was partially shaped by Rambo's and Gooren's definitions. Lewis Rambo defines a religious conversion as "a process of religious change that takes place in a

---

1. Barker and Currie, "Do Converts?," 305–13; Pew Research Center, "Muslim Americans: No Sign of Growth"; Pew Research Center, "Muslim Americans: Middle Class."

dynamic field of people, events, ideologies, institutions and orientations."[2] Henri Gooren defines conversion "as a comprehensive personal change of religious worldview and identity, based on both self-report and attribution by others."[3]

The term "conversion" is used in a broader sense in this study. The definition of conversion encompasses Gooren's stage of affiliation, that is, becoming a formal member "without change of identity."[4] Similarly, conversion encompasses pre-/post-affiliation stages. Additionally, conversion is understood as a dynamic and complex personal process of religious change that usually implies the construction of new identifies, and also the adoption of new values and beliefs. This understanding of conversion provides new opportunities to examine the nuances of religious conversion in various contexts.

Another contribution of the study is that it expands Rambo's understanding of the context. Rambo proposes seven stages in his model: context, crisis, quest, encounter, interaction, commitment, and consequences. According to Rambo, "context is the most comprehensive of all the stages, is the dynamic force field in which conversion takes place. Context encompasses the modes of access and transmission, provides the models and methods of conversion, and also contains sources of resistance."[5] This study utilized a multidisciplinary approach, focusing on personal, social, cultural, and religious contextual factors. In addition, the contextual factors were considered in the analysis throughout all the stages. This is a different perspective as related to Rambo's model. For Rambo, context is one of the stages of the model. Even though Rambo acknowledges the fact that "context is more than a stage this is passed through and it is the total environment in which conversion transpires,"[6] the understanding of context within this study is broader.

Regarding religious commitment, Rambo proposes that "commitment is the consummation of the conversion process, and it empowers the convert with a sense of connection with God and the community."[7] Also, he suggests that "commitment is the fulcrum of the change process. Following a period of intensive interaction, the potential convert faces the prospect,

---

2. Rambo, *Understanding Religious Conversion*, 5.
3. Gooren, *Religious Conversion and Disaffiliation*, 3.
4. Gooren, *Religious Conversion and Disaffiliation*, 48–51.
5. Rambo, *Understanding Religious Conversion*, 165.
6. Rambo, *Understanding Religious Conversion*, 20.
7. Rambo, *Understanding Religious Conversion*, 168–69.

the choice, of commitment."[8] The important elements of the commitment stage according to Rambo's model are decision-making, rituals, surrender, testimony manifested in language transformation, and biographical reconstruction, and motivational reformulation.[9]

Based on the findings in this study, there are additional factors that need to be considered. For instance, the overall context in which the choices about commitment take place. In this case, the Muslim-minority context is very significant. Also, the different levels of socialization of the converts, the diverse perspectives of the converts concerning religious commitment, and the levels of familiarity or estrangement with previous religious practices.

These factors which have emerged from this study create new opportunities to expand Gooren's conversion career approach, especially concerning the commitment and religious practices of individuals switching to different religions. Gooren's approach represents a systematic attempt to analyze the changes in levels of individual religious activity including pre-affiliation, affiliation, conversion, confession [commitment], and disaffiliation. According to Gooren, "a core member identity with a high level of participation inside the (new) religious community and a strong evangelism on the outside."[10] Based on the findings of this study, it is important to examine the nuances of individuals who are considered to have less commitment because they too make important choices regarding religious commitment. These individuals largely focus on more private rituals and practices.

As described in chapter 1, the research followed Gooren's typology with a minor distinction: using "pre-affiliation," "affiliation," "conversion," and "high commitment" instead of the term "confession." Since the focus of this research was on affiliation and conversion, the disaffiliation stage was omitted in this study.

Chapter 5 examined and challenged the position of scholars who make a critical distinction between low and high levels of religious commitment.[11] The findings of this study shed new light on conversion studies by adding new factors that need to be considered to have a more thorough understanding about the nuances of religious commitment and practice. The context needs to be taken into consideration, looking at multiple factors that shape the responses, tendencies, and preferences of the converts concerning religious commitment and practice.

8. Rambo, *Understanding Religious Conversion*, 124.
9. Rambo, *Understanding Religious Conversion*, 124.
10. Gooren, *Religious Conversion and Disaffiliation*, 49.
11. Barker and Currie, "Do Converts?"; Pew Research Center, "Muslim Americans: No Sign of Growth"; Pew Research Center, "Muslim Americans: Middle Class."

6.3.2 Literature Implications

The research setting of this study can help contribute to the existing literature on the religious conversion to Islam in the United States. As discussed in chapter 1, the existing literature pertaining to the religious conversion in the United States largely concentrates on Catholicism. Consequently, more research needs to be conducted to examine the nuances of religious conversion among minorities.

There are potential contributions in the field of conversion studies and sociology of religion. One of the vital contributions that this study could potentially achieve is regarding new typologies of conversion. It can also contribute to a new understanding of the prevailing debates among Muslims in Europe and the United States on the nature of Muslim minorities in the West and on diaspora studies in the United States.

Additionally, it may contribute to the body of literature on the identity of Hispanics and religion in the United States. Hispanic identity studies have been focused largely on the Catholic background of Hispanics, so this study may shed light on the construction of identities of Hispanic Muslim converts in these locations in the United States.

This research is significant because it addresses a gap in studies on the phenomenon of religious conversion in the United States. The question of the nature and extent of religious conversion is critical since it promises greater clarity on the process of conversion itself and, in this sense, promises something new and original to the existing research corpus. This research question will encompass the finer questions on the role of the agency in socialization (especially as seen by converts), as well as the role of the converts in strategically allowing the construction of new identities (or allowing this to the extent it serves their strategic purposes—their evident public and private responses).

This research can contribute to continuous theoretical and practitioner debates concerning the benefit of interfaith dialogue between Christians and Muslims. This research can contribute to theoretical debates about the role of culture and socialization in religious conversion among diverse ethnic groups. My aim is to make a modest contribution which provides new layers and approaches for the study of religious conversion among ethnic minorities based on the factors mentioned by Rambo and Gooren.[12] In addition, the finding of this study can contribute to religious conversion studies by proposing new patterns, nuances, and relationships between multiple factors that have been largely ignored in previous studies.

---

12. See Rambo, *Understanding Religious Conversion*; Gooren, *Religious Conversion and Disaffiliation*.

The inquiry as to why immigrant communities are more open to Islam is important. Furthermore, this research may bring new insights into immigrant religions in North America. Finally, this research may contribute to the implementation of diverse methods to study religious conversion.

6.4 MY ROLE AS RESEARCHER AND REFLEXIVITY

My approach was to understand the religious conversion process based on the local contexts and locations of the converts. There is a level of reflexivity in this process as well. Therefore, my role as a researcher becomes important as I try to understand these conversions from the perspectives of the converts. In doing this, there is a combination of roles as both an outsider and an insider.

First, as an outsider, I am not a Muslim, and I do not live in an area where there are a lot of interactions between Muslims and Christians. I observed and analyzed the conversion of the individuals with respect, focusing on the converts' point of view. William Paden proposes a comparative study of religions whose goals are "understanding and description."[13] Paden's approach attempts to have one step outside of their own religious world into that of the world they are studying. Considering many other comparisons on religious studies, it is without biases and presuppositions. The comparative method, therefore, allows understanding without judgment. Paden based his approach on the following cornerstones: starting with respect for each religion and relying on observable facts. Paden takes these facts and arranges them in observable patterns. He also places them in a context in which the reader can understand.

Second, as an insider, I am a Hispanic immigrant currently living in the United States. I understand some of the challenges that immigrants face when they move to a different country. I came to the United States in 1997. Thus, the level of reflexivity in the process needs to be considered.

There is also the role of observer-as-participant; in this role, there is some observation, but very little of it involves any participation. However, I have been able to participate in some activities such as Islamic courses on Saturdays, prayer meetings on Fridays, and special activities such as the celebration of Hispanic Day at Islamic centers. Usually, these special activities are open to the community.

---

13. Paden, *Religious Worlds*, 168.

6.5 LIMITATIONS OF THE STUDY

This research faces several limitations. First, there are some limitations regarding the methods used in this research, especially concerning the initial interviews that shape the data collection. The biggest initial challenge was to find informants who were willing to share their stories. The background of the researcher has some strengths and weaknesses. Because I was teaching at a Christian university and I was not a Muslim, some of the imams were suspicious of the research. Thus, I was interviewed by several imams that I met in the initial stages of the research. I am grateful that I was able to build genuine relationships with these imams. They asked me questions about my motivation and the purpose of the research. Once they understood the purpose of the research, they began to refer potential informants for interviews. Some of the imams suggested that I should travel to different locations. Thus, I began to attend different services at several Islamic centers in Hampton Roads, then in Richmond, Virginia. By building more relationships, I was also advised to go to Alexandria and the Metropolitan DC area.

Second, I was unable to enhance the validity of the data by interviewing parents, siblings, or close friends of the participants. The purpose was to validate some of their responses to facilitate the triangulation of the data. Dealing with participants that are not fully familiar with research culture also poses some limitations on the process of data collection. Some of the informants recommended that I contact their friends who were willing to be interviewed, but later these potential informants decided not to follow through. They refused the invitation to participate, mainly because of their fear of saying the wrong things in their interviews. Some of them were very timid, so they did not have the confidence to speak with a person that they did not know well. Despite the explanation given and the provision of confidentiality and anonymity, four individuals declined the invitations to participate in this study.

Another significant challenge is that most of the relatives and siblings of the informants live in different locations. Some of them even expressed that there is still tension with their families because of their conversion to Islam. Thus, the opportunity to interview relatives and siblings was very limited in this study. Sampling is a crucial factor in the methodology and depending on the research, there can be unexpected limitations and challenges that affect the process of sampling. There is a need to implement different strategies to strengthen the validity of the research by using multiple layers in the process of interpretation and analysis of the data.

Third, there are some limitations concerning the location. Most of the informants are from the Metropolitan DC area, and few of them live in New

Jersey. In order to do a comparative study, there is a need to conduct more extensive interviews including both males and females in these locations. I tried to include more informants from the New Jersey area, but at the time of the interviews several of the referrals were traveling or had two jobs and their time was very limited. Another challenge was that I was able to travel only during the weekends. Time and availability of the informants need to be considered in the planning for interviews. As I stated in the introduction previously, the general observations and applications related to Hispanic Muslims are based on these particular locations and contexts. Thus, the implications for different Muslim minorities in other locations in the United States requires careful analysis, looking at the social, cultural, and religious contexts in these settings.

Fourth, there is a limitation regarding the scope of the study. As I described in the introduction, this research did not address in-depth, important theological themes that emerged in the interviews. For example, the concept of oneness (*Tawhid*) was important for several informants and shaped their perspective regarding Islam as a way of life. Informants who highlight this theological concept of Islam tend to have a more holistic approach, seeing Islam not as mere religion but as an integrated pattern of life. Theological concepts will need further exploration to examine the way in which these concepts shape their choices concerning commitment and practice in a Muslim-minority context.

6.6 PROSPECTS FOR FURTHER RESEARCH

There are several avenues of future research that can be undertaken in the fields of conversion studies and sociology of religion. For instance, there is a need for further research on the conversion of minorities to Islam in general. As previously mentioned, minimal research exists in the United States concerning conversion to Islam among Hispanics. Thus, it is important to focus on states where there is a large population of Hispanics such as Florida, Texas, California, and New York. Having more research in different locations will contribute to the understanding of the complexities and nuances of conversion from Christianity to Islam in different settings. Additionally, generational differences and challenges need further examination.

Furthermore, there is a need for more comparative studies on conversion to Islam. It would be worthwhile to explore the different dynamics of both men and women from different religious backgrounds who converted to Islam in Latin America. According to studies conducted in Latin America, Islam is growing in countries such as Argentina, Brazil, Mexico, and Colombia. What are the patterns of religious conversion? What are the similarities and differences between converts in Latin America and converts in the United States? How does the minority-Muslim country context shape the experiences of Latinos switching to Islam? How do Latino Muslims in these countries manage different challenges of rejection and isolation by their parents, close relatives, coworkers, and friends?

The answers that most of the informants in this study gave regarding the reactions of parents and friends after they decided to follow Islam were very limited because they were unwilling to elaborate. Some of them provided shorter answers or decided not to reflect much on this question. This was very surprising because most of the informants reported challenges and negative experiences regarding their relatives and friends. It is necessary to further explore this issue, looking at the minority-religion context in the United States. How do the honor and shame values that are emphasized in most Arab countries shape the reactions of the Hispanic Muslim converts? What are the negotiations that take place between converts and their parents, siblings, and friends?

Another important issue to examine is the link between politics in these countries and the significant aspects of sharia law that Islamic organizations promote. How do these tensions and dynamics shape the way that Muslim converts practice their religion? How do they reconstruct their new identities as Latino Muslims in a Muslim-minority context?

6.7 QUESTIONS RAISED IN THE STUDY

There is also a need for further studies of Hispanic Muslims considering converting to other religions, including Buddhism and Hinduism. What are the commonalities among these converts? What are the contributions of Muslim minorities? How do Muslim minorities shape the local Islamic culture and practice in the United States?

It is important to analyze the disaffiliation process among some Muslim converts who decide to leave Islam and are willing to switch back to the previous religion or to explore a new religion (conversion career). What are the dynamics and nuances of the disaffiliation? How do these individuals make sense of the disaffiliation process? What are the reactions and responses of born-Hispanic Muslims? It is important to analyze the dynamics and the process of negotiation that takes place.

Other questions that emerged from this study are the following: What are the newer local expressions, commitments, and practices of Islam in these locations? To what extent do Hispanic Muslim converts shape local

Islamic practices (devotional and rituals)? What role do Hispanic Muslim converts play in fashioning their local Islamic identity in different geographical locations in the United States?

Methodologically, there is a need to conduct more research using multidisciplinary approaches. How can theology contribute to the sociology of religion and conversion studies? How can different disciplines contribute to new approaches to expand the examination of religious conversion studies? Further studies should include multidisciplinary approaches, including sociology, anthropology, theology, missiology, and psychology.

6.8 REGARDING THEORY AND APPROACHES (SOCIALIZATION)

Individual agency has been highlighted in this thesis. However, as mentioned earlier, the institutional agency is significant particularly in the context of the United States. It is important to research more about the role that imams and community leaders play in the socialization of new converts.

There is a need also to explore further the different principles and applications based on Rambo's model and Gooren's conversion career. More research needs to be done looking at Muslim minority converts who choose to disaffiliate from Islam and reembrace Christianity. What are the nuances of disaffiliation? How do these converts make sense of disaffiliation? What are the dynamics with parents, siblings, relatives, and friends? What are the most significant challenges that they face with close Muslim friends? These kinds of questions will add new perspectives and understanding to the study of religious conversion among minorities.

6.9 IDENTITY, COMMUNITY, AND BELIEFS

Furthermore, there is a need to explore more deeply issues of identity, community, and religious beliefs and doctrines emphasized by different religions. How do the converts become part of the *Ummah* (Muslim community)? How do the new converts interact with born Muslims? How do born Muslims interact with and perceive Muslim minority converts? What are some of the challenges within the Muslim community in the United States? Both Latinos and Muslims greatly value community, yet some converts expressed the challenges presented by the lack of integration within the Muslim community. Thus, it is important to research more about the role of imams in terms of facilitating or encouraging the integration of Muslim minorities with the wider Muslim community. How do they do this, and by what means do they facilitate this integration?

This integration is also relevant for the converts because their identities contain several layers: the American culture, their ethnicity as Hispanics, and their religion as Muslims. How do converts self-identify, especially when they have to face significant challenges with non-Muslims in the marketplace, with the coworkers, and with classmates? To what extent do they compromise or negotiate religious beliefs and practices to be able to build community and relate with their families and friends?

6.10 MUSLIM REFUGEES IN THE UNITED STATES

Finally, there are new trends and challenges concerning the exile of Muslims from different countries who have been largely forced to leave everything behind for different reasons, including violence and social and political turmoil. What are the new realities of the Muslim refugees? How are the interactions with other Muslims in general? To what extent do Muslim refugees reconstruct their Muslim identities now that they live in Muslim-minority countries? How do they practice their faith in Muslim-minority countries such as the United States, Canada, and Mexico? What are the negotiations and adaptations that take place when they live in a different culture and context? Do they remain in their faith, or are they open to new opportunities to embrace different religions? These are significant questions that need to be explored in future research.

6.11 FINAL REMARKS

The Identity of the Converts: Why Is it Important?

Considering the previous analysis included in chapter 4 regarding assimilation and integration, I propose that this dynamic process of selectively making choices as the converts construct their identities cannot be entirely explained by full assimilation or full integration. Rather, it is a complex network of processes that are shaped by multiple contextual factors, including ethnicity, culture, and religious experiences.

Most of the converts (the second-generation Hispanics in particular) made their choices based on previous values and beliefs. Sometimes these were based more on Catholicism, sometimes on core Hispanic values like the importance of family and hugging. There was a selective process of assimilation and selective isolation in some cases. In most of the cases, there was not a drastic rupture with the previous religion. Some previous values and beliefs were retained by the converts, such as family values, respect for parents, community life, and the significance of prayer. There was neither full assimilation nor full isolation.

It was a complicated process of negotiation and decision-making that interplayed with culture, religion, and ethnicity. Most of the converts oscillated between assimilation and isolation. As Yang framed it,[14] we cannot understand the identity construction of immigrants by opposing the conceptualizations of assimilation and ethnic preservation. "Instead of choosing either American or ethnic identities," Yang wrote, "immigrants may construct adhesive identities that integrate both together."[15]

The integration of religious and ethnic identities is reflected by several informants who participated in this research. Most individuals in this study experienced different levels of selective integration and partial translation. Consequently, the reconstruction of the identities is an important process to consider in further research.

To conclude this thesis, it is pertinent to highlight the significance of the nuances and the fluid dynamics that take place in the religious conversion. Rambo astutely conveys the complexities of conversion. He states,

> Conversion is paradoxical. It is elusive. It is inclusive. It destroys, and it saves. Conversion is sudden, and it is gradual. It is created totally by the action of God, and it is created totally by the action of humans. Conversion is personal and communal, private and public. It is both passive and active. It is a retreat from the world. It is a resolution of conflict and an empowerment to go into the world and to confront, if not create, conflict. Conversion is an event and a process. It is an ending and a beginning. It is final and open ended. Conversion leaves us devastated and transformed.[16]

---

14. See also Kim and Hurh, "Beyond Assimilation and Pluralism."
15. Yang, *Chinese Christians in America*, 17.
16. Rambo, *Understanding Religious Conversion*, 176.

Appendix 1

Summary of Similarities and Differences Difference between *Wasatiyya* (centrist) and *Salafiyya* Approaches

Issues of sociojuristic worldviews	*Wasatiyya* (centrist) approach Moderates try to understand the text and the context	*Salafiyya* approach (followers of the first three generations of Islam)
Ideology	Represents a flexible approach to *fiqh* to harmonize rights and duties: material and spiritual issues, individualism, and communalism	Represents a strict rigid *fiqh* and follows traditions. No separation materials and spirituals since it may lead to imitation of infidels
Approach to traditional four schools of *fiqh*	Emphasizes systematic search in all four legal schools of *fiqh* for the most suitable answer and beyond them the liberal application of *ijtihad* (independent juristic effort)	Emphasizes the concept of *al-wala wa 'l-bara* (loyalty and disavowal) and imitation of the past and refrains from *ijtihad* (independent juristic effort)
Need for balanced adjusted *fiqh* for minorities	Encourages to create presence in the West and modifies some Islamic religious laws to enable Muslims facing the religiosocial challenges of modernism and to remain culturally independent	Legitimize voluntary move Rejects permissibility of adjusting *fiqh* in order to accommodate minorities' conditions
Residence and interaction with non-Muslims	Legitimizes residence in non-Muslim lands on the condition of religious freedom, encouraging participation in European life that does not conflict with Islamic ideologies	Permits residence in the West in more restrictive terms and discourages interactions or integration in the West, rather promotes segregation from non-Muslim majorities
Objectives	Links two objectives together: *al-taysir fi al –fatwa wa'l-tabshir fi al-da'wa*: *al-taysir fi al –fatwa* (facilitation in legal opinion) and *al-tabshir fi al-da'wa* (promoting Islam)	Stresses the importance of pure and total devotion to Islam and to *tawhid* (Unitarianism) and encourages literal interpretations

Methodology	An interest or a necessity could legitimize something that could be otherwise prohibited in order to accommodate manmade Western laws	May suspend the prohibited so that divine Islamic laws at the end overpower manmade Western norms and legislations
Application of Shar'ia for Minorities	Shar'ia needs adjustments in search for the most suitable applications Differentiation between *'ibadat* (rituals) and *mu'amalat* (social transactions)	No adjustments to Shar'ia, rather it must be strictly obeyed whatever the difficulties may be, and Muslims must not imitate infidels
Non-Muslims' considerations	Non-Muslims are the *dar al da'wa* (the abode of proselytizing) a mission field for Islam. and not to be considered *dar al-harb* (abode of war) Encourages participations that may promote the case of Islam	Non-Muslims are enemies, Muslims may deal justly with non-Muslims who do not fight against Muslims Emphasizes that it is permissible to live under the rule of infidels only if Muslims can manifest their religion and demonstrate animosity towards non-Muslims
Initialization of Minorities' presence	Favors the formation of Islamic organizations, etc. in the West	*Salafi* European ruling on minorities has not been institutionalized. *Salafi* are based mainly in Muslim majority countries
Future perspective	The gradual creation of "European Islam" or the transformation of Islam by the Western environment to create type of Islam which is at peace with modernity	Islam in Europe for the sake of *da'wa* even if leads to transplanted entities in conflict/at odds with modernity

Appendix 2

DEMOGRAPHIC INFORMATION

Demographic Information about Converts and Parents

Pseudonym	Birth Year	Age	Age at Conversion	Birth Country	Generation	Father Birth Country	Mother Birth Country
Lucía	1988	24	22	USA	2nd	Colombia	Colombia
Martina	1987	25	17	USA	2nd	Chile	Chile
Catalina	1985	27	20	USA	2nd	Puerto Rico	Puerto Rico
Simón	1988	24	19	USA	2.5	Virginia, US	Texas, US (Mexican American)

Religious Background, Occupation, and Education Level of the Converts

Pseudonym	Religious Background	Occupation before Islam	Current Occupation	Highest Level of Education	Education before Islam
Lucía	Catholic	Selling cars	Housewife	High School	High School
Martina	Baptist	Student	Program coordinator	BA in Religion	One year of college
Catalina	Nominal Catholic	Student	Housewife	Associate degree	First year of college
Simón	Episcopalian, et al	College Student	Resources Information Affairs	BA in Global Affairs	Mid College

Appendix 3

Summary of Conversion Motifs (Lofland and Skonovd 1981)

Pseudonym	Conversion Motifs	Degree of Social Pressure	Temporal Duration	Level of Affective Arousal	Affective Content	Belief-Participation Sequence
Martina	Intellectual	Low	1 year	Medium	Illumination	Belief-participation
Catalina	Affectional	Medium	6 months	High	Affection	Participation-belief
Simón	Experimental	Low	2 years	Low	Curiosity	Participation-belief
Lucía	Intellectual/ Affectional	None	6–8 months	Medium	Illumination/ Affection	Belief-participation

Appendix 4

Summary of the Findings of the 12 Categories

Categories	Martina
Agency: Individual vs. Institutional	Individual.
Role of the converts: more active vs. more passive	More active.
Life Course Agency (More or less influence of the individuals at important turning points in their own lives)	More life course agency (strategic decisions in life: studying and reading the Qur'an).
Contextual Factors (personal, cultural, social, and religious)	Personal, religious/social.
Conversion Motifs & Belief-Participation Sequence	Intellectual. Belief-participation.
Conversion Motives (Push Factors)	She was searching for truth; very interested in religion. Her questions were answered by imams and Muslim friends.
Reasons/Most Appealing Aspects of Islam (Pull factors)	Believed that the Qur'an was true and so had no choice but to act on that. Believed that God had communicated to her and to humanity and so she could not continue to be Christian. Prayer, community (Friday's services), and sermons. Emphasis on good deeds. For example, in Islam there is a greater emphasis on being aware of your own mortality and having this sort of acceptance that God can take you back at any moment. You have no guarantee that you will reach old age and should make every single moment count in terms of your good deeds while here on earth. That is the most profound thing that changed right after conversion. Cuartas/Martina 2012:7–8 Muslim friends and Internet.

Family Background & Structure: more structure vs. less structure; stable vs. unstable.	Less structure, stable family. Middle class. "She was very happy." Cuartas/Martina 2012:2 "Never tested the boundaries." She relied on the family support system. Parents were never really strict in the approach to parenting. She has one brother.
Previous Religious Commitment of the Converts (high vs. low)	She grew up Baptist. More participation (Sundays, Wednesdays, and VBS). Active with the Christian community only at church.
Parental Previous Religious Commitment (high vs. low)	"Very spiritual." "Family have a spiritual nature without rhetoric." Cuartas/Martina 2012:3. Less committed, just Sundays.
Contact with Muslims (more friends vs. less or no Muslim friends at all)	Met a Bengali Muslim girl at middle school.
Crises (experience or absence)	She had a crisis during senior year in high school. "I don't know if I want to elaborate on it too much." Cuartas/Martina 2012:17

Categories	Catalina
Agency: Individual vs. Institutional	Some degree of institutional agency by contact with her husband; a second-generation Hispanic Muslim.
Role of the converts: more active vs. more passive	More passive, quick conversion.
Life Course Agency (More or less influence of the individuals at important turning points in their own lives)	Less life course agency (focus on family and home, married a Muslim, raising Muslim children).
Contextual Factors (personal, cultural, social, and religious)	Social/cultural, personal. Everything is based on family.
Conversion Motifs & Belief-Participation Sequence	Affectional. Participation-belief.
Conversion Motives (Push Factors)	It was a convenient decision so that children can have Muslim parents. She wanted to be a good wife and a good mother. Her questions were answered by her husband. She wanted to maintain her personal and social values and Islam was a good fit for her.
Reasons/Most Appealing Aspects of Islam (Pull factors)	Emphasis on family. Questions were answered. "Islam was so simple, straight forward, it made sense, it was just clear, there was one God." Cuartas/Catalina 2012:7 "You can pray in the privacy of your home...no need to go to church." Cuartas/Catalina 2012:7
Family Background & Structure: more structure vs. less structure; stable vs. unstable.	Big and typical Puerto Rican family, close relationship with extended family. Middle class. Less structure, stable family. "She was happy." Cuartas/Catalina 2012:1 She has two sisters.

Previous Religious Commitment of the Converts (high vs. low)	She was a nominal Catholic.
	Less commitment.
	"We didn't go to church, just on Christmas and Easter." Cuartas/Catalina 2012:2
	Say prayers at night. Cuartas/Catalina 2012:3
	She considered herself inactive at church.
Parental Previous Religious Commitment (high vs. low)	Parents were nominal, less commitment.
	"Mother was more religious than the father." Cuartas/Catalina 2012:2
Contact with Muslims (more friends vs. less or no Muslim friends at all)	Her husband is a second-generation Hispanic Muslim.
	"He was very open about his religion." Cuartas/Catalina 2012:5
Crises (experience or absence)	No mention of crisis.

APPENDIX 4   221

Categories	Simón
Agency: Individual vs. Institutional	Institutional/individual.
Role of the converts: more active vs. more passive	More passive than active. Passive personality but very active role in making choices.
Life Course Agency (More or less influence of the individuals at important turning points in their own lives)	More life course agency (traveling, studying, relationships with Muslims).
Contextual Factors (personal, cultural, social, and religious)	Social/personal or Personal/social.
Conversion Motifs & Belief-Participation sequence	Experimental. Participation-belief.
Conversion Motives (Push Factors)	He was interested in and curious about Islam. He had a "show me" mentality and curiosity. Try new things. Influenced by friends but always active in his decisions. Level of comfort and acceptance. Structural availability and several contacts with Muslims in Saudi Arabia and Istanbul.
Reasons/Most Appealing Aspects of Islam (Pull factors)	He converted to Islam in Turkey & Istanbul in Dec 2007. Cuartas/Simón 2012:7. Sense of community and friendships. It was an "interesting" experience. He observed Muslims in UAE noticing integrity, taking care, conduct of students, brotherhood, Cuartas/Simón 2012:10. He practices Islam more privately than publicly.
Family Background & Structure: more structure vs. less structure; stable vs. unstable	Middle class, mother's family from Air Force, Father's profession is geology. Less structure, a lot of traveling. He had many diverse friends from other countries. He has one younger sister.

Previous Religious Commitment of the Converts (high vs. low)	Less commitment, public activism though. He considered himself "inactive."
	He grew up Episcopalian.
	He tried different religions, such as Buddhism and Hinduism.
	African-American Episcopalian church with grandparents.
	He also went to a Presbyterian church.
Parental Previous Religious Commitment (high vs. low)	Little commitment.
	Parents stopped going to church.
	He was influenced by grandparents in Texas.
Contact with Muslims (more friends vs. less or no Muslim friends at all)	More contacts with Muslims. Several contacts with Muslim friends and imams. Experience in the Middle East, Arabic course at Nova.
	English Muslim in Turkey encouraged him to perform the *Shahadah*.
	German Muslim gave him a Qur'an.
Crises (experience or absence)	He had several crises.
	His grandfather passed away while he was in high school.
	Another crisis was that he was frustrated because he was unable to exercise his talents musically and artistically. He went to a school to specialize in Science in Technology.

Categories	Lucía
Agency: Individual vs. Institutional	Individual.
Role of the Converts: more active vs. more passive	More active than passive.
Life Course Agency (More or less influence of the individuals at important turning points in their own lives)	A lower degree of life course agency than Martina. She was highly impacted by the decisions of her parents.
Contextual Factors (personal, cultural, social, and religious)	Personal, social, and religious. Very close interplay of social and religious factors.
Conversion Motifs & Belief-Participation Sequence	Intellectual/affectional.
Conversion Motives (Push Factors)	She contrasted Catholicism and Islam. She experienced dissatisfaction with the Catholic church (theology and doctrine). She was also disappointed with the pastor's lifestyle from the evangelical church. Cuartas/Lucía 2012:4. "My mother passed away when I was twelve and then there was the big gap between then and me having my son which led me to try to find more structure." Cuartas/Lucía 2012:2. After having her first son, she became more intentional about religion. She was very influenced by the sudden passing of her mother: Belief in Islam about Janna ...Going to heaven (paradise) at the feet of her mother. Cuartas/Lucía 2012:6.
Reasons/Most Appealing Aspects of Islam (Pull factors)	Islamic values. She liked the emphasis on one God, family, and the idea of seeing her mother in heaven- "Jannah." Cuartas/Lucía 2012:6. She wanted to give her children a religion (legacy). Getting together with the sisters. Islam is very strict—"you need to be a certain type of person" (following morals... example: getting drunk is fine in Catholicism.

Family Background & Structure: more structure vs. less structure; stable vs. unstable.	She grew up in a big family: she has nine sisters and one brother. Her mother did not really play her role as a mom. She was raised by her nannies, Cuartas/Lucía 2012:1.
	She went to live with her aunts when she was fifteen.
	No structure, unstable home. She experienced a lot of crises, including the passing of her parents.
Previous Religious Commitment of the Converts (high vs. low)	She grew up as nominal Roman Catholic.
	At the age of thirteen, she was forced by her aunts to be baptized.
	She was very antagonistic about the Catholic church.
	She went to Catholic church with her mom only during Easter or weddings.
	Her nannies were evangelical Christian.
	They invited her, so she went more often to an evangelical church during weekends to play the tambourine, Cuartas/Lucía 2012:2.
	After the passing of her mom, she participated in an evangelical church for eighteen months.
	She considered herself a devoted Catholic but did not follow rules.
	She was very active in the evangelical church. Later, she was disappointed about some things about the pastor, Cuartas/Lucía 2012:4.
Parental Previous Religious Commitment (high vs. low)	Parents were very nominal Catholics. Her mother went to church with her children only during Easter, weddings, etc.
Contact with Muslims (more friends vs. less or no Muslim friends at all)	A Colombian female Muslim friend introduced her to Islam.
Crises (experience or absence)	She had several crises:
	Her father was arrested when she was ten.
	Dramatic death of her mother when she was twelve, Cuartas/Lucía 2012:1. The lifestyle of her parents was difficult. Her mother was a heroin addict and her father was a drug lord, Cuartas/Lucía 2012:1.
	She had two sons when she was only seventeen and twenty years old (previous relationship).

Appendix 5

Variables Considered for Selected Cases

226   APPENDIX 5

Variables	María	Camila	Héctor	Martín
Agency of the Converts	Learned about the philosophy of Islam and the law system of Islam before she learned about what needed doing. Before pronouncing the *Shahadah*, she visited the mosque near her work regularly while she decided	Agency is involved because she often went during her process of learning. She met her husband through Islam and converted after she got married, though he had no influence over her decision	Regularly attended mosque for Friday meetings once he began to determine that he believed what Islam believed	Brother of his friend gave him all of the information that would be needed
Role of the Converts	More active than passive. Very involved in the process of learning about Islam. Took her fifteen years to convert, but she was the one who noticed the Muslims were different and proceeded to ask everybody questions. When the one family could not answer, she moved on to others that could answer	More active than passive. Studied Islam and the Bible at the same time so that she understood what it was that she was leaving when she decided to become a Muslim. Took an Islam class, bought a Qur'an, and learned that the Nation of Islam and Islam are not the same thing	More active than passive. Studied the history of the Bible and everything he could about Christianity to try and determine the reality of Jesus and who he is and what he did. He walked into a Muslim student meeting and began listening to discussions and meeting friends through those discussions	More passive than active. He himself did not really pursue his own conversion. He settled in with his friend and his friend's brother who had converted to Islam and kind of learned about it through him

Contextual Factors	Religion – She did not like the influence that her mother's family seemed to have on their church, because it influenced the way that she viewed Catholicism (despised the arrogance that she saw in that family) Social – like the above stated. She found the few Muslims that she could find and began talking to them and asking a lot of questions. Personal – I think that she had a lot of questions and because her father was a major influence in her life, he did a lot to help open her view of the world. Being Muslim has given her a level of comfort Cultural – I think that part of her wanted to be counter-cultural because of the influence of her father. Ultimately, she discovered that Islam had a major influence on Hispanic culture	Religion – stopped believing in God and became an atheist, which means that she had many spiritual questions that had her questioning what it is that she believed in. Social – strong interest in social justice issues and it was this interest that brought her into contact with the Nation of Islam and then into contact with Islam. Personal – World religion was her minor, so it was because she was interested in learning more about Islam that led her to taking the Islam class and buying the Qur'an so that she could begin to study it for herself. I think that for her, it brought her back to a lot of the questions that she had in the past. Cultural – Being Hispanic is something that is very important to her and even while she did her study, she made sure that she was able to find other Hispanics that were also Muslim	Religion – Had some disagreements with some of the Catholic beliefs and so wanted to do some study to discover the truth that can be seen. Social – Social justice issues motivated him and led him to experiencing friendships and conversations with people that were not just Christian but were of other religions as well. Personal – I think that he was bothered by the discrepancies that he noticed in Catholicism and in how the world treated Christianity in general (evidenced by his problems with Santa Claus being used at times of Christmas) Cultural – It fits into a lot of his Hispanic beliefs in the first place and so he finds no real tensions with his Hispanic background (especially because he finds that there is a respect for women)	Religion – He didn't like Catholicism and found it to be painful and a punishment when he was a child. Even though he tried finding a church later on, he kept coming upon the same problem Social – Settled him in to how he viewed the world (acceptance). Personal – his friend's brother kept giving him things to view and listen to. I think for the most part he just wanted to get the brother off his back and to a large degree, he did desire to change his life. He wanted to step away from the life that he once lived. Cultural – It gave him something to believe in and settle his issues with his culture

228   APPENDIX 5

Most appealing aspects about Islam	Islam is full/ holistic. I feel that it is a religion for every day, sense of justice. Importance of women. I feel I can be who I really am. p. 7	Scientific, intellectual approach of Islam. I was encouraged to ask questions. As a thinker, I appreciate it, p. 5	Tawhid in Arabic, unity of God, strict monotheism and social justice, p.8	That Jesus was just another prophet from God that was the main problem. I could never understand Trinity until I learned about Islam, p. 10.
Family background and structure	Grew up in Panama and each parent had children from a previous marriage. She is the only child of her parents. Normal childhood, but special in that her father opened her eyes to the world around her	Typical American upbringing, even though she was Latina. She comes from a close family in a middle-class background	Parents divorced when he was young, mother remarried when he was about 10 or 11. His mother was Catholic by conviction rather than by any real religious intentions. Father is agnostic. He was influenced more by his grandparents being very religious but admits to questioning things	Grew up in Bolivia. Parents divorced. Three brothers. Mother did not marry a man that treated him well, so unstable family structure
Socialization by Muslim friends/ imams	Introduced to Islam through friends of the family	Did not meet Latina Muslim friends but she did meet and know friends that were Muslims.	Built friendships in his quest to study other religions	His friend's brother
Factors that shapes Hispanic Catholic identity: migration, mobility, marginality, dysfunctionality, religious experience, etc.	Mother remained Catholic, but father became Episcopalian. Arrogance of mother's family influenced the way that she viewed Catholicism. Father (love of her life) was always a free thinker and bought her a Qur'an when he saw that she was interested. Lost her favorite nephew at 17 and then her father at 29. Grew up in Panama, but later immigrated to the US when older	Family were marginal Catholics who went to church only during the holidays. Mentioned that she and her sister fought the whole time in services that her mother stopped taking them	Grandparents are very religious. He enjoyed reading the Bible and studying it, but he also enjoyed reading Malcolm X's biography and determined to be more open to new things in college. He started the trend in his family of reading the story of Jesus during Christmas. He did not really feel any level of marginality or dysfunctionality or anything like that. Went to the University of Michigan. Did have a concern for his family in his process of converting.	Came to the US as an adult. Mother moved them a lot in his youth and he only stabilized when he went to college. Catholic as his culture rather than being something he really decided

APPENDIX 5   229

Significant pre and post-affiliation choices	Does not wear the hijab and sees no need to do so. She joined the interfaith discussions and became a leader in the mosque	Does not wear the hijab at work	To change the dynamic of how he dealt with his family. To have read the autobiography of Malcolm X and to go to his school's club fair to discover what sort of clubs he could join to learn about different religions	Did not change his clothing or grow his beard
Degree of tension between ethnicity, culture and religion	Finds no tension because of the influence of Islam on Spain	She does not see any tensions between them, but her culture is very important to her (in truth, I do believe that if she had not found other Hispanic Muslims, she might not have converted because she would have felt strange about it)	Finds no tension because of Islam's influence on Spain he does acknowledge, though that breaking into friendships can be a bit difficult between different ethnicities but that does not mean that there is not acceptance (the idea that sometimes, culture does not translate between cultures)	Feels that there is a major discord between his Hispanic culture and his Islamic beliefs
Significant choices post-affiliation (e.g., dress, dietary, relationships, etc.)	Does not wear the hijab. Has close male friends and is not a fan of gender separation. Involved in Interfaith. Teach classes about Islam	Does not wear the hijab at work. Did not change her name. Changed his interactions with his family to suit his new religion (i.e. Not hugging female members of his family)	Did not change his name. Does not care about the conversion/reversion argument. Involved in interfaith activities	Has not changed himself outwardly. Does not attend Friday prayers or read the Qur'an. Considers his instant change being about his prayer and believing that Islam is correct
Responses of parents and friends	Family had no problems. Only one aunt asked for reasoning. Some of her friends stopped having a friendship with her, but most had no issues	Confused, but supportive of her choice	Family showed some concern because they wondered what would change. Father is agnostic and was more concerned about the rules rather than the doctrine of Islam	Parents did not speak to him for months

	Muslim/ Latina/ Hispanic/ American	Muslim/ Latina/ Hispanic/ American	Muslim/ Puerto Rican/ American/ Latino	Hispanic/ Muslim/ American
Self-identification based on the demographic survey				
Values and beliefs before conversion (more emphasis vs. less emphasis)	No original sin, sense of community, sense of family, direct relationship with God, sense of responsibility to the world	Community and lack of hierarchy (rules against racism) giving to charity and social justice	Belief in one God without the Trinity, and dealing with social justice issues	Islam is about a way of life (living life through your actions)

Appendix 6

General Information about the Converts

Convert	Age	Generation	Current Occupation	Highest Level of Education
Lucía	24	2	Housewife	High School
Martina	25	2	Islamic Society of North America (ISNA); American Muslim Health Professionals- Muslim organization	BA in Religion
Catalina	27	2	Housewife	Associate Degree
Simón	24	2.5	Resources Information Affairs-American company	BA Global Affairs
Claudia	31	2	Information technology recruiter- American company	BS in Sociology
Teresa	23	1.5	Financial broker- American company/business owner	Associate Degree in Business
Vicente	31	2	Mechanical engineer/ martial arts at the masjid	Mechanical Engineering
Jaime	30	2	Software developer- American government	BS Information Technology
María	49	1	Public relations/Interfaith dialogue/Chaplain	College Degree
Camila	28	2	Health educator, Zumba instructor/ private company	BA in Sociology
Héctor	36	2	Youth Director Islamic Center	BA in History and Sociology; MA in Education
Martín	31	1	Lead repair technician- American company	4 years of Systems Engineering

Appendix 7

Summary of Levels of Commitment in Different Dimensions

Convert	Religious Activity	Level of Religious Commitment PRC 2011	Ritualistic Dimension (More or less commitment)					Devotional Dimension (More or less commitment)	
			Daily Prayers	Charity	Fasting	Pilgrimage to Mecca		Private Prayers	Consulting the Qur'an more often
María	More active	High	More	More	More	No		Less	Less
Héctor	More active	High	More	More	More	No		Less	Less
Vicente	More active	High	More	More	More	No		Less	Much More
Teresa	More active	High	More	More	More	No		Less	Less
Simón	More active	High	More.	More	More	No		Less	Less
Claudia	Less active	Moderate	Moderate	Moderate	More	Yes		More	More
Jaime	Less active	Moderate	Moderate.	Moderate	Less	No		More	Less
Martina	Less active	Moderate	Moderate	Moderate	More	No		More	More
Catalina	Less active	Low	Less	Less	More	Yes		More	Less
Camila	Less active	Low	Less	More	More	No		More	Less
Lucía	Less active	Very Low	Less	Less	Less	No		More	Much more.
Martín	Less active	Nominal	Less. He does not attend Friday Praye	Less	Less	No		More	Less

Bibliography

Abalos, David T. *Latinos in the United States: The Sacred and the Political.* Notre Dame: University of Notre Dame Press, 1986.
Abd-Allah, Umar F. *A Muslim in Victorian America: The Life of Alexander Russell Webb.* Oxford: Oxford University Press, 2006.
Abdo, Geneive. *Mecca and Main Street: Muslim Life in America After 9/11.* Oxford: Oxford University Press, 2006.
Abdullah, Omer bin. "Reflecting on Islam in America." *American Journal of Islamic Social Sciences* 19 (2002) 154–56.
Ahmed, Akbar. *Journey into America: The Challenge of Islam.* Washington D.C.: Brookings Institution Press, 2010.
Ahmed-Ghosh, Huma. "Ahmadi Women Reconciling Faith with Vulnerable Reality through Education." *Journal of International Women's Studies* 8 (2006) 36–51.
Akram, Susan M., and Kevin R. Johnson. "Race, Civil Rights, and Immigration Law after September 11, 2001: The Targeting of Arabs and Muslims." *New York University Annual Survey of American Law* 58 (2001) 295–356.
Alamillo, José M. "Bibliographic Essay on U.S. Latino/a History." https://www.nps.gov/parkhistory/resedu/ LatinoFinal.pdf.
Al-Azmeh, Aziz, and Effie Fokas, eds. *Islam in Europe: Diversity, Identity and Influence.* Cambridge: Cambridge University Press, 2007.
Alba, Richard, and Nancy Denton. "Old and New Landscapes of Diversity." In *Not Just Black and White: Historical and Contemporary Perspectives on Immigration, Race, and Ethnicity in the United States*, edited by Nancy Foner and George M. Fredrickson, 237–61. New York: Russell Sage Foundation, 2004.
Alba, Richard, and Victor Nee. "Rethinking Assimilation Theory for a New Era of Immigration." *International Migration Review* 31 (1997) 826–74.
Alba, Richard, et al. "The Changing Neighborhood Contexts of the Immigrant Metropolis." *Social Forces* 79 (2000) 587–621.
Allah, Wakeel. *In the Name of Allah, Vol. 1: A History of Clarence 13X and the Five Percenters.* Atlanta: A-Team, 2007.
Allensworth, Elaine M. "Earnings Mobility of First and '1.5' Generation Mexican-Origin Women and Men: A Comparison with US-born Mexican Americans and Non-Hispanic Whites." *International Migration Review* 31 (1997) 386–410.
Allievi, Stefano. "Pour Une Sociologie des Conversions: Lorsque des Européens Deviennent Musulmans." *Social Compass* 46 (1999) 283–300.
———. "The Shifting Significance of the Halal/Haram Frontier: Narratives on the Hijab and Other Issues." In *Women Embracing Islam: Gender and Conversion in*

the West, edited by Karin van Nieuwkerk, 120–49. Austin: University of Texas Press, 2006.
Al-Qaradawi, Yusuf. *The Lawful and the Prohibited in Islam*. Plainfield, NJ: Islamic, 1997.
Al-Shingiety, Abubaker. "The Muslim as the 'Other': Representation and Self-Image of the Muslims in North America." In *The Muslims of America*, edited by Yvonne Yazbeck Haddad, 53–61. New York: Oxford University Press, 1991.
Alston, Jon P. "Three Measures of Current Levels of Religiosity." *Journal for the Scientific Study of Religion* 14 (1975) 165–68.
Altemeyer, Bob. *Enemies of Freedom: Understanding Right-Wing Authoritarianism*. San Francisco: Jossey-Bass, 1988.
Althoff, Andrea. "Migration and the Transformation of Latino Religious Identities in the US." Lecture at Calvin College, Grand Rapids, MI. April 17, 2007. https://www.calvin.edu/henry/archives/lectures/althoff.pdf.
Ameli, Saied Reza. *Globalization and British-Muslim Identity*. London: Icas, 2002.
Ammerman, Nancy T. *Sacred Stories, Spiritual Tribes: Finding Religion in Everyday Life*. Oxford: Oxford University Press, 2014.
———. "Spiritual but Not Religious? Beyond Binary Choices in the Study of Religion." *Journal for the Scientific Study of Religion* 52 (2013) 258–78.
An-Na'im, Abdullah. *What Is an American Muslim?: Embracing Faith and Citizenship*. New York: Oxford University Press, 2014.
Anthias, Floya, and Nira Yuval-Davis. "Contextualizing Feminism: Gender, Ethnic and Class Divisions." *Feminist Review* 15 (1983) 62–75.
Anthony, Francis-Vincent, et al. "Religious Practice and Religious Socialization: Comparative Research among Christian, Muslim and Hindu Students in Tamilnadu, India." *Journal of Empirical Theology* 20 (2007) 100–28.
Aponte, Edwin D. *Santo!: Varieties of Latino/a Spirituality*. Maryknoll, NY: Orbis, 2012.
Aponte, Edwin D., and Miguel De La Torre. *Handbook of Latina/o Theologies*. St. Louis: Chalice, 2006.
Archer, Margaret. *Structure, Agency and the Internal Conversation*. Cambridge: Cambridge University Press, 2003.
Armstrong, Rose-Marie. "Turning to Islam: African-American Conversion Stories." *Christian Century* 120 (2003) 18–23.
Arrington, Carolyn. *Estevanico, Black Explorer in Spanish Texas*. 1st ed. Austin: Eakin, 1986.
Audi, Robert. *Rationality and Religious Commitment*. Oxford: Oxford University Press, 2011.
Avalos, Hector. *Introduction to the U.S. Latina and Latino Religious Experience*. Boston: Brill Academic, 2004.
Bader, Christopher, et al. *American Piety in the 21st Century: New Insights to the Depth and Complexity of Religion in the US*. Waco, TX: Baylor Institute for Studies of Religion, 2006.
Badran, Margot. "Feminism and Conversion: Comparing British, Dutch, and South African Life Stories." In *Women Embracing Islam: Gender and Conversion in the West*, edited by Karin van Nieuwkerk, 192–232. Austin: University of Texas Press, 2006.
Bagby, Ihsan A., *The American Mosque 2011: A National Portrait*. Washington DC: Council on American-Islamic Relations (CAIR), 2012.

———. "The American Mosque in Transition: Assimilation, Acculturation and Isolation." In *Muslims and the State in the Post-9/11 West*, edited by Erik Bleich, 120–37. Abingdon, UK: Routledge, 2013.

Bagby, Ihsan A., et al. *The Mosque in America: A National Portrait*. Washington DC: Council on American-Islamic Relations (CAIR), 2001.

Bagheri, Elham. "A Qualitative Investigation of Religion, Gender Role Beliefs, and Culture in the Lives of a Select Group of Muslim Men." PhD diss., University of Iowa, 2012.

Balch, Robert W., and David Taylor. "Seekers and Saucers." In *Conversion Careers: In and Out of the New Religions*, edited by James T. Richardson, 43–64. Beverly Hills: SAGE, 1977.

Barker, Irwin R., and Raymond F. Currie. "Do Converts Always Make the Most Committed Christians?" *Journal for the Scientific Study of Religion* 24 (1985) 305–13.

Barnard, Alan, and Jonathan Spencer. *Encyclopedia of Social and Cultural Anthropology*. London: Routledge, 1998.

Bartkowski, John P. "Religious Socialization among American Youth: How Faith Shapes Parents, Children, and Adolescents." In *The SAGE Handbook of the Sociology of Religion*, edited by James A. Beckford and Jay Demerath, 511–25. Los Angeles: Sage, 2007.

Beckford, James A. "Accounting for Conversion." *British Journal of Sociology* 29 (1978) 249–62.

———. "The Restoration of 'Power' to the Sociology of Religion." *Sociological Analysis* 44 (1983) 11–31.

Beito, David T., and Linda Royster Beito. *Black Maverick: T.R.M. Howard's Fight for Civil Rights and Economic Power*. Urbana: University of Illinois Press, 2009.

Bellinger, Larry. "A New Farrakhan? The Nation of Islam Leans Toward the Mainstream." *Sojourners* 31 (2002) 16–17.

Beniflah, Jake. "The Effects of Acculturation on the Cognitive Structure of Foreign-Born U.S. Hispanics." DBA thesis, Golden Gate University, 2011.

Berg, Herbert. *Elijah, Muhammad and Islam*. New York: New York University Press, 2009.

Bergad, Laird W., and Herbert S. Klein. *Hispanics in the United States: A Demographic, Social, and Economic History, 1980–2005*. Cambridge: Cambridge University Press, 2010.

Berger, Peter L. "The Desecularization of the World: A Global Overview." In *The Desecularization of the World: Resurgent Religion and World Politics*, edited by Peter L. Berger, 1–18. Washington D.C.: Ethics and Public Policy Center, 1999.

———. *Invitation to Sociology: A Humanistic Perspective*. New York: Anchor, 1963.

———. *The Sacred Canopy: Elements of a Sociological Theory of Religion*. New York: Anchor, 1969.

Berger, Peter L., and Thomas Luckmann. *The Social Construction of Reality: A Treatise in the Sociology of Knowledge*. Garden City, NY: Doubleday, 1966.

Bernard, H. Russell. *Research Methods in Anthropology: Qualitative and Quantitative Approaches*. 4th ed. Lanham, MD: AltaMira, 2006.

Beyer, Peter. *Religion and Globalization*. London: Sage, 1994.

Bilgrami, Akeel. "What is a Muslim? Fundamental Commitment and Cultural Identity." *Critical Inquiry* 18 (1992) 821–42.

Booth, Alan, and Ann C. Crouter, eds. *Does it Take a Village?: Community Effects on Children, Adolescents, and Families*. Mahwah, NJ: Psychology, 2001.

Bouhdiba, Abdelwahab, and M. Maruf Dawalibi. *The Different Aspects of Islamic Culture*. Paris: UNESCO, 1998.

Bourque, Nicole. "How Deborah Became Aisha: The Conversion Process and the Creation of Female Muslim Identity." In *Women Embracing Islam: Gender and Conversion in the West*, edited by Karin van Nieuwkerk, 233–49. Austin: University of Texas Press, 2006.

Bowen, John R. "Islamic Adaptations to Western Europe and North America: The Importance of Contrastive Analyses." *American Behavioral Scientist* 55 (2011) 1601–15.

Bowen, Patrick D. "Conversion to Islam in Colorado." MA thesis, University of Denver, 2009.

———. "Conversion to Islam in the United States: A Case Study in Denver, Colorado." *Intermountain West Journal of Religious Studies* 1 (2009) 41–64.

———. "Early U.S. Latina/o-African-American Muslim Connections: Paths to Conversion." *The Muslim World* 100 (2010) 390–413.

———. "The Latino American Da'wah Organization and the Latina/o Muslim Identity in the United States." *Journal of Race, Ethnicity and Religion* 1 (2010) 1–23.

———. "The Search for Islam: African-American Islamic Groups in NYC, 1904–1954." *The Muslim World* 102 (2011) 264–83.

Bowker, John. *The Cambridge Illustrated History of Religions*. Cambridge: Cambridge University Press, 2002.

Bréchon, Pierre. "Cross-National Comparisons of Individual Religiosity." In *The SAGE Handbook of the Sociology of Religion*, edited by James A. Beckford and Jay Demerath, 463–89. Los Angeles: Sage, 2007.

Bromley, David G., and Anson D. Shupe. "Just a Few Years Seem Like a Lifetime: A Role Theory Approach to Participation in Religious Movements." In *Research in Social Movements Conflicts and Change: A Research Annual*, edited by Louis Kriesberg, 159–85. Greenwich, CT: JAI, 1979.

Brown, Eric. "After the Ramadan Affair: New Trends in Islamism in the West." *Current Trends in Islamist Ideology* 2 (2005) 7–29.

Brunner, Rainer. "Forms of Muslim Self-Perception in European Islam." *Hagar* 6 (2005) 75–86.

Bryman, Alan. *Social Research Methods*. 3rd ed. Oxford: Oxford University Press, 2008.

Buckser, Andrew, and Stephen D. Glazier. *The Anthropology of Religious Conversion*. Lanham, MD: Rowman & Littlefield, 2003.

Buxant, Coralie, et al. "Free-Lance Spiritual Seekers: Self-Growth or Compensatory Motives?" *Mental Health: Religion & Culture* 13 (2010) 209–22.

Caballero, Chamion, et al. "Parenting 'Mixed' Children: Difference and Belonging in Mixed Race and Faith Families." Report, London South Bank University, 2008.

Cadaval, Olivia. "The Latino Community: Creating an Identity in the Nation's Capital." In *Urban Odyssey: A Multicultural History of the Nation's Capital*, edited by Francine Cary, 231–49. Washington, DC: Smithsonian, 2003.

Cafferty, Pastora San Juan, and William C. McCready. *Hispanics in the United States: A New Social Agenda*. New Brunswick, NJ: Transaction, 1985.

Camarillo, Albert. *Latinos in the United States: A Historical Bibliography*. Santa Barbara, CA: ABC-Clio, 1986.

Campo, Juan E. *Encyclopedia of Islam*. New York: Facts On File, 2009.
Capet, Race. "Created Equal: Slavery and America's Muslim Heritage." *Cross Currents* 60 (2010) 549–60.
Carson, Clayborne. *Malcolm X: The FBI File*. New York: Skyhorse, 2012.
Carvalho, Jean-Paul. "A Theory of the Islamic Revival" (working paper, Department of Economics, University of Oxford, 2009).
Cavalcanti, H.B. and Debra Schleef. "The Case for Secular Assimilation? The Latino Experience in Richmond, Virginia." *Journal for the Scientific Study of Religion* 44 (2005) 473–83.
Chapman, Thandeka K. "Foundations of Multicultural Education: Marcus Garvey and the United Negro Improvement Association." *The Journal of Negro Education* 73 (2004) 424–34.
Chaves, Mark. "Family Structure and Protestant Church Attendance: The Sociological Basis of Cohort and Age Effects." *Journal for the Scientific Study of Religion* 30 (1991) 501–14.
Chen, Carolyn, and Russell Jeung. *Sustaining Faith Traditions: Race, Ethnicity, and Religion among the Latino and Asian American Second Generation*. New York: New York University Press, 2012.
Ciment, James. "*Atlas of African-American History*. New York: Facts On File, 2007.
———. *Encyclopedia of American Immigration*. Armonk, NY: Sharpe, 2001.
Civil Rights Under Federal Programs: An Analysis of Title VI of the Civil Rights Act of 1964. Clearinghouse Publication No. 1. U.S. Washington, DC: Commission on Civil Rights, 1968.
Clark, John. "Cults." *JAMA* 242 (1979) 279–81.
Clayton, Richard R. "5-D or 1?" *Journal for the Scientific Study of Religion* 10 (1971) 37–40.
Clayton, Richard R., and James W. Gladden. "The Five Dimensions of Religiosity: Toward Demythologizing a Sacred Artifact." *Journal for the Scientific Study of Religion* 13 (1974) 135–43.
Cohen, Robin, et al. *Global Sociology*. London: Macmillan, 2000.
Comas-Diaz, Lillian. "Hispanics, Latinos, or Americanos: The Evolution of Identity." *Cultural Diversity and Ethnic Minority Psychology* 7 (2001) 115–20.
Cone, James H. "Demystifying Martin and Malcolm." *Theology Today* 51 (1994) 227–37.
Conway, Flo, and Jim Siegelman. *Snapping: America's Epidemic of Sudden Personality Change*. New York: Lippincott, 1978.
Cook-Huffman, Celia. "The Role of Identity in Conflict." In *Handbook of Conflict Analysis and Resolution*, edited by Dennis J. D. Sandole et al., 19–31. London: Taylor & Francis, 2008.
Corbett, Julia M. *Religion in America*. Upper Saddle River, NJ: Prentice Hall, 2001.
Cornwall, Marie. "The Influence of Three Agents of Religious Socialization: Family, Church, and Peers." In *The Religion and Family Connection: Social Science Perspectives*, edited by Darwin L. Thomas, 207–31. Provo, UT: Religious Studies Center, Brigham Young University, 1988.
———. "The Social Bases of Religion: A Study of Factors Influencing Religious Belief and Commitment." *Review of Religious Research* 29 (1987) 44–56.
Creswell, John W. *Qualitative Inquiry & Research Design: Choosing among Five Approaches*. Thousand Oaks, CA: Sage, 2007.

Cristian, Viviana. *Who are We?: Cultural Identity among Latino College Students in Northern Virginia*. PhD diss., The Catholic University of America, 2009.

Crockett, Lisa J. "Agency in the Life Course: Concepts and Processes." *Faculty Publications, Department of Psychology. Paper 361* (2002) 1–30. https://digitalcommons.unl.edu/cgi/viewcontent.cgi?article=1355&context=psychfacpub.

Curtis, Edward E, IV. "African-American Islamization Reconsidered: Black History Narratives and Muslim Identity." *Journal of the American Academy of Religion* 73 (2005) 659–84.

———. *Black Muslim Religion in the Nation of Islam, 1960–1975*. Chapel Hill: The University of North Carolina Press, 2006.

———. *The Columbia Sourcebook of Muslims in the United States*. New York: Columbia University Press, 2008.

———. *Encyclopedia of Muslim-American History*. New York: Infobase, 2010.

———. *Islam in Black America: Identity, Liberation, and Difference in African-American Islamic Thought*. Albany: State University of New York Press, 2002.

———. *Muslims in America: A Short History*. Oxford: Oxford University Press, 2009.

Dana, Karam, et al. "Mosques as American Institutions: Mosque Attendance, Religiosity and Integration into the Political System among American Muslims." *Religions* 2 (2011) 504–24.

David, Barbara, and John C. Turner. "Studies in Self-Categorization and Minority Conversion: Is Being a Member of the Out-Group an Advantage?" *British Journal of Social Psychology* 35 (1996) 179–99.

Dávila, Alberto, et al. "Income, Earnings and Poverty." In *Latinas/os in the United States: Changing the Face of América*, edited by Rodriguez Havidan et al., 181–98. New York: Springer, 2008.

Dawson, Lorne. "Self-Affirmation, Freedom, and Rationality: Theoretically Elaborating 'Active' Conversions." *Journal for the Scientific Study of Religion* 29 (1990) 141–63.

Day, Jennifer. *Population Projections of the United States by Age, Sex, Race, and Traditions, Diversity, and Popular Expressions*. Volume 1. Santa Barbara, CA: ABC-CLIO, 1996.

DeCaro, Louis A., Jr. *On the Side of My People: A Religious Life of Malcolm X*. New York: New York University Press, 1997.

De Jong, Gordon F., et al. "Dimensions of Religiosity Reconsidered: Evidence from a Cross-Cultural Study." *Social Forces* 54 (1976) 866–89.

De La Torre, Miguel A. *Hispanic American Religious Cultures*. 2 vols. Santa Barbara, CA: ABC-CLIO, 2009.

———. "Religion and Religiosity." In *Latinas/os in the United States: Changing the Face of América*, edited by Rodriguez Havidan et al., 225–40. New York: Springer, 2008.

De La Torre, Miguel A., and Edwin David Aponte. *Introducing Latino/a Theologies*. Maryknoll, NY: Orbis, 2001.

De La Torre, Miguel A., and Gaston Espinosa. *Rethinking Latino(a) Religion and Identity*. Cleveland: Pilgrim, 2006.

Del Pinal, Jorge. "Demographic Patterns: Age Structure, Fertility, Mortality, and Population Growth." In *Latinas/os in the United States: Changing the Face of América*, edited by Rodriguez Havidan et al., 57–71. New York: Springer, 2008.

De Vos, George. *Ethnic Pluralism: Conflict and Accommodation: The Role of Ethnicity in Social History*. Palo Alto, CA: Mayfield, 1995.

DeWalt, Kathleen M., and Billie R. DeWalt. *Participant Observation: A Guide for Fieldworkers*. 2nd ed. Lanham, MD: Altamira, 2011.
Diaz McConnell, Eileen. "U.S. Latinos/as and the American Dream: Diverse Populations and Unique Challenges in Housing." In *Latinas/os in the United States: Changing the Face of América*, edited by Rodriguez Havidan et al., 87–100. New York: Springer, 2008.
Díaz-Stevens, Ana María. "A Case for the Puerto Ricans, the Forgotten People." *Union Seminary Quarterly Review* 56 (2002) 178–86.
———. "Colonization Versus Immigration in the Integration and Identification of Hispanics in the United States." In *Religion and Immigration: Christian, Jewish, and Muslim Experiences in the United States*, edited by Yvonne Yazbeck Haddad et al., 61–84, Walnut Creek, CA: AltaMira, 2003.
———. "Ethnoreligious Identity as Locus for Dialogue Between Puerto Rican Catholics and American Jews." *Religious Education* 91 (1996) 473–79.
———. "Memory, Imagination, and Tradition: Diasporic Latino Spirituality." *Union Seminary Quarterly Review* 53 (1999) 1–18.
Díaz-Stevens, Ana María, and Anthony M. Stevens-Arroyo. *Recognizing the Latino Resurgence in U.S. Religion: The Emmaus Paradigm*. Boulder, CO: Westview, 1998.
Dickson, Rory. "The Tablighi Jama'at in Southwestern Ontario: Making Muslim Identities and Networks in Canadian Urban Spaces." *Contemporary Islam* 3 (2009) 99–112.
Downton, James V. "An Evolutionary Theory of Spiritual Conversion and Commitment: The Case of Divine Light Mission." *Journal for the Scientific Study of Religion* 19 (1980) 381–96.
———. *Sacred Journeys: The Conversion of Young Americans to Divine Light Mission*. New York: Columbia University Press, 1979.
Droogers, André, et al. "Conversion Careers and Culture Politics in Pentecostalism: A Comparative Study in Four Continents." Proposal submitted to the thematic program *The Future of the Religious Past* of the Netherlands Organization for Scientific Research (NWO), 2003.
Durkheim, Émile. *The Elementary Forms of the Religious Life*. London: Allen and Unwin, 1966.
Dutton, Yasin. "Conversion to Islam: The Qur'ranic Paradigm." In *Religious Conversion Contemporary Practices and* Controversies, edited by Christopher Lamb and M. Darroll Bryant, 151–65. New York: Cassell, 1999.
Earle, Jonathan. *The Routledge Atlas of African American History*. London: Routledge, 2000.
Eaton, Richard M. *Islamic History as Global History*. Washington, DC: American Historical Association, 1990.
Edgell, Penny. "A Cultural Sociology of Religion: New Directions." *Annual Review of Sociology* 38 (2012) 247–65.
Eid, Paul. "The Interplay between Ethnicity, Religion, and Gender among Second-Generation Christian and Muslim Arabs in Montreal." *Canadian Ethnic Studies* 35 (2003) 30–60.
El Azayem, Gamal Abou, and Zari Hedayat-Diba. "The Psychological Aspects of Islam: Basic Principles of Islam and Their Psychological Corollary." *The International Journal for the Psychology of Religion* 4 (1994) 41–50.

Elizondo, Virgilio P. *Galilean Journey: The Mexican-American Promise*. Maryknoll, NY: Orbis, 1983.

El Kacimi, Said. "Identity and Social Integration: Exploratory Study of Muslim Immigrants in the United States." PhD diss., Claremont Graduate University, 2008.

Ellis, Carl. "How Islam is Winning Black America." *Christianity Today* 44 (2000) 52–53.

Ellis, Mark, and Jamie Goodwin-White. "1.5 Generation Internal Migration in the US: Dispersion from States of Immigration?" *International Migration Review* 40 (2006) 899–926.

Emirbayer, Mustafa, and Ann Mische. "What Is Agency?" *American Journal of Sociology* 103 (1998) 962–1023.

Enroth, Ronald M. *Youth, Brainwashing, and the Extremist Cults*. Grand Rapids: Zondervan, 1977.

Erikson, Erik H. *Identity: Youth and Crisis*. New York: Norton, 1968.

Escarce, José J., et al. "The Health Status and Health Behaviors of Hispanics." In *Hispanics and the Future of America*, edited by Marta Tienda and Faith Mitchell, 362–409. Washington, DC: National Academies, 2006.

Espinosa, Gastón, et al. *Hispanic Churches in American Public Life: Summary of Findings*. Indianapolis: Institute for Latino Studies, University of Notre Dame, 2003.

———. *Latino Religions and Civic Activism in the United States*. Oxford: Oxford University Press, 2005.

Espiritu, Yen. *Asian American Panethnicity: Bridging Institutions and Identities*. Philadelphia: Temple University Press, 1992.

———. *Homebound: Filipino American Lives Across Cultures, Communities and Countries*. Berkeley: University of California Press, 2003.

Esposito, John. "Contemporary Islam." In *The Oxford History of Islam*, edited by John Esposito, 643–90. 1st ed. Oxford: Oxford University Press, 1999.

———. *The Islamic Threat: Myth or Reality?* New York: Oxford University Press, 1999.

———. *Islam: The Straight Path*. 4th ed. Oxford: Oxford University Press, 2011.

———. "Muslims in America or American Muslims." In *Muslims on the Americanization Path?*, edited by Yvonne Yazbeck Haddad and John L. Esposito, 3–18. Atlanta: Scholars, 1998.

———. *The Oxford Dictionary of Islam*. New York: Oxford University Press, 2003.

———. "Religious Life: Belief and Practice." In *Islam: The Straight Path*, edited by John Esposito, 85–140. 4th ed. Oxford: Oxford University Press, 2011.

———. *What Everyone Needs to Know about Islam*. 2nd ed. New York: Oxford University Press, 2011.

Esposito, John, et al. *World Religions Today*. 3rd ed. New York: Oxford University Press, 2008.

Evanzz, Karl. *The Judas Factor: The Plot to Kill Malcolm X*. New York: Thunder's Mouth, 1993.

———. *The Messenger: The Rise and Fall of Elijah Muhammad*. New York: Pantheon 1999.

Eve, Michael. "Integrating Via Networks: Foreigners and Others." *Ethnic & Racial Studies* 33 (2010) 1231–48.

Falkenberg, Steve. *Psychological Explanations of Religious Socialization: Religious Conversion*. Richmond, KY: Eastern Kentucky University Press, 2009.

Fernández-Shaw, Carlos M. *The Hispanic Presence in North America from 1492 to Today*. New York: Facts on File, 1991.

Fetterman, David M. *Ethnography: Step by Step.* Applied Social Research Methods Series Vol. 17. 51 vols. Thousand Oaks, CA: Sage, 1998.
Fichter, Joseph H. *Sociology.* 2nd ed. Chicago: University of Chicago Press, 1973.
Fields, A. Belden. "Human Rights and Social Movements (Review)." *Human Rights Quarterly* 32 (2010) 454–57.
Fisher, Humphrey J. "Conversion Reconsidered: Some Historical Aspects of Religious Conversion in Black Africa." *Africa* 43 (1973) 27–40.
Fishman, Shammai. *Fiqh al-Aqalliyyat: A Legal Theory for Muslim Minorities.* Washington DC: Hudson Institute, 2006.
Fitzpatrick, Joseph, and Lourdes Parker. "Hispanic-Americans in the Eastern United States." *The Annals of the American Academy of Political and Social Science* 454 (1981) 98–110.
Flores, Juan. *From Bomba to Hip-hop: Puerto Rican Culture and Latino Identity.* New York: Columbia University Press, 2000.
Foner, Nancy, and George M. Fredrickson. *Not Just Black and White: Historical and Contemporary Perspectives on Immigration, Race, and Ethnicity in the United States.* New York: Russell Sage Foundation, 2004.
Ford Foundation. *Hispanics: Needs and Impact of this Growing Population.* New York: Ford Foundation, Office of Reports, 1984.
Frey, William H., and Reynolds Farley. "Latino, Asian, and Black Segregation in US Metropolitan Areas: Are Multiethnic Metros Different?" *Demography* 33 (1996) 35–50.
Fry, Richard. "Hispanic College Enrollment Spikes, Narrowing Gaps with Other Groups." *Pew Hispanic Center* (August 2011). http://www.pewhispanic.org/2011/08/25/hispanic-college-enrollment-spikes-narrowing-gaps-with-other-groups.
Fuchs, Lawrence H., et al. "Comment: 'The Invention of Ethnicity': The Amen Corner [with Response]." *Journal of American Ethnic History* 12 (1992) 53–63.
Fullerton, J. Timothy, and Bruce Hunsberger. "A Unidimensional Measure of Christian Orthodoxy." *Journal for the Scientific Study of Religion* 21 (1982) 317–26.
Gallup Center for Muslim Studies. "Muslim Americans: Faith, Freedom, and the Future" *Abu Dhabi Gallup Center* (August 2011). https://news.gallup.com/poll/148931/presentation-muslim-americans-faith-freedom-future.aspx.
Gann, Lewis H., and Peter Duignan. *The Hispanics in the United States: A History.* Boulder, CO: Westview, 1986.
Gans, Herbert J. "Symbolic Ethnicity: The Future of Ethnic Groups and Cultures in America." *Ethnic and Racial Studies* 2 (1979) 1–20.
Gardell, Mattias. *In the Name of Elijah Muhammad: Louis Farrakhan and the Nation of Islam.* Durham: Duke University Press, 1996.
Garoogian, David, ed. *The Hispanic Databook: Detailed Statistics and Rankings on the Hispanic Population, including 23 ethnic backgrounds from Argentinian to Venezuelan, for 1,266 US counties and cities.* Amenia, NY: Grey House, 2004.
Gartrell, C. David, and Zane K. Shannon. "Contacts, Cognitions, and Conversion: A Rational Choice Approach." *Review of Religious Research* 27 (1985) 32–48.
Geertz, Clifford. *The Interpretation of Cultures.* Vol. 5019. New York: Basic, 1973.
GhaneaBassiri, Kambiz. *A History of Islam in America: From the New World to the New World Order.* New York: Cambridge University Press, 2010.
Ghatas, Ishak M. "Muslims in Europe or European Muslims?" Paper presented at the Oxford Centre for Mission Studies, Oxford, United Kingdom, November 19, 2013.

Gimenez, Martha E. "U.S. Ethnic Politics: Implications for Latin Americans." *Latin American Perspectives* 19 (1992) 7–17.
Glazer, Nathan, and Daniel P. Moynihan. *Beyond the Melting Pot: The Negroes, Puerto Ricans, Jews, Italians and Irish of New York City*. Cambridge: Massachusetts Institute of Technology Press, 1963.
Gleason, Philip. "Identifying Identity: A Semantic History." *The Journal of American History* 69 (1983) 910–31.
Glock, Charles Y., and Rodney Stark. *Religion and Society in Tension*. Chicago: Rand McNally, 1965.
Gomez, Michael A. *Black Crescent: The Experience and Legacy of African Muslims in the Americas*. Cambridge: Cambridge University Press, 2005.
———. "Muslims in Early America." *Journal of Southern History* 60 (1994) 671–710.
González, Juan. *Harvest of Empire: A History of Latinos in America*. New York: Penguin, 2000.
González, Justo L. *Mañana: Christian Theology from a Hispanic Perspective*. Nashville: Abingdon, 1990.
Goody, Jack. "Religion, Social Change, and the Sociology of Conversion. In *Changing Social Structure in Ghana*, edited by Jack Goody, 91–106. London: International African Institute, 1975.
Gooren, Henri. "Conversion Careers and Culture Politics in Pentecostalism: Time, Space and Mobility in Four Continents." *PentecoStudies* 9 (2010) 229–50.
———. "Conversion Careers in Latin America: Entering and Leaving Church among Pentecostals, Catholics, and Mormons." In *Conversion of a Continent*, edited by Timothy J. Steigenga and Edward L. Cleary, 52–71. New Brunswick, NJ: Rutgers University Press, 2007.
———. "Conversion Narratives." In *Studying Global Pentecostalism: Theories and Methods*, edited by Allan Anderson et al., 93–112. Berkeley: University of California Press, 2010.
———. "Reassessing Conventional Approaches to Conversion: Toward a New Synthesis." *Journal for the Scientific Study of Religion* 46 (2007) 337–53.
———. "Reconsidering Protestant Growth in Guatemala, 1900–1995." In *Holy Saints and Fiery Preachers: The Anthropology of Protestantism in Mexico and Central America*, edited by James W. Dow and Alan R. Sandstrom, 169–203. Westport, CT: Praeger, 2001.
———. *Religious Conversion and Disaffiliation: Tracing Patterns of Change in Faith Practices*. New York: Palgrave-Macmillan, 2010.
———. "The Religious Market Model and Conversion: Towards A New Approach." *Exchange* 35 (2006) 39–60.
Gordon, Milton. *Assimilation in American Life: The Role of Race, Religion, and National Origins*. New York: Oxford University Press, 1964.
Gracia, Jorge J. E. *Hispanic Latino Identity: A Philosophical Perspective*. Malden, MA: Blackwell, 2000.
———. *Latinos in America: Philosophy and Social Identity*. 1st ed. Malden, MA: Wiley-Blackwell, 2008.
Grant, Ken A. "Living in the Borderlands—An Identity and a Proposal." *Dialog* 49 (2010) 26–33.
Greeley, Andrew. "Defection among Hispanics." *America* 159 (1988) 61–62.
———. "Defection among Hispanics (Updated)." *America* 177 (1997) 12–13.

———. *The Denominational Society: A Sociological Approach to Religion in America*. Glenview, IL: Scott, Foresman, 1972.

Green, Tim. "Conversion in the Light of Identity Theories." In *Longing for Community: Church, Ummah, or Somewhere in Between?*, edited by David Greenlee, 41–52. Pasadena, CA: William Carey Library, 2013.

Greil, Arthur, and Lynn Davidman. "Religion and Identity." In *The SAGE Handbook of the Sociology of Religion*, edited by James A. Beckford and Jay Demerath, 549–65. Los Angeles: SAGE, 2007.

Greil, Arthur, and David R. Rudy. "What Have We Learned from Process Models of Conversion? An Examination of Ten Case Studies." *Sociological Focus* 17 (1984) 305–23.

Grusec, Joan E., and Paul D. Hastings. *Handbook of Socialization: Theory and Research*. New York: Guilford, 2008.

Gudykunst, William B., and Young Yun Kim. *Communicating with Strangers: An Approach to Intercultural Communication*. Boston: McGraw-Hill, 2003.

Guzik, Elysia. "The Search for Meaning: Information Seeking and Religious Conversion." *Advances in the Study of Information and Religion* 3 (2013) 1–24.

Haddad, Yvonne Yazbeck. "A Century of Islam in America." *Hamdard Islamicus* 21 (1998) 88–96.

———. "The Globalization of Islam." In *The Oxford History of Islam*, edited by John Esposito, 601–41. 1st ed. Oxford: Oxford University Press, 1999.

———. "The Quest for Peace in Submission: Reflections on the Journey of American Women Converts to Islam." In *Women Embracing Islam: Gender and Conversion in the West*, edited by Karin van Nieuwkerk, 19–47. Austin: University of Texas Press, 2006.

Haddad, Yvonne Yazbeck, and John L. Esposito. *Muslims on the Americanization Path?* New York: Oxford University Press, 2000.

Haddad, Yvonne Yazbeck, and Adair T. Lummis. *Islamic Values in the United States: A Comparative Study*. New York: Oxford University Press, 1987.

Haddad, Yvonne Yazbeck, and Jane I. Smith. *Mission to America: Five Islamic Sectarian Communities in North America*. Gainesville: University Press of Florida, 1993.

———. *Muslim Communities in North America*. Albany: State University of New York Press, 1994.

Haddad, Yvonne Yazbeck, et al. *The Contemporary Islamic Revival: A Critical Survey and Bibliography*. New York: Greenwood, 1991.

———. *Muslim Women in America: The Challenge of Islamic Identity Today*. Reprint Edition. New York: Oxford University Press, 2011.

———. *Religion and Immigration: Christian, Jewish, and Muslim Experiences in the United States*. Walnut Creek, CA: AltaMira, 2003.

Haley, Alex. *The Autobiography of Malcolm X*. New York: Ballantine, 1999.

Hall, Stuart. "The Question of Cultural Identity." In *Modernity and its Futures*, edited by Stuart Hall et al., 273–326. Cambridge, UK: Polity, 1992.

Hammond, Philip E. "Religion and the Persistence of Identity." *Journal for the Scientific Study of Religion* 27 (1988) 1–11.

Hammoudi, Abdellah. *A Season in Mecca: Narrative of a Pilgrimage*. New York: Hill and Wang, 2006.

Haniff, Ghulam M. "The Muslim Community in America: A Brief Profile." *Journal of Muslim Minority Affairs* 23 (2003) 303–31.

Harris, Marvin. "History and Significance of the Emic/Etic Distinction." *Annual Review of Anthropology* 5 (1976) 329–50.

Hashmi, Nadia. "From Ethnicity to Religion: The Shifting Identities of Young Muslims in Britain and France." PhD diss., European University Institute, 2003.

Hassan, Riaz. "On Being Religious: Patterns of Religious Commitment in Muslim Societies." *Muslim World* 97 (2007) 437–78.

Heelas, Paul, et al. *The Spiritual Revolution: Why Religion Is Giving Way to Spirituality.* Malden, MA: Blackwell, 2005.

Hefner, Robert W. "Of Faith and Commitment: Christian Conversion in Muslim Java." In *Conversion to Christianity: Historical and Anthropological Perspectives on a Great Transformation*, edited by Robert W. Hefner, 99–125. Berkeley: University of California Press, 1993.

Helbling, Marc. *Islamophobia in the West: Measuring and Explaining Individual Attitudes.* London: Routledge, 2012.

Herberg, Will. *Protestant-Catholic-Jew: An Essay in American Religious Sociology.* 2nd edition. Garden City, NY: Doubleday, 1960.

Hermansen, Marcia. "Keeping the Faith: Convert Muslim Mothers and the Transmission of Female Muslim Identity in the West." In *Women Embracing Islam: Gender and Conversion in the West*, edited by Karin van Nieuwkerk, 250–75. Austin: University of Texas Press, 2006.

———. "Roads to Mecca: Conversion Narratives of European and Euro-American Muslims." *Muslim World* 89 (1999) 56–89.

———. "Two-way Acculturation: Muslim Women in America between Individual Choice (Liminality) and Community Affiliation (Communitas)." In *The Muslims of America*, edited by Yvonne Yazbeck Haddad, 188–201. Oxford: Oxford University Press, 1991.

Hill, Peter C., and Ralph W. Hood, Jr. *Measures of Religiosity.* Birmingham, AL: Religious Education, 1999.

Hill, Peter C., and Kenneth I. Pargament. "Advances in the Conceptualization and Measurement of Religion and Spirituality: Implications for Physical and Mental Health Research." *American Psychologist* 58 (2003) 64–74.

Hill, Peter C., et al. "Conceptualizing Religion and Spirituality: Points of Commonality, Points of Departure." *Journal for the Theory of Social Behaviour* 30 (2000) 51–77.

Hill, Ronald Paul. "A Primer for Ethnographic Research with a Focus on Social Policy Issues Involving Consumer Behavior." In *Advances in Consumer Research Volume 20*, edited by Leigh McAlister and Michael L. Rothschild, 59–62. Provo, UT: Association for Consumer Research, 1993.

Hill, Samuel S., and Charles H. Lippy. *Encyclopedia of Religion in the South.* Macon, GA: Mercer University Press, 2005.

Himmelfarb, Harold S. "Agents of Religious Socialization among American Jews." *The Sociological Quarterly* 20 (1979) 477–94.

Hitlin, Steven, and Glen H. Elder. "Time, Self, and the Curiously Abstract Concept of Agency." *Sociological Theory* 25 (2007) 170–91.

Hitlin, Steven, and Charisse Long. "Agency as a Sociological Variable: A Preliminary Model of Individuals, Situations, and the Life Course." *Sociology Compass* 3 (2009) 137–60.

Hodge, David R. "Social Work and the House of Islam: Orienting Practitioners to the Beliefs and Values of Muslims in the United States." *Social Work* 50 (2005) 162–73.

Hopkins, Jack W. *Latin America: Perspectives on a Region.* New York: Holmes & Meier, 1998.
Houtepen, Anton. "Conversion and the Religious Market: A Theological Perspective." *Exchange* 35 (2006) 18–38.
Howard, Judith A. "Social Psychology of Identities." *Annual Review of Sociology* 26 (2000) 367–93.
Hunt, Larry L. "Religion and Secular Status among Hispanics in the United States: Catholicism and the Varieties of Hispanic Protestantism." *Social Science Quarterly (University of Texas Press)* 81 (2000) 344–62.
Iannaccone, Laurence R. "Voodoo Economics? Reviewing the Rational Choice Approach to Religion." *Journal for the Scientific Study of Religion* 34 (1995) 76–88.
Isaacs, Harold R. *Idols of the Tribe: Group Identity and Political Change.* New York: Harper Colophon, 1975.
Itzigsohn, José. "The Formation of Latino and Latina Panethnic Identities." In *Not Just Black and White: Historical and Contemporary Perspectives on Immigration, Race, and Ethnicity in the United States*, edited by Nancy Foner and George M. Fredrickson, 197–216. New York: Russell Sage Foundation, 2004.
James, William. *Principles of Psychology.* New York: Holt, Rinehart, and Winston, 1890.
Jindra, Ines W. "How Religious Content Matters in Conversion Narratives to Various Religious Groups." *Sociology of Religion* 72 (2011) 275–302.
———. *A New Model of Religious Conversion: Beyond Network Theory and Social Constructivism.* Leiden: Brill, 2014.
Jung, Jong Hyun. "Islamophobia? Religion, Contact with Muslims, and the Respect for Islam." *Review of Religious Research* 54 (2012) 113–26.
Kaba, Amadu J. "Religion, Immigration and Assimilation: The Hispanic/Latino Population in the United States and the North African/Muslim Population in Europe." *Asian Journal of Latin American Studies* 21 (2008) 69–102.
Kepel, Gilles. *Allah in the West: Islamic Movements in America and Europe.* Stanford: Stanford University Press, 1997.
Khan, Muqtedar. "Islam and the New Europe: The Remaking of a Civilisation." *Global Dialogue: Europe and its Muslims* 9 (2007) 19–32.
Kidder, Louise H., and Charles M. Judd. *Research Methods in Social Relations.* 5th ed. New York: Holt, Rinehart and Winston, 1986.
Kilbourne, Brock, and James T. Richardson. "Paradigm Conflict, Types of Conversion, and Conversion Theories." *Sociology of Religion* 50 (1988) 1–21.
Kim, Bryan S. K., et al. "Latino/a Values Scale: Development, Reliability, and Validity." *Measurement & Evaluation in Counseling & Development* 42 (2009) 71–91.
Kim, Kwang Chung, and Won Moo Hurh. "Beyond Assimilation and Pluralism: Syncretic Sociocultural Adaptation of Korean Immigrants in the US." *Ethnic and Racial Studies* 16 (1993) 696–713.
King, Morton B. "Measuring the Religious Variable: Nine Proposed Dimensions." *Journal for the Scientific Study of Religion* 6 (1967) 173–90.
King, Morton B., and Richard A. Hunt. "Measuring the Religious Variable: Amended Findings." *Journal for the Scientific Study of Religion* (1969) 321–23.
———. "Measuring the Religious Variable: Final Comment." *Journal for the Scientific Study of Religion* (1990) 531–35.
———. "Measuring the Religious Variable: National Replication." *Journal for the Scientific Study of Religion* 14 (1975) 13–22.

---. "Measuring the Religious Variable: Replication." *Journal for the Scientific Study of Religion* 11 (1972) 107–17.
King, Valarie. "The Influence of Religion on Fathers' Relationships with Their Children." *Journal of Marriage and Family* 65 (2003) 382–95.
King, Yesenia. "Latina Muslims: In the Borderlands." MA thesis, California State University, 2009.
Klein, Herbert S. *The Atlantic Slave Trade: New Approaches to the Americas.* 2nd ed. Cambridge: Cambridge University Press, 2010.
Kose, Ali, and Kate Miriam Loewenthal. "Conversion Motifs among British Converts to Islam." *International Journal for the Psychology of Religion* 10 (2000) 101–10.
Köszegi, Michael A., and J. Gordon Melton. *Islam in North America: A Sourcebook.* New York: Garland, 1992.
Kraft, Kathryn. "Faith Is Lived Out in Community: Questions of New Community for Arab Muslims Who Have Embraced a Christian Faith." *St. Francis Magazine* 6 (2010) 954–82.
---. "Relationships, Emotion, Doctrine, Intellect—and All That Follows." In *Longing for Community: Church, Ummah, or Somewhere in Between?*, edited by David Greenlee, 11–18. Pasadena, CA: William Carey Library, 2013.
---. *Searching for Heaven in the Real World: A Sociological Discussion of Conversion in the Arab World.* Oxford: Regnum, 2012.
Kramp, Mary K. "Exploring Life and Experience through Narrative Inquiry." In *Foundations for Research Methods of Inquiry in Education and the Social Sciences*, edited by Kathleen B. deMarrais and Stephen D. Lapan, 1–21. Mahwah, NJ: Erlbaum, 2004.
Krauss, Steven Eric, et al. "The Muslim Religiosity-Personality Measurement Inventory (MRPI)'s Religiosity Measurement Model. Towards Filling the Gaps in Religiosity Research on Muslims." *Pertanika Journal of Social Sciences & Humanities* 13 (2005) 131–45.
---. "Religious Socialization among Malaysian Muslim Adolescents: A Family Structure Comparison." *Review of Religious Research* 54 (2012) 499–518.
Kuburic, Zorica, and Srdan Sremac. "Conversion and its Context: Toward Human Divinity." *Politics & Religion Journal* 4 (2010) 317–20.
Laderman, Gary, et al. *Religion and American Cultures: An Encyclopedia of Traditions, Diversity, and Popular Expressions.* Vol. 1. 3 vols. Santa Barbara, CA: ABC-CLIO, 2003.
Lakhdar, Mounia, et al. "Research: Conversion to Islam among French Adolescents and Adults: A Systematic Inventory of Motives." *International Journal for the Psychology of Religion* 17 (2007) 1–15.
Lapidus, Ira M. *A History of Islamic Societies.* Cambridge: Cambridge University Press, 2002.
Laurence, Jonathan, and Justin Vaïsse. *Integrating Islam: Political and Religious Challenges in Contemporary France.* Washington, DC: Brookings Institution, 2006.
Lecesse, Francesco A. "Islam, Sufism, and the Postmodern in the Religious Melting Pot." In *Routledge Handbook of Islam in the West*, edited by Roberto Tottoli, 411–54. New York: Routledge, 2014.
Leon, Ana M. "Latino Cultural Values in the United States: Understanding Their Impact on Toddler Social and Emotional Development." *International Journal of Interdisciplinary Social Sciences* 4 (2010) 13–25.

Leonard, Karen I. *Muslims in the United States: The State of Research*. New York: Russell Sage Foundation, 2003.
Lester Murad, Nora. "The Politics of Mothering in a 'Mixed' Family: An Autoethnographic Exploration." *Identities: Global Studies in Culture and Power* 12 (2005) 479–503.
Levin, Kevin M. "Until Every Negro Has Been Slaughtered: Did Southerners See the Battle of the Crater as a Slave Rebellion?" *Civil War Times* 49 (2010) 32–37.
Lichter, Daniel T., et al. "Immigration and Intermarriage among Hispanics: Crossing Racial and Generational Boundaries." *Sociological Forum* 26 (2011) 241–64.
Lieblich, Amia, et al. "The Holistic-Content Perspective." In *Narrative Research: Reading, Analysis, and Interpretation,* edited by Amia Lieblich et al., 62–87. London: Sage, 1998.
———. *Narrative Research: Reading, Analysis, and Interpretation*. London: Sage, 1998.
Lin, Nan, and Mary Dumin. "Access to Occupations through Social Ties." *Social Networks* 8 (1986) 365–85.
Lincoln, C. Eric. *The Black Muslims in America*. 3rd ed. Grand Rapids: Eerdmans, 1994.
Lippy, Charles H. *Faith in America: Changes, Challenges, New Directions*. Vol 1. 3 vols. Westport, CT: Praeger, 2006.
Loewenthal, Kate. "Marriage and Religious Commitment: The Case of Chabad Chasidic Women." *Journal of Contemporary Religion* 5 (1988) 8–10.
Lofland, John. "Becoming a World-Saver, Revisited." *American Behavioral Scientist* 20 (1977) 805–18.
Lofland, John, and Norman Skonovd. "Conversion Motifs." *Journal for the Scientific Study of Religion* 20 (1981) 373–85.
Lofland, John, and Rodney Stark. "Becoming a World-Saver: A Theory of Conversion to a Deviant Perspective." *American Sociological Review* 30 (1965) 862–75.
Long, Norman. *Development Sociology: Actor Perspectives*. London: Routledge, 2001.
Long, Theodore E., and Jeffery K. Hadden. "Religious Conversion and the Concept of Socialization: Integrating the Brainwashing and Drift Models." *Journal for the Scientific Study of Religion* 22 (1983) 1–14.
Lynch, Frederick R. "Toward a Theory of Conversion and Commitment to the Occult." In *Conversion Careers: In and Out of the New Religions,* edited by James T. Richardson, 91–112. Beverly Hills: SAGE, 1977.
Magida, Arthur J. *Prophet of Rage: A Life of Louis Farrakhan and His Nation*. New York: HarperCollins, 1996.
Mahoney, Annette. "Religion in Families, 1999–2009: A Relational Spirituality Framework." *Journal of Marriage and Family* 72 (2010) 805–27.
Maldonado, Jorge. "Immigration and the Family: The Dynamics and Processes of Hispanic Immigrant Families." *Journal of Latin American Theology* 3 (2008) 39–53.
Malony, H. Newton, and Samuel Southard. *Handbook of Religious Conversion*. Birmingham, AL: Religious Education, 1992.
Manstead, Antony S.R., and Miles Hewstone. *The Blackwell Encyclopedia of Social Psychology*. Malden, MA: Blackwell, 1996.
Marable, Manning. *Malcolm X: A Life of Reinvention*. New York: Viking, 2011.
March, Andrew F. "Sources of Moral Obligation to Non-Muslims in the 'Jurisprudence of Muslim Minorities' (Fiqh Al- Aqalliyyat) Discourse." *Islamic Law and Society* 16 (2009) 34–94.

Marín, Gerardo, and Barabara V. Marín. *Research with Hispanic Populations: Applied Social Research Method Series.* Vol. 23. 51 vols. London: Sage, 1991.

Marsh, Clifton E. *From Black Muslims to Muslims: The Resurrection, Transformation, and Change of the Lost-Found Nation of Islam in America, 1930–1995.* 2nd ed. Lanham, MD: Scarecrow, 1996.

Martínez, Juan F. *Walk with the People: Latino Ministry in the United States.* Nashville: Abingdon, 2008.

Martínez-Vázquez, Hjamil A. "Alianza Islámica." In *Encyclopedia of Muslim-American History,* edited by Edward E. Curtis IV, 48. New York: Facts On File, 2010.

———. "Finding Enlightenment: US Latina/o's Journey to Islam." *The Journal of Latino-Latin American Studies* 3 (2008) 59–73.

———. *Latina/o y Musulmán: The Construction of Latina/o Identity among Latina/o Muslims in the United States.* Eugene, OR: Pickwick, 2010.

———. "Latino American Dawah Organization." In *Encyclopedia of Muslim-American History,* edited by Edward E. Curtis IV, 365. New York: Facts On File, 2010.

———. "PIEDAD." In *Encyclopedia of Muslim-American History,* edited by Edward E. Curtis IV, 453. New York: Facts On File, 2010.

Maslim, Audrey A., and Jeffery P. Bjorck. "Reasons for Conversion to Islam Among Women in the United States." *Psychology of Religion and Spirituality* 1 (2009) 97–111.

Massey, Douglas S. "Latinos, Poverty, and the Underclass: A New Agenda for Research." *Hispanic Journal of Behavioral Sciences* 15 (1993) 449–75.

Matza, David. *Delinquency and Drift.* New York: Wiley, 1964.

Mazumdar, Shampa, and Sanjoy Mazumdar. "The Articulation of Religion in Domestic Space: Rituals in the Immigrant Muslim Home." *Journal of Ritual Studies* 18 (2004) 74–85.

M'Bow, Amadou Mahtar, and Ali Kettani. *Islam and Muslims in the American Continent.* Beirut: Center of Historical, Economical and Social Studies, 2001.

McCaffrey, Paul. *Hispanic Americans.* Bronx: Wilson, 2007.

McCloud, Aminah Beverly. *African American Islam.* New York: Routledge, 1995.

McGuire, Meredith. *Religion: The Social Context.* 3rd ed. Belmont, CA: Wadsworth, 1992.

Mead, George Herbert, and Charles W. Morris. *Mind, Self & Society from the Standpoint of a Social Behaviorist.* Chicago: University of Chicago Press, 1934.

Medina, José. "Hispanic/Latino Identity: A Philosophical Perspective (Review)." *Journal of Speculative Philosophy* 17 (2003) 139–41.

———. "Women: The U.S. Latina Religious Experience." In *Introduction to the U.S. Latina and Latino Religious Experience,* edited by Hector Avalos, 280–300. Danvers, MA: Brill Academic, 2004.

Melville, Margarita B. "Hispanics: Race, Class, or Ethnicity?" *Journal of Ethnic Studies* 16 (1988) 67–83.

Migration Policy Institute. "United States: Inflow of Foreign-Born Population by Country of Birth." *MPI,* 2007. http://www.migrationinformation.org/datahub/countrydata/country.cfm.

Miles, Matthew B., and A. Michael Huberman. *Qualitative Data Analysis: An Expanded Sourcebook.* 2nd ed. Thousand Oaks, CA: Sage, 1994.

Mol, Hans. *Identity and the Sacred: A Sketch for a New Social-Scientific Theory of Religion.* Oxford: Blackwell, 1976.

Moore, Joan W., and Harry Pachon. *Hispanics in the United States*. Englewood Cliffs, NJ: Prentice-Hall, 1985.

Moore, Kathleen. "American Muslim Associational Life from 1950 to the Present." In *Routledge Handbook of Islam in the West*, edited by Roberto Tottoli, 137–53. New York: Routledge, 2014.

Morales, Ed. *Living in Spanglish: The Search for Latino Identity in America*. New York: LA Weekly, 2002.

Morawska, Ewa. "The Sociology and Historiography of Immigration." In *Immigration Reconsidered: History, Sociology, and Politics*, edited by Virginia Yans-McLaughlin, 187–238. New York: Oxford University Press, 1990.

Morris, Aldon D. *The Origins of the Civil Rights Movement: Black Communities Organizing for Change*. New York: Free Press, 1984.

Morton, Jeffery Jay. "Embracing Islam: Conversion Narratives of American Muslims Living in Southern California." PhD diss., School of Intercultural Studies, Biola University, 2003.

Muhammad, Elijah. *Message to the Blackman in America*. Phoenix: Secretarius MEMPS Ministries, 1973.

Nabhan-Warren, Kristy. "Hispanics and Religion in America." https://oxfordre.com/religion/view/10.1093/acrefore/9780199340378.001.0001/acrefore-9780199340378-e-79.

Nasr, Seyyed Vali R. "Democracy and Islamic Revivalism." *Political Science Quarterly* 110 (1995) 261–85.

Natambu, Kofi. *The Life and Work of Malcolm X*. Indianapolis: Alpha, 2002.

National Center for Education Statistics. "The Condition of Education." Washington DC: U.S. Government Printing Office, 2003.

National Commission on Terrorist Attacks upon the United States, et al. *The 9/11 Commission Report*. Washington DC: US Government Printing Office, 2004.

Neusner, Jacob. *World Religions in America: An Introduction*. Louisville: Westminster John Knox, 2009.

Nock, Arthur D. *Conversion*. Oxford: Oxford University Press, 1933.

Norris, Rebecca S. "Converting to What? Embodied Culture and the Adoption of New Beliefs." In *The Anthropology of Religious Conversion*, edited by Andrew Buckser and Stephen D. Glazier, 171–81. Oxford: Rowman and Littlefield, 2003.

Novas, Himilce. *Everything You Need to Know about Latino History*. New York: Plume, 2007.

Nyang, Sulayman. *Islam in the United States of America*. Chicago: ABC International Group, 1999.

Orlov, Ann, and Reed Ueda. "Central and South Americans." In *Harvard Encyclopedia of American Ethnic Groups*, edited by Philip Gleason et al., 210–17. Cambridge: Belknap Press of Harvard University, 1980.

Ozorak, Elizabeth Weiss. "Social and Cognitive Influences on the Development of Religious Beliefs and Commitment in Adolescence." *Journal for the Scientific Study of Religion* 28 (1989) 448–63.

Ozyurt, Saba Senses. "The Selective Integration of Muslim Immigrant Women in the United States: Explaining Islam's Paradoxical Impact." *Journal of Ethnic & Migration Studies* 39 (2013) 1617–37.

Paden, William E. *Religious Worlds: The Comparative Study of Religion*. Boston: Beacon, 1994.

Padilla, Felix. *Latino Ethnic Consciousness*. Notre Dame: University of Notre Dame, 1985.
Paloutzian, Raymond F., et al. "Religious Conversion and Personality Change." *Journal of Personality* 67 (1999) 1047–79.
Pantoja, Segundo. *Religion and Education among Latinos in New York City*. Leiden: Brill, 2005.
Paredes, Mario J. "La Presencia Hispana en los Estados Unidos (Spanish)." *Humanitas* 16 (2011) 320–25.
Park, Robert Ezra. *Race and Culture*. Glencoe, IL: Free Press, 1950.
Patton, Michael Quinn. *Qualitative Research & Evaluation Methods*. 3rd ed. Thousand Oaks, CA: Sage, 2002.
Peek, Lori. "Becoming Muslim: The Development of a Religious Identity." *Sociology of Religion* 66 (2005) 215–42.
Pellitero, Ramiro. "Los 'Hispanics' o 'Latinos' de los Estados Unidos: Su Realidad Teológica y Su Proyección Sobre la Sociedad Norteamericana." *Scripta Theologica* 34 (2002) 329–69.
Pement, Eric. "Louis Farrakhan and the Nation of Islam: Striking a Responsive Chord in the Black Community." *Christian Research Journal* 18 (1996) 6–7, 44.
Perea, Stan, and Cheryl A. Smith. *The New America: The America of the Moo-shoo Burrito*. 1st ed. Denver: His Ministries, 2004.
Perl, Paul, et al. "What Proportion of Adult Hispanics Are Catholic? A Review of Survey Data and Methodology." *Journal for the Scientific Study of Religion* 45 (2006) 419–36.
Perry, Bruce. *Malcolm: The Life of a Man Who Changed Black America*. Barrytown, NY: Station Hill, 1991.
Pew Forum on Religion & Public Life. "U.S. Religious Landscape Survey." http://religions.pewforum.org/pdf/report-religious-landscape-study-full.pdf.
Pew Hispanic Center. "Changing Faiths: Latinos and the Transformation of American Religion." http://pewhispanic.org/reports/report.php?ReportID=75.
———. "Characteristics of the 60 Largest Metropolitan Areas by Hispanic Population." http://www.pewhispanic.org/files/2012/09/Top_10_Metro_Area_Findings.pdf.
———. "Generational Differences." http://www.pewhispanic.org/files/2011/10/13.pdf.
———. "Hispanic Student Enrollments Reach New Highs in 2011." http://www.pewhispanic.org/files/2012/08/Hispanic-Student-Enrollments-Reach-New-Highs-in-2011_FINAL.pdf.
———. "The Rise of the Second Generation: Changing Patterns in Hispanic Population Growth." http://www.pewhispanic.org/2003/10/14/the-rise-of-the-second-generation.
———. "The 10 Largest Hispanic Origin Groups." http://www.pewhispanic.org/files/2012/06/The-10-Largest-Hispanic-Origin-Groups.pdf.
———. "U.S. Hispanic Country-of-Origin Counts for Nation, Top 30 Metropolitan Areas." http://pewhispanic.org/files/reports/142.pdf.
———. "U.S. Population Projections: 2005–2050." http://pewhispanic.org/reports/report.php?ReportID=85.
———. "When Labels Don't Fit: Hispanics and Their Views of Identity." http://www.pewhispanic.org/2012/04/04/when-labels-dont-fit-hispanics-and-their-views-of-identity.

Pew Research Center. "America's Changing Religious Landscape." Washington D.C., (May 2015). https://www.pewforum.org/2015/05/12/americas-changing-religious-landscape/.

———. "Muslim Americans: Middle Class and Mostly Mainstream." https://www.pewresearch.org/2007/05/22/muslim-americans-middle-class-and-mostly-mainstream/.

———. "Muslim Americans: No Sign of Growth in Alienation or Support for Extremism." http://www.people-press.org/files/legacypdf/Muslim%20American%20Report%202010-02-12%20fix.pdf.

———. "The Shifting Religious Identity of Latinos in the United States." http://www.pewforum.org/2014/05/07/the-shifting-religious-identity-of-latinos-in-the-united-states/.

Pfeifer, Samuel, and Ursula Waelty. "Psychopathology and Religious Commitment—A Controlled Study." *Psychopathology* 28 (1995) 70–77.

Polkinghorne, Donald. "Narrative Configuration in Qualitative Analysis." *International Journal of Qualitative Studies in Education* 8 (1995) 5–23.

Portes, Alejandro, and Dag MacLeod. "What Shall I Call Myself?: Hispanic Identity Formation in the Second Generation." *Ethnic and Racial Studies* 19 (1996) 523–47.

Portes, Alejandro, and Rubén G. Rumbaut. *Immigrant America: A Portrait*. 3rd ed. Berkeley: University of California Press, 2006.

Portes, Alejandro, and Min Zhou. "The New Second Generation: Segmented Assimilation and its Variants." *The Annals of the American Academy of Political and Social Science* 530 (1993) 74–96.

Poston, Larry. *Islamic Da'wah in the West: Muslim Missionary Activity and the Dynamics of Conversion to Islam*. New York: Oxford University Press, 1992.

Prevette, Bill. *Child, Church and Compassion: Towards Child Theology in Romania*. Oxford: Regnum, 2012.

Rahim, Abdur. *The Principles of Muhammadan Jurisprudence According to the Hanafi, Maliki, Shafi'i and Hanbali Schools*. Westport, CT: Hyperion, 1981.

Rahman, Fazlur. *Islam & Modernity: Transformation of an Intellectual Tradition*. Chicago: University of Chicago Press, 1982.

———. *Major Themes of the Qur'an*. Chicago: University of Chicago Press, 2009.

Rahnama, Ali. *Pioneers of Islamic Revival*. London: Zed, 1994.

Ramakrishnan, S. Karthick. "Second-Generation Immigrants? The '2.5 Generation' in the United States." *Social Science Quarterly (Blackwell Publishing Limited)* 85 (2004) 380–99.

Rambo, Lewis. "Theories of Conversion: Understanding and Interpreting Religious Change." *Social Compass* 46 (1999) 259–71.

———. *Understanding Religious Conversion*. 2nd ed. New Haven: Yale University Press, 1993.

Ramirez, Margaret. "New Islamic Movement Seeks Latino Converts." *Los Angeles Times*, March 15, 1999. https://www.latimes.com/archives/la-xpm-1999-mar-15-me-17467-story.html.

Read, Jen'nan Ghazal, and John P. Bartkowski. "To Veil or Not to Veil? A Case Study of Identity Negotiation among Muslim Women in Austin, Texas." *Gender & Society* 14 (2000) 395–417.

Richardson, James T. "The Active vs. Passive Convert: Paradigm Conflict in Conversion/Recruitment Research." *Journal of the Scientific Study of Religion* 24 (1985) 163–79.

———. *Conversion Careers: In and Out of the New Religions*. Contemporary Social Science Issues 47. Beverly Hills: Sage, 1978.
Richardson, James T., and Mary Stewart. "Conversion Process Models and the Jesus Movement." In *Conversion Careers: In and Out of the New Religions*, edited by James T. Richardson, 24–42. Beverly Hills: SAGE, 1977.
Richardson, James T., et al. "Conversion to Fundamentalism." *Society* 15 (1978) 46–52. https://doi.org/10.1007/BF02694711.
Rickford, Russell John. *Betty Shabazz: A Remarkable Story of Survival and Faith Before and After Malcolm X*. Naperville, IL: Sourcebooks, 2003.
Riessman, Catherine Kohler. *Narrative Methods for the Human Sciences*. Los Angeles: Sage, 2008.
Rinderle, Susana, and Danielle Montoya. "Hispanic/Latino Identity Labels: An Examination of Cultural Values and Personal Experiences." *Howard Journal of Communications* 19 (2008) 144–64.
Ritzer, George. *Blackwell Encyclopedia of Sociology*. Malden, MA: Blackwell, 2007.
Robbins, Thomas. "Constructing Cultist 'Mind Control.'" *Sociology of Religion* 45 (1984) 241–56.
Rodriguez, Clara. *Changing Race: Latinos, the Census and the History of Ethnicity*. New York: New York University Press, 2000.
Rodríguez, Havidan M., et al. *Latinas/os in the United States: Changing the Face of América*. New York: Springer, 2008.
Roll, Samuel, and Marc Irwin. *The Invisible Border: Latinos in America*. Boston: Intercultural, 2008.
Roof, Wade Clark. "Religion and Spirituality." In *Handbook of the Sociology of Religion*, edited by Michele Dillon, 137–50. Cambridge: Cambridge University Press, 2003.
Roof, Wade Clark, and Bruce Greer. *A Generation of Seekers: The Spiritual Journeys of the Baby Boom Generation*. San Francisco: Harper San Francisco, 1993.
Roof, Wade Clark, and Christel Manning. "Cultural Conflicts and Identity: Second-Generation Hispanic Catholics in the United States." *Social Compass* 41 (1994) 171–84.
Rounds, John C. "Curing What Ails Them: Individual Circumstances and Religious Choice among Zulu-Speakers in Durban, South Africa." *Africa* 52 (1982) 77–89.
Rouse, Roger. "Making Sense of Settlement: Class Transformation, Cultural Struggle, and Transnationalism among Mexican Migrants in the United States." *Annals of the New York Academy of Sciences* 645 (1992) 25–52.
———. "Mexican Migration and the Social Space of Postmodernism." *Diaspora* 1 (1991) 8–23.
Rumbaut, Ruben, and Alejandro Portes. "Introduction: Ethnogenesis: Coming of Age in Immigrant America." In *Ethnicities: Children of Immigrants in America*, edited by Rubén G. Rumbaut and Alejandro Portes, 1–19. Berkeley: University of California Press, 2001.
Saenz, Rogelio. "A Profile of Latinos in Rural America." *Carsey Institute* 35 (2008).
Salisbury, W. Seward. "Religious Identification, Mixed Marriage and Conversion." *Journal for the Scientific Study of Religion* 8 (1969) 125–29.
Sánchez, Samantha, and Juan Galván. "Latino Muslims: The Changing Face of Islam in America." *Islamic Horizons* (July/August 2002) 22–30.
Schein, Edgar H., et al. *Coercive Persuasion*. New York: Norton, 1961.

Schlehofer, Michèle M., et al. "How Do 'Religion' and 'Spirituality' Differ? Lay Definitions among Older Adults." *Journal for the Scientific Study of Religion* 47 (2008) 411–25.
Schlenker, Barry R. "Identity and Self-Identification." In *The Self and Social Life*, edited by Barry R Schlenker, 65–99. New York: McGraw-Hill, 1985.
———. "Self-Identification: Toward an Integration of the Private and Public Self." In *Public Self and Private Self*, edited by Barry R Schlenker, 21–62. New York: Springer-Verlag, 1986.
Schneider, Jens, and Maurice Crul. "New Insights into Assimilation and Integration Theory: Introduction to the Special Issue." *Ethnic and Racial Studies* 33 (2010) 1143–48.
Schumann, Christoph. "A Muslim 'Diaspora' in the United States?" *The Muslim World* 97 (2007) 11–32.
Schwartz, Seth J., et al. "Introduction: Toward an Integrative View of Identity." In *Handbook of Identity Theory and Research*, edited by Seth J. Schwartz et al., 1–30. London: Springer, 2011.
Searle, John. *The Construction of Social Reality*. New York: Free Press, 1995.
Sethi, Sheena, and Martin Seligman. "Optimism and Fundamentalism." *Psychological Science* 4 (1993) 256–59.
Shatzmiller, Maya. "Marriage, Family, and the Faith: Women's Conversion to Islam." *Journal of Family History* 21 (1996) 235–66.
Shavit, Uriya. "The Wasati and Salafi Approaches to the Religious Law of Muslim Minorities." *Islamic Law and Society* 19 (2012) 416–57.
Sheik, Christine S. "Religious and Ethnic Variation among Second-Generation Muslim Americans." PhD diss., The University of Arizona, 2007.
Siddiqi, Muzammil H. "Practicing Islam in the United States." In *The Oxford Handbook of American Islam*, edited by Yvonne Yazbeck Haddad and Jane I. Smith, 159–73. Oxford: Oxford University Press, 2014.
Simmons, Gwendolyn Z. "From Muslims in America to American Muslims." *Journal of Islamic Law and Culture* 10 (2008) 254–80.
Singer, Audrey, et al. *At Home in the Nation's Capital: Immigrant Trends in Metropolitan Washington*. Washington, DC: Brookings Greater Washington Research Program, 2003.
Singer, Margaret T. "Coming Out of the Cults." *Psychology Today* 12 (1979) 72–82.
Singh, David Emmanuel. *Islamization in Modern South Asia: Deobandi Reform and The Gujjar Response*. Berlin: de Gruyter, 2012.
Smilde, David. *Reason to Believe: Cultural Agency in Latin American Evangelicalism*. 1st ed. Berkeley: University of California Press, 2007.
Smith, Jackie, and Tina Fetner. "Structural Approaches in the Sociology of Social Movements." In *Handbook of Social Movements across Disciplines*, edited by Bert Klandermans and Conny Roggeband, 13–57. New York: Springer, 2010.
Smith, James P. "Assimilation across the Latino Generations." *The American Economic Review* 93 (2003) 315–19.
Smith, Jane I. *Islam in America*. 2nd ed. New York: Columbia University Press, 2009.
———. *Muslims, Christians, and the Challenge of Interfaith Dialogue*. Oxford: Oxford University Press, 2007.
———. "Muslim Communities: Patterns of Muslim Immigration." http://usinfo.state.gov/products/pubs/muslimlife/immigrat.htm.

Smith, Tom W. "Review: The Muslim Population of the United States: The Methodology of Estimates." *The Public Opinion Quarterly* 66 (2002) 404–17.

Snow, David A., and Richard Machalek. "The Sociology of Conversion." *Annual Review of Sociology* 10 (1984) 167–90.

Snow, David A., et al. "Social Networks and Social Movements: A Microstructural Approach to Differential Recruitment." *American Sociological Review* 45 (1980) 787–801.

Snyder, Thomas D., et al. "Digest of Education Statistics, 2011." http://nces.ed.gov/pubs2011/2011015.pdf.

Song, Miri. "What Happens after Segmented Assimilation? An Exploration of Intermarriage and 'Mixed Race' Young People in Britain." *Ethnic and Racial Studies* 33 (2010) 1149–1213.

Stake, Robert E. "Qualitative Case Studies." In *The SAGE Handbook of Qualitative Research*, edited by Norman K. Lincoln and Yvonna S. Denzin, 443–66. 3rd ed. London: Sage, 2005.

Stark, Rodney, and Roger Finke. *Acts of Faith: Explaining the Human Side of Religion*. Berkeley: University of California Press, 2000.

Stark, Rodney, and Charles Y. Glock. *American Piety: The Nature of Religious Commitment*. Berkeley: University of California Press, 1968.

Stevens-Arroyo, Antonio M. *Discovering Latino Religion: A Comprehensive Social Science Bibliography*. New York: Bildner Center for Western Hemisphere Studies, 1995.

Stevens-Arroyo, Antonio M., and Gilbert R. Cadena. *Old Masks, New Faces: Religion and Latino Identities*. New York: Bildner Center for Western Hemisphere Studies, 1995.

Stoner, Carroll, and Jo Anne Parke. *All God's Children: The Cult Experience–Salvation or Slavery?* Radnor, PA: Chilton, 1977.

Straus, Roger A. "Religious Conversion as a Personal and Collective Accomplishment." *Sociology of Religion* 40 (1979) 158–65.

Stryker, Sheldon, and Peter J. Burke. "The Past, Present, and Future of an Identity Theory." *Social Psychology Quarterly* 63 (2000) 284–97.

Suárez-Orozco, Carola, and Marcelo M. Suárez-Orozco. *Transformations: Immigration, Family Life, and Achievement Motivation among Latino Adolescents*. Stanford: Stanford University Press, 1995.

Suro, Roberto, et al. "Latino Growth in Metropolitan America: Changing Patterns, New Locations." *The Brookings Institution*, 2002. https://www.brookings.edu/wp-content/uploads/2016/06/surosinger.pdf.

Swidler, Ann. *Talk of Love: How Culture Matters*. Chicago: University of Chicago Press, 2003.

Talhami, Ghada Hashem. "America's Early Experience with the Muslim Faith: The Nation of Islam." *Middle East Policy* 15 (2008) 129–38.

Taves, Ann. *Religious Experience Reconsidered: A Building-Block Approach to the Study of Religion and Other Special Things*. Princeton: Princeton University Press, 2009.

Tellis, Winston. "Introduction to Case Study." *The Qualitative Report* 3 (July 1997) 1–19. http://www.nova.edu/ssss/QR/QR3-2/tellis1.html.

Terrill, Robert. *Malcolm X: Inventing Radical Judgment*. Lansing: Michigan State University Press, 2004.

Thumma, Scott L. "Seeking to Be Converted: An Examination of Recent Conversions Studies and Theories." *Pastoral Psychology* 39.3 (1991) 185–94.

Tinaz, Nuri. "Conversion of African Americans to Islam: A Sociological Analysis of the Nation of Islam and Associated Groups." PhD diss., University of Warwick, 2001.

Torres, Rodolfo D., and George Katsiaficas. *Latino Social Movements: Historical and Theoretical Perspectives*. New York: Routledge, 1999.

Tsoukalas, Steven. *The Nation of Islam: Understanding the "Black Muslims."* Phillipsburg, NJ: P & R, 2001.

Tunison, Emory H. "Mohammad Webb, First American Muslim." *The Arab World* 1 (1945) 13–18.

Turner, Richard Brent. *Islam in the African-American Experience*. Bloomington: Indiana University Press, 2003.

United States Commission on Civil Rights. *Report of the U.S. Commission on Civil Rights*. Washington, DC: First official report of the Commission, 1959.

U.S. Department of Commerce. "Hispanic Origin: 1995 to 2050." *U.S. Bureau of the Census, Current Population Reports*, P25–1130, U.S. Government Printing Office, Washington, DC. http://www.census.gov/prod/1/pop/p25-1130.pdf.

———. "The Hispanic Population: 2010." *U.S. Bureau of the Census*, U.S. Government Printing Office, Washington, DC. http://www.census.gov/prod/cen2010/briefs/c2010br-04.pdf.

Van der Maas, Eduard. "Hispanic Pentecostalism." In *The New International Dictionary of Pentecostal and Charismatic Movements*, edited by Stanley M. Burgess and Eduard M. Van der Maas, 715–23. Grand Rapids: Zondervan, 2002.

van Nieuwkerk, Karin. "Biography and Choice: Female Converts to Islam in the Netherlands." *Islam and Christian-Muslim Relations* 19 (2008) 431–47.

———. "Gender, Conversion, and Islam: A Comparison of Online and Offline Conversion Narratives." In *Women Embracing Islam: Gender and Conversion in the West*, edited by Karin van Nieuwkerk, 95–119. Austin: University of Texas Press, 2006.

———. "Gender and Conversion to Islam in the West." In *Women Embracing Islam: Gender and Conversion in the West*, edited by Karin van Nieuwkerk, 1–16. Austin: University of Texas Press, 2006.

———. "Introduction: Gender and Conversion to Islam in the West." In *Women Embracing Islam: Gender and Conversion in the West*, edited by Karin van Nieuwkerk, 1–16. Austin: University of Texas Press, 2006.

———. *Women Embracing Islam: Gender and Conversion in the West*. Austin: University of Texas Press, 2006.

Vélez, William. "The Educational Experiences of Latinos in the United States." In *Latinas/os in the United States: Changing the Face of América*, edited by Clara E. Rodriguez and Douglas S. Massey, 129–48. New York: Springer, 2008.

Vermeulen, Hans. "Segmented Assimilation and Cross-National Comparative Research on the Integration of Immigrants and their Children." *Ethnic and Racial Studies* 33 (2010) 1214–30.

Voas, David. "Surveys of Behaviours, Beliefs and Affiliation: Micro-Quantitative." In *The SAGE Handbook of the Sociology of Religion*, edited by James A. Beckford and Jay Demerath, 463–89. Los Angeles: Sage, 2007.

Voas, David, and Fenella Fleischmann. "Islam Moves West: Religious Change in the First and Second Generations." *Annual Review of Sociology* 38 (2012) 525–45.

Wang, Yuting. *An Uncertain Future: Negotiating Multiple Identities in a Racially and Ethnically Diverse Mosque in the Post-9/11 United States.* Notre Dame: University of Notre Dame Press, 2009.

Warner, R. Stephen, et al. "Islam Is to Catholicism as Teflon Is to Velcro: Religion and Culture among Muslims and Latinas." In *Sustaining Faith Traditions: Race, Ethnicity, and Religion among the Latino Asian American Second Generation*, edited by Carolyn Chen and Russell Jeung, 46–68. New York: New York University Press, 2012.

Warner, William L., and Leo Srole. *The Social Systems of American Ethnic Groups.* New Haven: Yale University Press, 1945.

Waters, Mary C., and Tomás R. Jiménez. "Assessing Immigrant Assimilation: New Empirical and Theoretical Challenges." *Annual Review of Sociology* 31 (2005) 105–25.

Webb, Alexander Russell. *Islam in America.* New York: Oriental, 1893.

Weyr, Thomas. *Hispanic U.S.A.: Breaking the Melting Pot.* New York: Harper & Row, 1988.

Wilson, Everett A., and Jesse Miranda. "Hispanic Pentecostalism." In *The New International Dictionary of Pentecostal and Charismatic Movements*, edited by Stanley M. Burgess and Eduard M. Van der Maas, 715–23. Grand Rapids: Zondervan, 2002.

Wohlrab-Sahr, Monika. "Symbolizing Distance: Conversion to Islam in Germany and the United States." In *Women Embracing Islam: Gender and Conversion in the West*, edited by Karin van Nieuwkerk, 71–94. Austin: University of Texas Press, 2006.

Worthington, Everett L., Jr. "Understanding the Values of Religious Clients: A Model and its Application to Counseling." *Journal of Counseling Psychology* 35 (1988) 166–74.

Worthington, Everett L., Jr., et al. "The Religious Commitment Inventory—10: Development, Refinement, and Validation of a Brief Scale for Research and Counseling." *Journal of Counseling Psychology* 50 (2003) 84–96.

X, Malcolm, and Alex Haley. *The Autobiography of Malcolm X.* New York: Ballantine, 1992.

Yadegari, Mohammad. "Liberation Theology and Islamic Revivalism." *Journal of Religious Thought* 43 (1986) 38–51.

Yamane, David. "Narrative and Religious Experience." *Sociology of Religion* 61 (2000) 171–89.

Yang, Fenggang. *Chinese Christians in America: Conversion, Assimilation, and Adhesive Identities.* University Park: Pennsylvania State University Press, 1999.

———. "Chinese Conversion to Evangelical Christianity: The Importance of Social and Cultural Contexts." *Sociology of Religion* 59 (1998) 237–57.

———. "Religious Conversion and Identity Construction: A Study of a Chinese Christian Church in the United States." PhD diss., Catholic University of America, 1997.

Yapp, Malcolm E. "Contemporary Islamic Revivalism." *Asian Affairs* 11 (1980) 178–96.

Yin, Robert K. *Applications of Case Study Research.* 2nd ed. Los Angeles: Sage, 2003.

———. *Applications of Case Study Research.* 3rd ed. Los Angeles: Sage, 2011.

———. *Case Study Research: Design and Methods.* 2nd ed. London: Sage, 1994.

———. *Case Study Research: Design and Methods.* 4th ed. Los Angeles: Sage, 2009.

Younis, Mohamed. "Muslim Americans Exemplify Diversity, Potential." Gallup Center for Muslim Studies, March 2009. https://news.gallup.com/poll/116260/muslim-americans-exemplify-diversity-potential.aspx.

Zambrana, Ruth Enid. *Latinos in American Society: Families and Communities in Transition*. Ithaca, NY: Cornell University Press, 2011.

Zebiri, Kate. *British Muslim Converts: Choosing Alternative Lives*. Oxford: Oneworld, 2008.

———. "'Holy Foolishness' and 'Crazy Wisdom' as Teaching Styles in Contemporary Western Sufism." *Religion and Literature* 44 (2012) 1–30.

www.ingramcontent.com/pod-product-compliance
Lightning Source LLC
Chambersburg PA
CBHW050343230426
43663CB00010B/1968